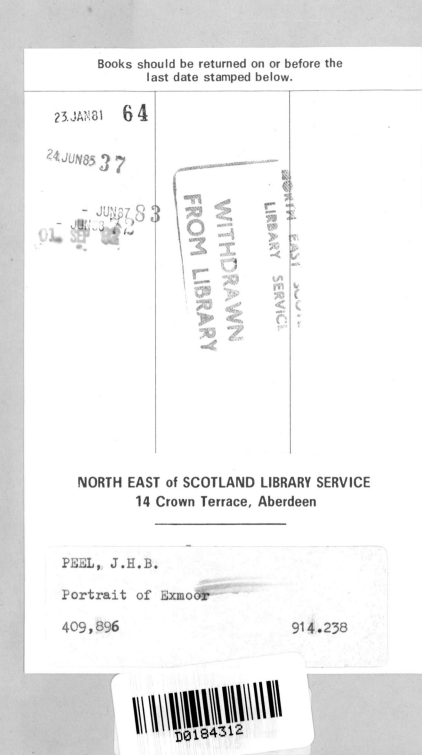

PORTRAIT OF EXMOOR

THE *PORTRAIT* SERIES

Portrait of
EXMOOR

J. H. B. PEEL

ILLUSTRATED
AND WITH MAP

ROBERT HALE · LONDON

914·238
H09,896
444305

PRINTED IN GREAT BRITAIN
BY EBENEZER BAYLIS AND SON LIMITED
THE TRINITY PRESS, WORCESTER, AND LONDON

10·40.

CONTENTS

CONTENTS

ILLUSTRATIONS

The photographs for this book were taken by the author.

For Mother
eighty-three years young
this portrait
of the land of her fathers

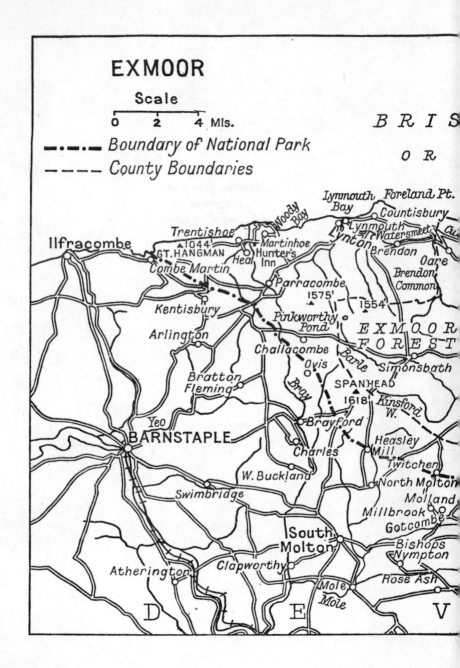

EXMOOR

Scale

0　2　4 Mls.

—·—·— Boundary of National Park
— — — — County Boundaries

B R I S

O R

Lynmouth Foreland Pt.
Bay
Countisbury
Woody Bay
Lynmouth
Watersmeet
Trentishoe
LYNTON
Cu
Martinhoe
Brendon
1044'
GT. HANGMAN
Hunter's
Oare
Ilfracombe
Heal Inn
Brendon
Combe Martin
Common
Parracombe
1575'
Kentisbury
1554'
Pinkworthy
E X M O O R
Arlington
Pond
F O R E S T
Challacombe
Ovis
Simonsbath
Barle
Bratton
SPANHEAD
Fleming
Bray
1618' Kinsford
W.
Yeo
Brayford
BARNSTAPLE
Heasley
Charles
Mill
Twitchen
W. Buckland
North Molton
Molland
Swimbridge
Millbrook
Gotcombe
South
Atherington
Clapworthy
Molton
Bishops
Nympton
Mole
Rose Ash
Mole

D　　　E　　　V

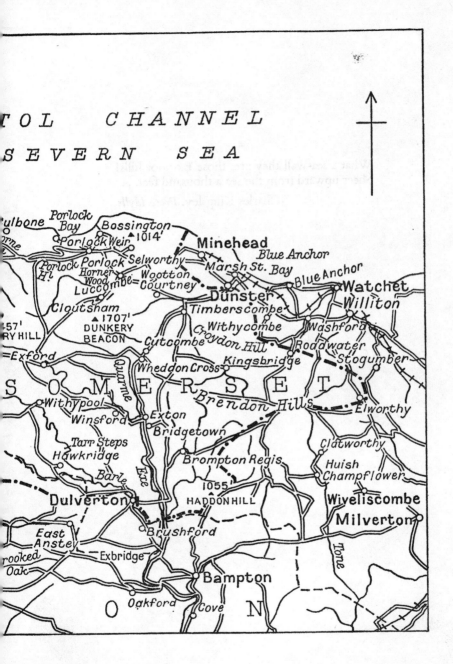

TOL CHANNEL

SEVERN SEA

What a sea-wall they are, those Exmoor hills!
Sheer upward from the sea a thousand feet. . . .

Charles Kingsley, *Prose Idylls*.

SPRINGTIME

Two arcs of Exmoor almost intersect beyond the window of this Haven. On a bright spring morning I feel that I have only to stretch an arm in order to touch the halo of green and gold and wool-white sheep which crowns the further hill. But the hill itself is a little more distant than that—perhaps four minutes' walk. I have no need to walk to the nearer hill; the Haven is partway up it. Here, like another Devon poet, Robert Herrick, I may say:

> We blesse our Fortunes, when we see
> Our own beloved privacie. . . .

The lane to the nearest village is long and steep. When you do arrive you find two churches but only four shops. The lane itself —it may be the steepest in England—is separated from the Haven by a coppice. If I walk a short way down the lane I reach an inn. There are two cottages further on, but you cannot see them. All around, the moor carves a horseshoe, densely wooded except where the tips almost touch; and there, nearly 1,000 feet up, the land is as bare as Moussorgski's mountain. Only bracken and broom withstand the wind. Below lie the Severn Sea and a glimpse of the Atlantic.

If I stop short of the inn, I find a path which enters a wood, and then emerges and follows a little river to the sea. The river arrives there before I do; partly because it takes more exercise, partly because it has passed from old age into a second and perpetual childhood, and partly because it can leap over boulders, whereas I must tread warily unless I would slither into the water. Daffodils grow beside this river, and primroses pave the path. The walk to the cove takes about twelve minutes.

As the lane may be the steepest, so the cove could be the smallest in England. You would call it pebbly, were it not that many of the pebbles are larger than cannon balls, and some too heavy to lift. On each side the twin arcs of Exmoor rise sheer from the sea; gorse-girt and Kendal-green, dappled with sheep, glidesome with gulls. When spring steps ashore smiling, you lie full-length in the sun, with the cliff for pillow, feeling the warmth between your shoulder-blades. But when spring scowls, you keep your distance because spray shrouds the beach, and should you walk through it, your jacket will bristle with brine. If you approach too close, you may be knocked down and buried at sea with a broken skull. When J. W. L. Page wrote *The Coast of Devon* in 1895 he spun a true tale of this Sea: "I have heard of a pilot boat . . . while lying in a dead calm, suddenly thrown on her beam ends by one of these moorland gusts."

Across the water, Wales is sometimes invisible and at other times so vivid that the last snow of spring winks from the hilltop at a naked eye. And between Saison and Cymry all manner of ships ply their lawful occasions. Seeing them, and the hills of Pembrokeshire, I extend Sir William Watson's greeting:

> . . . Wild Wales, whose kindred swayed
> This island, ages ere an English word
> Was breathed in Britain—let an English voice
> Hail and salute you here at England's heart.

A stream flows through the garden of the Haven, three feet beyond the window. For several years I tried to catch some modulation in the tenor—and in the bass—of its way. Surely a drought, or prolonged rainfall, must affect the volume of water? Science, no doubt, would compute a rise and fall, but neither the eye of intimacy nor the ear of old acquaintance can detect any change at all. Day and night, therefore, through fair weather and foul, the Haven is entertained by water music, the very voice of Exmoor, old as the hills from whence it flows. A purist may protest that Exmoor's voice is a wind instrument; and so indeed it is, on the heights; but among the combes the wind lowers its voice. In any event, a twice-purged purist will maintain that the voice of Exmoor is not one but many. "Up here", he will say, "even a virtuoso consents to sing in the choir." And that also is true. Yet the songsters are not condemned to anonymity. Each in turn performs a solo. At first light, for example, only the stream is heard, unless you follow it to the sea, and there only the waves are awake, plashing or plunging, in obedience to local conditions and to those other conditions that lie in mid-Atlantic.

But soon a lark leaps up, spiralling from sea-level to clifftop and thence into the last of the starlight and the first of the sun. Only your own ears will persuade you to believe the resonance of that Matins. As though they were a ball, the notes are bounced from one side of the ravine to the other, and back again, and then again back, tinkling and chiming with such persistence that you fancy the ravine itself has joined in, playing shuttlesong-and-battledore.

Through the half-light something moves on the summit—something white—for now the lambs add their own time of day, as though affirming that on Exmoor the sheep preceded the shepherd, and were before man was. By this time the news has got around. A primrose spreads it on the lawn; a blackbird lifts it to the sky. At first the hubbub can be sifted and identified—cuckoo, thrush, wren, dipper—but in a little while the day-spring so seizes each spectator that all are compelled to shout. Even the cliffside bracken looks up, visibly coaxed to shine by the sun's finger creeping downward like a wand. All creatures that on earth do dwell have received a summons, and are intent to answer Milton's ultimatum:

Awake, arise, or be forever fallen!

But not even the lark can dwell for long upon such heights. Vaughan's "world of light" gives way to Monday morning and the chores thereof. Birds unload their cargo of food into the holds of fledgling beaks. Flowers unfold. Clinging halfway up the ravine, stunted trees bend like the thorns at Wuthering Heights, "all stretching their limbs one way, as if craving alms of the sun". The postman arrives on his bicycle; the farmer trundles a tractor; the ecstasy of dawn has died.

But at twilight it revives, when the birds intone a calmer version of their songs before sunrise. There is a hill above Simonsbath where skylark and curlew sing long after their lowland brethren are silent. On and on they go, undaunted by the dark, and when at last all trace of daylight has disappeared, still the lark bears his blithe spirit into Meredith's realm:

. . . wide over many heads
The starry voice ascending spreads,
Awakening as it waxes thin
The best in us akin to him.

Suddenly the passion is spent. Faraway—far perhaps as Honey-mead—one lark still sings awhile, and then drops, dumb as a falling stone. Now only the voice of silence is heard. Exmoor sleeps.

Like many other venerables, Exmoor also snores; and this same silence, which had seemed eternal, is after all as transient as the climax of dawn; even on the mutest parts of the moor—atop Dunkery and beside Pinkworthy—even there, if you wait long enough, an owl will quaver, a vixen bark, the deer roar. Yet the true voice of Exmoor is stillness, that necessity which has become a luxury, hardly and expensively to be bought. Sometimes the stillness seems absolute, for many combes are bare of bushes and therefore of birdsong; not even a stream flows; on calm days, not even a breeze. Most people equate stillness with death, and then fall deeper into fallacy by equating noise with life. But noise is not life; it may become the opposite of life, inanimate and therefore lifeless, like aircraft, railways, conveyor-belts, cogs, fly-wheels and other cacophony. The earth is a womb; but pavements are a tomb. There is more life in one wren's song than in all the bulldozers that ever razed farmland into factories.

Meanwhile the moorfolk join with the rest of the kingdom as it greets the spring. W. H. Hudson said: "All weathers are good to those who love the open air." But he was far too wise to suppose that all weathers are of an equal goodness. Exmoor's northern rampart is the sea, which moderates the climate near the coast; but the heights inland are wild and wet. Neither the shepherd nor the sailor pays much attention to meteorologists. Like tribal law, our weather is conspicuously local. I have awakened in March to find an inch of snow on the path; and when I went uphill I found more than an inch, for the lane was blocked by drifts. Yet the roof of the inn, below the Haven, seemed scarcely white; and on the cove no trace of snow at all. At other times, standing by the brow of the lane, where all grew green, I have sighted snow above Parracombe and again beyond Countisbury.

Shirt-sleeved warmth on Christmas morning by the sea . . . oil-skinned twilight at noon in August near Exford . . . sleet at Withypool in June . . . farmers who never use anti-freeze . . . others who often take chains . . . is there such a thing as a typical spring day on Exmoor? Is there, on Exmoor, any typical day? There is indeed, and many of them. A typical March morning hides the river in mist, and then hits it with hail. A typical June afternoon melts the heather into honeycomb and deepens the tan on a shepherd's nape. The lower the milder; the higher the wilder; that seems to be our pattern. Exmoor, in short, has several climates, of which the wettest and wildest dwells among the summits inland. Coastwise, too, conditions vary. When a sea mist swathes Countisbury, the sky at Heddon's Mouth may be clear; and while Withypool winces under a south-easterly gale, Culbone may be calm. The Haven itself stands on a slope of a combe—reputedly the warmest in North Devon—that enjoys a climate which Charles Kingsley described as a blend of "the soft warmth of South Devon with the bracing freshness of the Welsh mountains . . ." Here is the place, and this the season, wherein the sea itself joins with Robert Bridges to greet the spring:

> Look! Look! the spring is come;
> O feel the gentle air,
> That wanders through the boughs to burst
> the green buds everywhere!

But Exmoor is not simply a theme for poets and weather-forecasters. It includes and also transcends the varied interests of stag-hunters, botanists, antiquarians, fishermen. Exmoor is a place where farmers earn their living; and the sound of that living seems never so loud as when the lambs bleat, the calves scamper, the ploughs drone. While townsfolk scan the stock market news, Exmoor quizzes the sky and then prods the earth. Says a farmer: "This yere'll do" . . . which is a terse paraphrase of Edward Thomas:

> It was a perfect day
> For sowing; just
> As sweet and dry was the ground
> As tobacco-dust.

While factory workers drive their new car to join the unofficial strike, an Exmoor shepherd digs his lambs from a March blizzard, or rescues them when the rivers rage with April rain. While others walk a barren moon, these men cultivate a rich earth. They are Exmoor. Tourists, cream teas, and charabancs are mere luxuries. The heart of the moor knows them not.

THE FOREST

The name Exmoor does not appear on any large-scale map. Instead, you will find Exmoor Forest, which may surprise some people who happen to know that at one time the forest was said to contain only two trees, Kite Oak and Hoar Oak. Both trees disappeared three centuries ago. The original Hoar Oak decayed and in 1658 collapsed. Its successor, planted in 1662, fell down on 26th December 1916. The present Oak, girt by iron railings, is more than half a century old; but a harsh climate has stunted it. Each of the trees had marked a forest boundary; one at Kittuck Hill, the other at the junction of Brendon and Lynton Commons. This paradox—a treeless forest—is apparent, not real, because the word forest connotes any large tract of wild or uncultivated land.

Where, then, ought we to begin? Must we return to what a Latin poet called the egg or inception . . . the moor's geological history? Or will it suffice to start with the earliest moorfolk, the Stone Age hunters? That would be interesting, certainly, but such pioneers scarcely stir my own imagination. They resembled the animals too closely. We pity their plight, and admire their stamina.

After them came Beaker Folk, Axe Folk, Iron Folk; probably they dwelt on the hilltops, wigwamming like Red Indians, obeying tribal chiefs whom they buried in graves and barrows, with rites that must forever elude us. What, for example, did the Longstone signify, that lonely plinth on Hawkridge Common?

The Romans reached Exmoor at a time when Devonshire formed part of the kingdom of the Dumnonii, a Celtic people whom the invaders quelled easily, for no major battle occurred in the South-west. Exmoor was bleak as well as barren, and since its natives were peaceable the Romans must have had a strong motive for keeping troops there. In a later chapter we shall examine that motive.

Meanwhile, I suggest that we begin in the year 1086, when William the Conqueror ordered a census or economic survey of his new kingdom. Four commissioners visited every shire, empowered to summon the sheriffs, barons, parish priests, reeves, and indeed any man—Norman or English—who could describe on oath and from his own knowledge how the land had been held in the reign of Edward the Confessor, and how it was being held in 1086. The commissioners recorded the names of the chief landowners, the number and status of their retainers and of their plough-teams, horses, cattle, service, rents. They recorded also the value of each manor in 1066 and in 1086, with a description of the meadows, pastures, woodlands, fishponds, mills. According to Bishop Robert of Hereford the returns were checked by a second body of commissioners. They were certainly resented by the English or Saxons, who, even in those years, felt reluctant to pay the Inland Revenue. One English chronicler described the survey as "shameful to tell and to do". The natives likened it to the Day of Doom or Judgement, and several lives were lost during disputes.

Domesday Book is a unique mediaeval document, but it never was infallibly omniscient. Some of the commissioners were misled, others were lazy. The rolls of parchment formed two volumes, now in the Records Office; the first volume concerned Suffolk, Norfolk, Essex; the second concerned the Southern and Midland counties. The North Country, which defied the Conqueror, had been so devastated that no survey of it was made. The South-west of England was covered by the so-called "Exon Domesday" (now in Exeter Cathedral), whose returns were made by twelve jurors from each hundred in Dorset, Wiltshire, Somerset, Devonshire, and Cornwall. Parts of the survey are written in Latin shorthand. Thus, *Rex habet* ("The King holds the land") may appear as *Rex hbt*. Sometimes a Saxon thane or squire retains his Exmoor land despite the Conquest. At Hawkwell, for instance, "Ulf holds Hauchewelle . . . he held it formerly." At other times the thane is now a Norman's servant, as at Bagley Manor, where the steward, Corflo, is described as the ex-lord: "He held it formerly."

During the Middle Ages Exmoor became one of five royal forests in Somerset; the others being Petherton, Mendip, Selwood, Neroche. W. H. Hudson said of Salisbury Plain that it is not "a precisely defined area, and may be made to include as much or as

little as will suit the writer's purpose." The area of Exmoor
Forest, by contrast, was defined closely and frequently. In 1279
twelve Somerset knights revised the boundaries that had been laid
down in 1219. Several other perambulations occurred during the
next twenty years, of which the last proved so drastic that Oare
became the only survivor of the former forest westward from
Porlock.

Men said of William the Conqueror that "he loved the tall
stags like a father"—which is a curious way of stating that he
enjoyed killing them. William, at all events, looked to his forests,
turning first to Hampshire, where, by adding 25,000 acres to an
uncultivated zone of 20,000 acres, he did indeed create a new
forest. As in Hampshire, so on Exmoor, every man's life was
dominated by the Forest Laws. Death became the usual penalty
for killing any wild creature in the forest; but if the offender were
fortunate he escaped with the loss of a limb or of his eyes. To
resist arrest might be fatal. In 1293 King Edward I decreed: "If
any forester do find any trespasser wandering within the Forest,
intending to do hurt or damage therein . . . and do flee or resist
. . . in this case, if the forester do kill any such offender, he shall
not be impeached for this felony." Some offenders were excom-
municated; in 1379 the Bishop of Durham anathematized "those
sons of iniquity who have abstracted stealthily and secretly from
our forest of Weardale certain birds called Merlin-hawks in the
vulgar tongue." Nevertheless it was not only in Lincolnshire
that a starry night delighted the poacher. A fourteenth-century
ballad, The Parlement of the Thre Ages, cites a man who killed a
deer, carved its meat, assembled the remains,

> And heaved all into an hole, and hid it with fern,
> That no forester of the fee shall find it thereafter.

Rivers, too, tempted all who dared "to go a-angling". A fifteenth-
century manual for fishermen—attributed to Lady Juliana
Berners—suggests that poachers sometimes plied their craftiness
rather for pleasure than for profit. Such a man was content even
when he had caught nothing, "for atte least he hath his wholsom
walk and mery at his ease, and swete ayre of the swete savoure of
the floures . . .".

On Exmoor the Forest Laws were enforced by various officials.
At their head stood the Justice of the Forest, who may or may not
have been a lawyer. In 1238 England had two such Justices; one

for the lands north of the Trent, the other for the lands south of it. The justiceship became a sinecure, and was abolished in 1846. The last holder, a Mr. Thomas Grenville, made a fortune from the southern justiceship, having held it for forty years.

Next in rank came the Chief Forester (on Exmoor they called him the Warden), who was required to maintain "the King's vert and venison" or pastures and deer. In 1289 "the Warden of Essemore" paid 14s. 6d. for his post; in return, he received £11. 11s. 4d. by sub-letting pasturage and other rights. The wardenship went always to a prominent local landowner. One of the fifteenth-century wardens was a woman, Sabina Pecche, who inherited the office from her brother, Richard de Plessey.

Below the warden were verderers and foresters (or game-keepers), and regarders whose task was to detect assart or unlawful cultivation of land within the forest. A mediaeval "Regard of Exemore" fined the vicar of Hawkridge ten shillings because he had sown four acres of forest to wheat.

There were four courts within the forest. The Court of Wood-warde or Attachment sat every forty days to try offences against vert and venison. The Court of Swaincote dealt chiefly with pasturage laws. The Court of Regard met triennially to enforce the laming of dogs lest they harried wild creatures in the forest. The Court of Justice Seat concerned itself with matters of higher policy within the forest. If a servant of those courts, or any other man, failed in his duties to them, he was heavily fined.

But the feud was not simply between the Crown and the peasantry; the barons, also, resented the enclosure of their land. When Henry III nibbled at the forests of his tenants-in-chief, the Earls of Chester and Pembroke sat with other of their peers at Stamford, where they compelled the King to give way. Yet still the Court went hunting. In 1298 Edward I held a Parliament in Sherwood Forest, and spent four weeks of the next year in the New Forest. Exmoor itself was a royal forest which the sovereign never visited.

Although the Forest Laws were mitigated, the men of Exmoor continued to suffer, and the rest of the kingdom with them. Their ordeals were aggravated during the seventeenth century, when Parliament refused to grant the subsidies that were needed for the maintenance of government. King Charles I thereupon required every owner of forestland to prove his title to possession; if an owner failed to comply, he was fined. In 1641 Parliament ordered the King to limit his purveyance of the forests. Thirty years later the same body—composed of very different members—passed an Act which forbade any man to kill game, even though it were on his own land, unless he enjoyed an income of £100 yearly (the equivalent, in modern devaluation, of several thousand sterling). And a century after that, Sir Roger de Coverley could still refer to a "yeoman of about a hundred pounds a year . . . just within the Game Act". Nor did the story end with the Game Act, for in 1970 there were men who had spoken with men whose fathers had been hanged for stealing a sheep. Game-owners and gamekeepers shared the evil reputation of lawyers. Thomas Carlyle set them among an unholy trinity: "Idlers, game-pre-servers, and mere human clothes-horses." Richard Jefferies casti-gated the tycoons who acquired an estate: "The farmers resented the town-bred insolence of people who aped the country gentle-man."

Throughout the Middle Ages the moor went its own way. The methods of farming did not change with the dynasties; the length of the latest gown, or the cut of a dandy's cap, passed like a comet at high noon. Even today there are parts of the moor on which only a ha'porth of star dust has settled. How often have I seen a shepherd wearing a sack over his head, and strips of cloth round his legs. Such men might have stepped out of the Middle Ages, or into Queen Victoria's Jubilee.

The farmers themselves were of two kinds, Free Suitors and Suitors-at-Large. The former, the aristocrats of their class, lived chiefly at Hawkridge and Withypool, retaining their forest rights by service. They were exempted from market tolls and from assize jury; they could cut turf, take fish, and graze their stock within the forest. In return, they attended the Swainmote, maintained the boundaries, supervised livestock, and assisted a coroner's inquest.

The Suitors-at-Large, who had no such obligations, paid cash for their rights of pasturage.

Beyond the moor, however, ways were changing rapidly, and not even Stoke Pero could escape their influence. England grew rich. Instead of selling her fleece, she took to weaving it and then exporting it as cloth. English ships plied and multiplied their brisk trade. Sir Thomas White, a seventeenth-century Secretary of State, speeded the export drive by "visiting most of the gentry of Devonshire, and giving them books and maps, showing how in six months the most of those ships had made their voyage". In short, the mediaeval manor's self-sufficiency gave way to a blend of cash-and-barter between towns and villages. But the going remained hard, wet, hazardous. Riding across the moor in 1538, John Leland scribbled a wayside memo: "From Dunster to Exford village a seven mile, of these seven four of the first were all hilly and rocky, full of brooks in every hill's bottom . . . ."

A century later Celia Fiennes noticed that the heavy goods were carried by pack-horses:

> They have their carriages on horseback, this being the time of harvest (tho' later in the yeare than usual being the middle of September) but I had the advantage of seeing their harvest bringing in, which is on a horse's backe, with sort of crookes of wood like cordes . . . they load them from the neck to the taile and pretty high and are forced to support it with their hands; so to a horse they have two people and the woman leads and supports them as well as men, and go through thick and thinn. . . .

Miss Fiennes met the same difficulties that had hindered Leland:

> I perceive they are very bleake in these countreys especially to this north ocean and the winds so troublesome they are forced to spin straw and so make a caul or net to worke to lay over their thatch on their ricks and out houses, with waites of straw to defend the thatch from being blown away by the greate winds.

Like a dove, she dared the floods ("which look'd so thick and troubled, as if they would clear all before a season after such rains . . ."), and Devon rewarded her courage ("I met with a very good Inn and accommodation, very good chamber and bed, and came by 5 of the clock so had good tyme to take off my wet cloaths and be well dryed and warme to eat my supper . . .").

One change she must have noticed, for it was already under way in Leland's time; the mud-and-wattle huts were being replaced by stone cottages and farmhouses so well-designed that some of them abide and are worth a fortune. A typical Tudor squire, Robert Fane, ripped the horn from his windows, set glass in its place, built a tennis court, and transformed his porch into a commodious shelter from the rain. Farmers on Exmoor were doing what Wordsworth observed among the Westmorland farmers a century later: "The storms and moisture of their climate induced them to sprinkle their upland property with out-houses of native stone, as places of shelter for their sheep, where

in tempestuous times, food was distributed to them." Wordsworth
cited another likeness between the Moor and his own fells:

Every family spun from its flock the wool with which it was
clothed; a weaver was here and there found among them; and the
rest of their wants was supplied by the produce of yarn, which
they carded and spun in their own houses, and carried to market,
either under their arms, or more frequently on pack-horses, a
small train taking their way down the valley or over the mountains
to the most commodious town.

The fell-folk went to Kendal, Windermere, Ambleside, Kirkby
Lonsdale, Appleby; the Exmoor-folk went to Dunster, Dulverton,
Bampton, Barnstaple, Lynton. The food and fodder of these
people scarcely changed throughout the Middle Ages.

Pigs were an important item of food, slaughtered in autumn,
and salted for winter. Nearly every manor had a swineherd who
kept watch while his pigs scoured the woodland for acorns. In
the South-west of England the name *dene* probably denoted a
swine pasturage; on Exmoor the *porcarii* were especially plentiful
at Bampton, which in 1086 had 353 pigs. Well into the nineteenth-
century the swineherd was a part of the English scene. John Clare,
who had been a swineherd, remembered the pigs that

. . . stretching in their slumbers lie
Beside the cottage in the sun.

Goats supplied milk and cheese. The small herd that grazes the
Valley of Rocks near Lynton may be descended from the goats
which the Domesday commissioners found there 1,000 years ago.
No doubt the peasants tried to weave the fleece, which must have
seemed a thankless task because even the Romans had regarded
goat's wool, *de lana capnina*, as a synonym for worthless.

Sheep must always have been the chief source of income. The
pure Exmoor Horn or Porlock—relics of a mountainous breed
—have white faces, black nostrils, and horns curling close to the
head. But cross-breeding created new definitions by destroying
old ones. Thus, in 1772 Arthur Young published an Exmoor
farmer's description of the Bampton breed: "They are generally
white-faced: the best-bred more like Leicestershire than any
other, but larger-boned and longer in the legs and body." A
century later, in 1855, the *Royal Agricultural Society's Journal*
stated: "It is very difficult to find the pure Bampton unmixed

with other blood, a few only remaining in Devonshire and West Somerset." However, a cross between Bamptons and Leicesters produced the famous Devon Longwool.

The North Devon cattle—the 'Rubies of the West'—may be seen in South Devon and so far to the east as Taunton; but they thrive best in their original habitat, which is on the edge of the moor, near North and South Molton. In 1903 F. S. Snell remarked: "nowhere do they appear to greater advantage than in the bleak region for which, owing to their active habits and hardy nature, they are especially developed".

The portrait, then, is of a wild region and a remote people. True, they did not have their own language, as the Cornish had; yet in the eyes of their bishop they seemed equally inaccessible and almost as uncouth. Both Henry VIII and Henry I would have accepted Leland's etching of the land between Exford and Simons-bath as "little or no Corne or Habitation". Heddon's Mouth and Hawkcombe Head had scarcely changed since William the Conqueror sent his commissioners to mind other people's business.

But the Moor was about to be invaded by another foreigner, scarcely less fiery than the Norman.

III

THE FOREST RECLAIMED

Sir Thomas Browne prefaced his study of ancient botany by remarking: "The Field of Knowledge hath been so traced, it is hard to spring any Thing New." Modern botanists may protest that Browne's dilemma arose less from a dearth of novelty than from a lack of knowledge. There is certainly no lack of knowledge about the history of Exmoor. Many books recount many aspects of it. A portrait, however, is not a pedigree. It will, of course, present its own background, but not a forest of genealogical trees. Nevertheless, the moor itself—its people, places, crafts, creatures, ships, customs, battles, sports, books, churches, schools ... the wind, the spray, the heather ... the postman plodding on foot from Parracombe, the child riding home from school on a pony—none can be savoured fully unless it is viewed in Time's perspective. That is why a chapter has been given to James Boevey, the man who influenced many chapters.

Boevey, a Dutch emigré, was a small imitation of his contemporary fellow-countryman, Cornelius Vermuyden, who, having come to England in 1621, bought the Yorkshire manor of Hatfield, transformed part of the Fens from a flood into a farm, and received a knighthood for his prowess as a civil engineer. Boevey himself was described by John Aubrey as "A person of great temperance and deep thought and a working head never idle ...". To start with, however, Boevey remained behind the scenes, as, for example, in 1652 when the Exmoor farmers were informed that an Oxfordshire gentleman had brought the forest or Chace, formerly "in the possession of Charles Stewart, late King of England". The size of the property was 20,000 acres; its price, £6,857 14s. 6d. No doubt the farmers shrugged their shoulders at this sign of a troubled time; and having shrugged their shoulders, they probably scratched their heads when the Oxfordshire buyer turned out to be an agent for James Boevey.

The new landowner came down from London to build a home, Simonsbath House, on a ridge above the River Barle. He built also a pound, larger and more efficient than Withypool's mediaeval prototype, for he was determined to make Simonsbath the capital of Exmoor, despite the fact that his nearest neighbour dwelt miles away, on the outskirts of Withypool. Installed at his solitary House, Boevey drained and tilled one hundred acres of moorland. There was no lack of textbooks to instruct him: *Essay for the advancement of husbandry learning* (1651), *English husbandman, nature of every soyle* (1613), *Countryman's instructor, remedies for the diseases, horse, sheepe and the cattle* (1636), *Feudigraphia, the synopsis of surveying* (1610), *Housewiferie of hennes* (1552), and, since he spoke French, *L'Agriculture et maison rustique* (1600). But he would have had to wait four years before ordering a copy of the new *Certain plaine demonstrations for improving barren land*. Although it was a century old, Thomas Tusser's *A Hundredth good pointes of husbandrie* remained popular, and on Exmoor it may still have been the latest news. Boevey's labourers used the tools which Tusser recommended:

A pitch-fork, a dung-fork, a skieve, skep, and a bin,
a broom and a pail to put water therein;
A hand-barrow, wheel-barrow, shovel, and spade,
a curry-comb, mane-comb, and whip for a jade.

At harvest-time, the new landlord may have observed that his men stole the grain:

Some pilfering thresher will walk with a staff;
will carry home corn as it is in the chaff.
And some in his bottle of leather so great
will carry home daily both barley and wheat.

Boevey had undertaken a stiff task, on ground which the modern botanist describes as "a lower upland zone" just short of 2,000 feet. Then as now, large areas of the moor produced only heather or ling (*Calluna vulgaris*) with fine-leaf and fox-leaf heath. Here and there the reclaimers would have found heath-sedge, hair-grass, crowberry, sheep's fescue, bilberry, and several kinds of lichen and moss. Having burned the heather slowly, in an effort to clear it, they may have been dispirited when some of the ashes revived and brought forth new flowers. On the other hand, they may have known that heather seeds, being very small (each seed weighs one ten-thousandth part of a gramme), can be blown from the flames and then back into the cinders, there to take root.

Peat was a valuable commodity in those years, and Exmoor its habitat, for the roots do best on high ground where heavy rainfall clogs a non-porous soil. Nordic immigrants called all such places a *meus* or Moss, as at Mossbrough in Derbyshire, Mosedale in Cumberland, Moseley in Staffordshire.

We know that several Scottish Highlanders worked at Simonsbath. On first arriving they must have glanced apprehensively when dusk fell, for they came from a land where wild animals so preyed on men and cattle that several Highland passes contained hospices or spittals, like the Spittal of Glenshee, where travellers could shelter at night. In Queen Elizabeth's reign the elk and brown bear roamed the Grampians; the last British wolf is said to have been killed by a Macqueen in 1743, long after Boevey had died. The red deer, by contrast, were already declining. During the Middle Ages they ranged throughout most of the high lands of Britain, from Exmoor and Wales to Cumberland and the Scottish mountains; but when Leland wrote his *Itineraries* in 1550 their numbers had so dwindled that he was able to mark the sites of the principal herds.

Exmoor farmers meanwhile felt the wind of change when Boevey's agent warned them that they must pay for pasturing their stock on the commons. The farmers replied that commons were by definition common property. The agent thereupon contradicted them, saying that all commons abutting onto the forest were an extension of it and therefore of Boevey's estate. Turning to their parsons for leadership, the people stood firm against intimidation. Boevey counter-attacked by suing them in the courts, which enriched the lawyers by impoverishing the litigants. But a great storm was about to break, not only over Exmoor but also throughout the kingdom.

In 1650, two years before Boevey had reached Simonsbath, Oliver Cromwell's decision to murder King Charles I was rewarded by Act of Parliament: "That Oliver Cromwell Esquire be constituted Captain-General and Commander-in-Chief of all the Forces raised or to be raised by the authority of Parliament within the Commonwealth of England." The military dictator wasted no time. Striding with his troops into the House of Commons, he mocked the Speaker's Mace ("Take away these baubles!")

and ordered the troops to chase the Members into the street. A
notice appeared on the door of the debating chamber: "House To
Let." The kingdom was then placed under martial law, administered regionally by eleven Major-Generals. The Prayer Book was
banned. Every loyal landowner was fined, and some were fined
into ruin. The death penalty was imposed on anyone who "speaks
against the government . . . or calls him tyrant or usurper".
The Genoese ambassador sent home a despatch.: "Cromwell is
the most hated man in England." Terrified of assassination, the
dictator would change bedrooms in the middle of the night.
While he slept, officers stood guard with drawn swords.

Boevey, in short, had taken a chance when he bought the
forest from the rebels, for if ever those rebels were ousted, his
own purchase would be declared invalid. His hopes must therefore
have risen when Cromwell accepted the title of King; and the
outlook remained bright even when Cromwell changed his
mind by accepting the style of Highness and the right to name
his sons as his successors. In 1660 Cromwell died and was succeeded by his younger son, His Highness Tumbledown Dick, a
pawn in the hands of ambitious generals. After a few months the
regime disappeared among its own dissensions. Even the worldly
Pepys was moved by the scenes which greeted the exiled king
when he landed at Dover: "The shouting and joy expressed by all
is past imagination . . . a day of rejoicing for our redemption
from tyranny."

As expected, the King decreed that "the late Usurping Powers"
had no right to sell property which did not belong to them. At
once the Exmoor farmers petitioned His Majesty that he would
eject the foreign interloper who had made their lives wretched
"by many long and tedious suits at Law". Boevey did indeed lose
his freehold of the forest, but he had already been astute enough
to acquire an interest in certain leases thereof; now, by bribing
London corruption, he secured other and longer leases. Gloom
settled above Simonsbath, and grew darker when Boevey re-
newed his war of writs.

In 1662 Boevey returned to Holland, where he set about suing
his fellow-countrymen, who hoisted him so high on his own
petard that the parabola landed him in jail. Again the gloom
lifted above Exmoor; and again it returned when, twelve years
later, Boevey reappeared, more than ever litigious. At one time
seventeen law suits ran concurrently. Having profited from

Boevey's Exmoor tenure for forty-three years, the lawyers deeply mourned his decease in 1696. If the Dutchman ever did find himself before the bar of a Supreme Court, he may have overheard St. Peter quoting Doctor Johnson: "I am afraid he is an attorney."

Had Boevey kept his hand to the plough, instead of turning aside to threaten his neighbours, he would certainly have been a happier husbandman, and might have brought true prosperity to every farmer who followed his good example. As it was, he died in a vengeful hour, and the weeds soon covered the grave of his moorland reclamation. Yet the title of this chapter was not meant to sound ironic. Glance again at some of the books which were nibbling the rind of mediaeval agriculture: *Adam out of Eden, experiments touching the advance of agriculture* (1699), *Aphorisms upon new ways of improving cider* (1684), *Designe for plentie, fruit trees* (1652), *England's happiness increased, potatoes* (1664), *Farm and grazier's complete instructor* (1697), *Treatise of wool and cattel* (1677), all summed up in the husbandman's *Ways to get wealth* (1625).

Boevey left the moor as he had found it, a mediaeval menage despite the times. Both in appearance and in outlook a Trentishoe shepherd or a Brayford swineherd were much as their forebears had been when Henry V pitied "the gentlemen in England now a-bed". Except that they would have spoken a different language, swineherd and shepherd could have rubbed along well enough with the farmfolk who had heard rumours of a battle at the other end of the world, near a place called Hastings. In 1666 as in 1066 the Parracombe pedlars held naïve notions of Heaven and Hell. When the parson at Brompton Regis recited *Quicunque Vult*—"neither confusing the persons nor dividing the substance. The Father incomprehensible, the Son incomprehensible: and the Holy Ghost incomprehensible"—then indeed the milkmaids might have murmured "Amen". Neither medicine nor surgery had advanced noticeably since the years when a mediaeval lord of Bampton sought hospital treatment from the monks at Glastonbury. The daily bread tasted the same as in the days when Chaucer's miller had swindled his customers. Illiteracy remained the rule. The population of some of the villages had scarcely changed since Domesday; and most men died where they had been born, not a few in the same room and on the same bed. A typical peasant's cottage was a one-room hovel, made of mud and wattle and wood, having a bonfire in the middle of the floor, with a hole in the roof for chimney. Writing in 1570, William Harrison remarked on "The multitude of chimnies lately erected". But on Exmoor the hole in the roof remained the rule. As late as 1688 Gregory King, in his survey of the population, used "cottager" and "pauper" as synonyms for each other. A century earlier, in 1589, Parliament had passed an Act against the Erecting and Maintaining of Cottages, which was intended to check "the great inconveniences which are found to grow by the creating ... of great numbers and multitudes of cottages". No cottage might be built unless the occupier of it owned at least four acres of land. The Act was not repealed until 1775. On Exmoor, however, the number of dwelling houses scarcely at all increased. John Taylor, the Caroline jingler, described a night he had spent in a peasant's cottage:

> ... no lodging (but the floor),
> No stool to sit, no lock upon the door,
> No straw to make us litter in the night,
> Nor any candlestick to hold the light.

The squire and the parson, on the other hand, were beginning to hear news from a wider and a kindlier world. During the famine of 1594 the Privy Council required Justices of the Peace to control the price of grain and to distribute supplies among those who most needed relief. In 1601 the Overseers of the Poor in the parish of North Molton were required to help the unemployed by supplying "flax, hemp, wool, thread, iron and other stuff to set the poor to work". The manor houses now had clear glass windowpanes. Gentlemen were privileged to wear a sword as part of their full dress. Never before had they moved so freely up or down the higher grades of society. Boevey, in fact, lived on the gentry's rising tide. In the late sixteenth century the area of land held by the nobility was less than it had been in the thirteenth century and than it would be during the eighteenth. When a yeoman, or a lawyer, or a merchant grew rich enough, he either bought or married his way into the lesser gentry: "Many of them," wrote William Harrison, "are able and do buy the lands of unthrifty gentlemen, and often setting their sons to the schools and to the Universities and to the Inns of Court. ..." The youngest son of a South Molton squire became a Tiverton wool merchant; the eldest daughter of a Barnstaple shopkeeper married the heir to a North Molton estate. And everywhere the Devon sea dogs were widening the horizon, pushing it further and further away. Again William Harrison came to the point:

> And whereas in times past their chief trade was into Spain, Portingall, France, Danske, Norwaie, Scotland and Iceland only, now in these days . . . they have sought out the east and west Indies, and made voyages not only into the Canaries and New Spain, but likewise into Cathaia, Moscovia, Tartaria and regions thereabouts, from whence (they say) they bring home great commodities.

Yet down on Exmoor the shape of things to come seemed very much the same as the shape of things that would never go. Of every five men, four worked on the land; and the fifth was up to his neck supplying their needs; the rest of him being a mixture of squire, parson, lawyer, poacher, soldier, seaman, schoolmaster.

The Exmoor harbours were also shipyards whose imports and exports sailed the Severn Sea with a speed and assurance that would have been impossible on Exmoor roads. Combe Martin, Lynmouth, Porlock, Minehead, Watchet . . . all were the ears that heard, the voice that spoke, the hand that sent, the belly that received. And at the inn on Saturday night the customer said: "I'll take a pint of ale, thankee. *And* I've earned 'en. There's two feet o' snow on Trentishoe Common. Instead o' finding my sheep, I near lost myself. By the way, have 'ee heard who's King today? Is it young Charlie yet, or still that old bastard Oliver?"

Unable to read, the shepherd had not heard of a new book, entitled *Invention of engines of motion*. Nor did he hear that in 1662 "young Charlie" had granted a charter to the Royal Society for Improving Natural Knowledge. It is unlikely that even the most literate Exmoor farmer ever knew that one of the earliest Fellows, the Hon. Robert Boyle, was not content simply to state that, at constant temperature, the volume of a given quantity of gas is inversely proportional to the pressure upon it. Men must put their thoughts into action. That is why Robert Boyle retired to the Oxford home of Apothecary Cook, there to write his first scientific treatise, announcing the invention of "a new Pneumaticall Engine".

The ways to Arcady
Exmoor National Park signpost

IV

THE FOREST ENCLOSED

If rumours of the "new Pneumaticall Engine" ever did reach Exmoor, the farmers were less impressed by it than by the news of Boevey's death; and less impressed by his death than by the respite from litigation which occurred when his widow announced that she would henceforth farm the land without enriching the lawyers.

After eight years Mrs. Boevey sold the lease to a man who lived near Timberscombe; and in 1750 the Earl of Orford acquired the forest. Seventeen years later he sold the lease to Sir Thomas Dyke Acland, who in 1785 was succeeded by his grandson, Warden of the Forest and Master of its Staghounds. Under the Aclands the land was well cared for, the rights of the farmers respected, the lot of the labourer improved. In short, the Aclands did not regard Exmoor solely as a source of personal profit, to be reaped and razed without regard to anything except the state of the market.

In 1808 a third Sir Thomas Acland sought to extend his lease. But what might have been the continuation of a good old regime, became the start of a bad new one; bad in the sense that, having begun well, it subjected the moor to an even newer "new Pneumaticall Engine". Briefly, what happened was this: when the third Sir Thomas sought to renew his lease, the newly-formed Commission of His Majesty's Woods, Forest and Land Revenues sent a certain Richard Hawkins to survey and value the moor. As a result of his report, the Crown enclosed six-elevenths of the moor for itself; Sir Thomas received one-eighth; the rest was allotted to the Free Suitors and the Borderers. There was nothing amiss in all this, unless it were Richard Hawkins' naïve illusion that the Crown could create oak woods on land where even the bilberry had to struggle for existence. In 1819, however, matters took a turn for the worse. The Crown was advised to sell its share

3

Springtime in Horner Woods

of the forest. And at that point the "Pneumaticall Engine" was joined by another sign of the times, Trade *alias* Frederick Knight, a Worcestershire industrialist.

Here a brief halt is necessary, to remind ourselves that few people were more perversely pitiful than the curate's Edwardian daughter who spoke of so-and-so as being "in trade". Every man is in trade. Even the poet hawks his visions for a hunk of bread. And none is so deeply in trade as the squire whose independent means depend on stocks and shares. The word 'trade' has a bold and honourable ancestry, for it comes from an earlier word, meaning to tread or march forward. A trader, in short, was an explorer, a pioneer, an adventurer. What we call an old-established family business became the Victorian heir of the mediaeval knight who hacked his way to Heaven via the Infidel. In trade— that vast network of manufacture and commerce—there adventure lived again. There courage and enterprise lived; there chivalry and sheer hard labour. And when the adventurers bought an estate of their own, the best of them shamed many a landed family by the compassionate expertise with which they managed the land and its people. Trade is harmful only when it becomes too heavy to carry and so crushes its victims.

John Knight, at all events, began well. Having bought several other Exmoor estates—notably from the Crown, Sir Charles Bampfylde, Sir Thomas Acland, and Sir Arthur Chichester— he enclosed most of the forest by means of a stone wall; gave the moor its first metalled roads; ploughed and burned thousands of acres; and built several farmsteads that wore well, looked well, worked well. If he had kept his hand to that plough, the moor would have prospered indeed. Unfortunately, like Boevey, he distracted both himself and his neighbours by obsessive greed. The first symptom of the disease was Pinkworthy Pool, which he built as a source of water-power. Water for what? For transforming Exmoor into a Black Country. But Pinkworthy was only a symptom. Soon an army of Irish navvies began to lay waste for the foundations of what was to be an industrial area, created without thought for the true well-being of its people; without thought of anything at all except private profit. Ruskin arraigned the attitude, in the opening sentence of *Unto This Last*:

> Among the delusions which at different periods have possessed themselves of the minds of large masses of the human race, perhaps the most curious—certainly the least creditable—is the modern

science of political economy, based on the idea that an advantageous code of social action may be determined irrespectively of the influence of social affection.

In 1850 John Knight was succeeded by his son, Frederick, an even more ruthless 'developer', who spent most of his time in London. For nearly half a century he was Member of Parliament for a Worcestershire constituency, and in the end they gave him a knighthood. Sir Fred persuaded a number of other industrialists that they could all wax fat by consuming the moor in the flames of factories, docks, railways, mines, traffic, housing estates. Four hundred years ago, in his fantasy *Utopia*, Sir Thomas More, Lord High Chancellor of England, had described a comparable devouring of the land, not by factories, but by the farmers' myopic policy of putting all their eggs into a Continental wool basket: "Your shepe", cried Sir Thomas, "that were wont to be so meke and tame, and so smal eaters, now, as I hear say, be become so great devowrers and so wylde, that they eate up, and swallow downe the very men themselfes. They consume, they destroye, and devoure whole fields, howses, and cities. . . ." Meanwhile the plot to desecrate Exmoor was hastened and enlarged; how widely and at what speed we shall discover when we explore the moorland mines.

For the present, let us consider the real moor, the rural moor. The question "How did a Victorian farmhand fare?" must be answered by a second question: "Which Victorian farmhand?" In 1870 as in 1970 conditions of work and rates of pay were not everywhere the same. Appalled by the widespread poverty in pre-Beveridge Britain, historians have compiled a mountain of statistics which, if they were swallowed whole, would be a miracle because, according to their thesis, nine-tenths of the British people long ago starved to death, and the remainder perished from a lack of servants. The problem is aggravated by the purchasing power of money, which has dwindled sharply during the past fifty years. A few facts may dispel some of the bias and much of the illusion. Thus, during the 1870s Edward Girdlestone examined the daily life of a North Devon farmhand. Wages, he said, were 8s. or 9s. a week: "carters and shepherds got 1s. a week more, or else a cottage rent free." The difficulty of understanding how any man could feed himself, let alone his family, on eight or nine shillings a week, is lessened by studying the price of food and other domestic items. For example, the annual budget of a typical North Somerset farmhand's family included £5. 4s. od. for rent; £2. 12s. od. for two-and-a-half tons of coal; 17s. 4d. for butter; 7s. 6d. for lighting; and 1s. 8d. for cutlery. A large loaf of bread cost 4d.; eggs fetched ½d. each; suits of clothes were made-to-measure from 30s.; the children's education cost 1d. per week per pupil. Such are the facts, and therefore indisputable.

When we try to discover what the Exmoor farmhand ate, we find dissension. Girdlestone stated that the worker's breakfast was "hot water poured on bread flavoured with onions". But Francis Heath's *The English Peasantry*, which appeared in 1874, stated that the worker's breakfast was "bread and bacon or dripping, with fried potatoes. . . ". There is a difference of many calories between those two menus. The same disagreement occurs at suppertime. According to Girdlestone, the worker ate "potatoes or cabbage greased with a tiny bit of fat bacon". According to Heath, the worker ate "hot vegetables, with meat or fish . . . and tea and bread and butter . . . the whole making a grand total of no inconsiderable amount and which only fairly hard work and fresh air enables him to digest". Experience compels me to reject Girdlestone and to accept Heath. I can walk twenty miles a day without adequate diet, but neither I nor anyone else can continue to do so, week after week, month by month, year in year out. If the Exmoor farmhand really had fared so badly—even half so badly—as Girdlestone suggested, then the moor could never have been farmed, because the labourer would have collapsed and died. But there is no need to regard Exmoor as an especially depressed area. Any fifth-form schoolboy knows that, until recent times, poverty was universal, not because men were heartless (charity abounded, beginning at home, and ending, it was hoped, in Heaven), but because they accepted it as part of the natural order of things. Just so, our remote descendants may be appalled by an era in which Sir Goalkeeper earned more than a parish priest, and the Queen of England spent less than a drug-addicted whine-merchant.

As for the Exmoor farmfolk, which is to say most of the Exmoor folk, the arrival of the Knight family confronted them with a question which we ourselves have failed to answer: can the moorland villages survive as farming communities with a summer tourist trade, or must they become dormitories for machine-minders in a new and nearby town? That twofold problem will be solved by the mysterious blend of apparent choice and apparent determinism which we call the destiny of man. Farming may become an unrecognizable phalanx of self-steering machines, an abattoir of self-slaughtering sheep, a zone of dehydrating factories, a vortex of vitamin pills which 'save' more time in order that men may have more leisure in which to wonder what to do.

My own hope for a less distant future is this: if young people cannot or will not live in our villages, then let those villages become the homes of people who can and will live in them. And if such people are elderly, even that is better than a population whose tastes and numbers transmute the village into a light-industries housing estate. Exmoor is one of the few truly dramatic landscapes in England. It deserves to be defended against the City of Dreadful Knights.

As I have said, we do not understand, because we have not identified, the dynamics of our destiny. Men may one day evolve into creatures that spend most of their lives doing nothing much, and most of it indoors. If that does happen, it will invalidate my belief that mankind cannot indefinitely endure the routine of contemporary industrial life. At present, relatively few people are able to escape from that routine; but those who have escaped, wish to preserve their liberty and to help others to do the same.

THE NATIONAL PARK

The word 'park' has several meanings. In the year 1440 it was used of a field; in 1579, of a tract of ornamental land, with woods and water, near a country mansion; in 1681, of a public park, such as St. James's; and in 1871, of the Yellowstone National Park in America, where country life was protected against the grosser assaults of Mammon. When Wordsworth watched the beginnings of the desecration of Lakeland, he expressed a hope which almost defines the National Parks. Lakeland, he said, must be treated as though it were "a sort of national property, in which every man has a right and interest who has an eye to perceive and a heart to enjoy".

There are ten such parks in England and Wales: Peakland, Lakeland, Snowdonia, Dartmoor, Pembrokeshire, Brecon Beacons, North Yorkshire, Yorkshire Dales, Northumberland, Exmoor. The largest of these is the Lake District National Park (816 square miles); the smallest is the Exmoor National Park (265 square miles). Together the parks cover 5,200,000 acres or 9 per cent of England and Wales, including nearly one-tenth of their coastline.

The nature and purpose of a National Park are widely unknown. Despite the expensive warnings offered by railways, coal-mines and electricity boards, many people still suppose that National Parks are nationalized and therefore in some mystical sense a public property. This illusion is so strong that, when they do enter a National Park, a considerable number of people behave as though they were at home: leaving litter on the lawn, setting fire to the trees, breaking down fences, and—if admonished for their misconduct—retorting: "It's a free country." But National Parks do not belong to everyone. They belong to their owners, who may be smallholders with five acres, or sheep farmers with 5,000 acres. The administration of these parks is something more than a feature of the portrait; it is a matter of public concern.

In 1949 a National Parks Commission—now known as The Countryside Commission—was established by Act of Parliament, to assist the State to choose and designate National Parks and other areas of outstanding natural beauty. The commission has defined its twofold aim: "To ensure that the control of development shall be conducted with special regard to the preservation and enhancement of its natural beauty and the promotion of facilities for open air recreation."

The first of those aims is a war against the Philistines. On Exmoor, for example, several unsightly advertisements have been removed, and many lesser placards reduced in size. Little can be done to cure the motor trade, whose horrors harry the kingdom from Land's End to John o'Groats; but the commission may stop anyone from building a new garage to compete with an old one across the road. Not even the farmers are allowed to disfigure the park.

Facilities for open-air recreation have been enhanced by courtesy of landowners who grant access across their property. Here the commission utters a warning: "Visitors have no right of entry to private land or property; the farmer's fields remain private inside the National Parks just as they are elsewhere." Among civilized people—the Eskimo, for instance, or the tribes of Equatorial East Africa—such warnings would be unnecessary; but among the British people they are so necessary that duplicates have to replace the originals which motorists destroy. At Luccombe I have seen a motor car unload itself into a field where ewes were grazing, heavy with lambs. Three children and one dog then chased the ewes while Dad set the grass afire by way of brewing tea.

In an admirably lucid pamphlet, explaining its *raison d'être*, the Countryside Commission emphasizes that it neither owns nor administers the National Parks. Who, then, does administer them? The answer varies with the region. Thus, the Lake District National Park is administered by a joint planning board; Dartmoor, by a planning committee of the Devon County Council; Exmoor (which lies partly in Devon and partly in Somerset), by planning committees of those two County Councils, each working within its own area, and by a joint advisory committee for the whole park. This wise division of labour acknowledges that the needs and traditions of Somerset are not the same as those of Devon.

The park's perimeter is so variously indented that to define it would demand a litany of place-names. The northern frontier is Foreland Point at Countisbury in Devon; the eastern, near Wiveliscombe in Somerset; the southern, at Brushford in Somerset; the western, at Combe Martin in Devon. Dulverton lies within the park—rather by yards than by miles—but Minehead does not. Bampton, too, was excluded, and now lies three miles beyond the park. One wishes that this market town had been granted its rightful place, for the ancient fair is still a red-letter day, when the ponies are sold at the October sales. However, a line had to be drawn somewhere, and the present boundaries encompass a cross-section of every aspect of the portrait—its highest hill, smallest church, finest walk—cattle country around Dulverton, sheepwalks above Simonsbath, combes below Brendon, heather beyond Exford, waves against Lynmouth.

Both sectors of the moor have their own warden and information centre, at Lynton in Devon and at Minehead in Somerset.

I have shared some memorable days with the Park Wardens, not only on Exmoor but also in Northumberland and Wales. Sometimes we were up before dawn, Landrovering to a mountainous bird sanctuary; sometimes we stood breathless while a fawn dappled its shadow down a sunlit glade; sometimes we marched through high-summer heather; and once we walked like Wenceslas by starlight.

The warden's warrant card defines his duties: "to inform and assist the public. He is authorized to investigate all breaches of the bye-laws and Statutes for the time being in force within the Park affecting public behaviour." That sounds stern, and is meant to deter all who would break the eight commandments which the commission has compiled and publicized, as follows: "Guard against all risk of fire; fasten all gates; keep dogs under proper control; keep to the paths across farmland; avoid damaging fences, hedges and walls; leave no litter; go carefully on country roads; respect the life of the countryside." Again, such exhortation would seem superfluous among civilized people; and again the British defy it. Year after year I watch strangers uprooting armfuls of the daffodils that grow beside the pathway to the cove. Year after year they skid at thirty miles an hour around corners which grown-ups would take at walking pace. Year after year they foul the streams, damage the fences, set their dogs among sheep, and answer back when a farmer's wife points out that the footpath (granted by her husband) does not cross her garden, but is clearly signposted 200 yards away.

There is some rivalry between the two Exmoors, and it can be explained by rivalry itself, a Latin word, *rivalis*, which connoted people who lived on opposite sides of a river. Later the word became a synonym for competitiveness and, later still, for enmity. Exmoor's rivalry, by contrast, is amiable. The greater part of the moor belongs to Somerset, but the most majestic lies in Devon, along and inland from the coast between the border at County Gate and the sea at Great Hangman. Nowhere else in Britain will you find such a kaleidoscope of towering cliffs, pastoral combes, wooded hills, heathery moorland.

In *Lorna Doone* our rivalry was recorded fairly. The book's first sentence sets the scene: "I, John Ridd, of the parish of Oare, in the county of Somerset...". When a Taunton reader protested that the story spoke too often of Devon, Blackmore replied: "Nowhere, to the best of my remembrance, have I said, or even implied, that Exmoor is mainly in Devon. Having known that country from my boyhood ... I have always borne in mind the truth that the larger part of the moor is within the county of Somerset." One wonders, in fact, whether Blackmore set Ridd's farm on the frontier in order to keep the peace. Jan himself declared: "Now I try to speak impartially, belonging no more to Somerset than I do to Devon, living upon the borders, and born of either county." Only once does Blackmore tilt his scales toward Devon, and even then he speaks for Cornwall, to whom the whole of Exmoor is alien and therefore inferior. Lorna's maid, you remember—the dauntless Gwenny Carfax—believed that one Cornishman was "better than any two men to be found in Devonshire, or any four in Somerset".

Somerset men have complained that we in Devon are slow to fulfil our park duties. Years ago, they say, Somerset erected signposts on paths and tracks across its own sector of the moor; but Devon dallied and erected none. That was true until 1969, when we posted our own sector with signs as handsome as Somerset's, which is not surprising, because each county employed the same Somerset craftsman to carve and inscribe its posts. However, the fact that a sign says *Dunkery Beacon 3 miles* does not guarantee that you will get there. Our climate is not a respecter of persons.

No native walks to Pinkworthy Pond after three days' rainfall in February. Even during August a footpath may let you down, suddenly and without warning, into a knee-deep quagmire.

Here a postscript may be added, summarizing the work of the Forestry Commission and its role on Exmoor. In 1916 a member of an ancient Exmoor family, the Right Honourable F. D. Acland, served as chairman of a committee whose task was "to consider and report upon the best means of conserving and developing the woodland and forestry of the United Kingdom, having regard to the experience gained during the war". Three years later the Forestry Commission was formed, to enlarge and improve Crown Forests and to offer guidance to the owners of private woodlands. In 1970 the Commission employed nearly 11,000 woodmen in 1,600,000 acres of its forests. Its task is to supervise a small and scattered area of Exmoor, in consultation with the Countryside Commission. The forester's aim is commercial, not aesthetic. In plainer language, he plants as many as possible of the species of trees that will earn the most profit in the least time. Such trees are conifers. The mountains of Scotland and Wales are strong enough to bear those regimented aliens; but Exmoor is not, and the Commission has wisely refrained from planting too many of them. In some of its plantations the Commission has designed glades, attractively signposted, where visitors may stroll, or rest, or have their picnic. An impenetrable core of those visitors ravage the plantations by setting fire to the trees (in 1965 more than 45,000 acres of the commission's woodlands were burned alive).

Finally, it seems necessary to point out that the National Parks are not the National Trust. The former, a public body, owns no land, and charges no fees; the latter, a private body, is among the largest landowners in Britain, partly because it does charge fees. Sometimes their interests clash. I could name National Trust Wardens who disliked, and were disliked by, National Park Wardens. There have been moments when the policy of one declined the requests of the other. But—at any rate in my own experience—those were personal antipathies, dabbling in minor matters. We must feel thankful that two such powerful bene-factors work together so harmoniously in a good cause. Nor is our thankfulness a gesture of sentimentality. In 1970 Britain's 56,000,000 acres were occupied by 54,000,000 people; so, if Utopia ever did achieve universal equality, each would occupy about one acre. Fortunately for all—though unhappily for many

—most of the population occupies less than 11 per cent of the total area. But that mixed blessing is not eternal. Every year increases the population, and decreases the area of countryside. Words, however, cannot mend the malaise. So long as the population multiplies, for so long the green acres will disappear beneath houses, offices, factories, roads. In 1969 the *Daily Telegraph* published a letter from the Society for the Preservation of Rural England, which diagnosed the disease, and suggested a palliative:

all these things spring from the same root cause—an arrogant and short-sighted materialism, and this is proved by their apologists' arguments. They are claimed to be "inevitable" "the price of progress" "essential to the balance of payments and the export drive", "part of technology", or—crowning humbug—"in the national interest". The people of this country are no longer taken in by this cant and would welcome some signs that official opinion recognizes the dangers.

Oliver Goldsmith said the same thing, saddened by the hordes of countryfolk whom industry was coaxing and compelling into the new factories: "In regretting the depopulation of the country, I inveigh against the increase of our luxuries; and here also I expect the shout of modern politicians against me." Goldsmith said the same thing again, in the poem itself, much to the amusement of our own "modern politicians":

Princes and lords may flourish, or may fade;
A breath can make them, as a breath has made;
But a bold peasantry, their country's pride,
When once destroy'd, can never be supplied.

In 1944 the same warning was repeated when H. J. Massingham said of a modern deserted village "Only one thing can ever re-people it—the restoration of the peasantry. But that industrialism does not understand. Catastrophe alone can teach it to understand." The question is, how many abortions, drug-addicts, murders, motorways, sonic booms, students and BBC plays do constitute a modern catastrophe? Do they create one at all? Are they not rather a symptom of progress and therefore in all ways admirable?

However, the moor is not without friends. An Exmoor Society leads the defence against State intrusion, public apathy, private misenterprise. Not even the most far-sighted businessman can discern a Bingo Bar on Dunkery Beacon nor a garage at County Gate. The Exmoor National Park is still a place where farmers go quietly about their work, and, as in Lorna Doone's day, "the land lies softly".

VI

SUMMER

Now the moor reaps its richest harvest, the sun itself, gold as the gorse that greets it. Daniel Defoe, who believed that reality is best expressed as an equation, would have turned his back on the sun, preferring to reflect it via a graph, as follows: every year The Haven receives more sunshine than does London, or Birmingham, or Edinburgh; more also than Llandudno, Weston-super-Mare, Tynemouth, Scarborough, Bath. The starkest comparison is the briefest: The Haven is half as sunny again as Manchester—1,542 hours against a murky 967. Our brightest month, June, receives 222 hours of sunshine. The rainfall is less than Malvern's, Matlock's, Swansea's—and only a third of Borrowdale's.

At The Haven, however, all such *minutiae* seem irrelevant, for they resemble Walter de la Mare's opinion of what he called "writing *about* poetry. . . . It can do little but attempt to give reasons for a delight that needs none." What is it to me, basking beside the stream, that Ventnor enjoys more sunlight, or Shrewsbury less? It suffices to know that the skin is pressed-down and overflowing with stooks of warmth from a harvest which began at dawn:

> The jackdaws prate; the cuckoos call;
> And shrill enough to reach the spheres
> Resounds the brazen madrigal
> Of half a hundred chanticleers.

As though shamed by John Davidson's choir, the sun rises out of the sea, and covers its own tardiness by calling on others, even as Ralph Hodgson called:

> Now one and all, you Roses,
> Wake up, you lie too long!
> This very moment closes
> The nightingale his song . . .

At noon only the hardiest worshipper remains at his devotions, bareheaded and perhaps supine before the god. As many of the rest as can, seek the shade, and will not emerge therefrom until the heat of the day subsides, and they say, "It seems cool enough to go for a stroll."

At teatime the bareness of a brilliant sky is swept by squadrons white as Masefield's

> Stately Spanish galleon coming from the Isthmus,
> Dipping through the Tropics by the palm-green shore. . . .

When the squadrons bear abeam of the cove, its yellow gorse, purple heather, grey scree and sparkling sheep incline you to believe that the Armada has sprinkled the moor

> With a cargo of diamonds,
> Emeralds, amethysts,
> Topazes, and cinnamon, and gold moidores.

In spring we awake; in autumn we learn to grow mellow; and in winter the firelight thereof is sufficient unto the day. But young summer caps them all and wears them as a feather. For one memorable fortnight June is as fresh as May, gayer than July. After a six-month labour, the moor has scaled the peak of its perfection, and pauses there, as though to assure itself before resuming the fruition of a cycle.

Each man has his own favourite corner of the moor, yet summer shortens all odds so closely that everywhere seems as good as anywhere. On setting out for Molland, with a view to walking as far as Bottreaux Mill, I begin to wonder whether I would not have done better to bathe from Dunster Beach, or cast the River Heddon at Kittitoe, or gallop on Withycombe Ridge, or do a hundred other things, any one of which would be incompatible with walking from Molland to Bottreaux Mill. In a little while, however, the nature of reality reasserts itself and is so agreeable that I wonder why ever I chose to forget it. Having reached Friendship Farm, I change my mind and with it my course, making instead for the cul-de-sac that leads to Ovis, and there becomes a track via Five Cross Way to Great Vint-combe. The woods are apple-green-dappled, and whenever I walk among shadows, they tread on my toes, irrepressible as a black jack-in-the-box. I see the heather—the pink and the white and the purple—warm as a heat-haze that has gone to earth, but without losing its grip on the sky.

Are you saying to yourself: "This is all very fine, but it over-looks the fact that the sun does *not* always shine in summer. Gales arrive, and days damp as the mist that dims them. Skies grow cloudy at breakfast-time, and then at twilight they clear, when it is too late to catch the day that never came?" Well, I have said it for you. Yet the best of summer remains beautiful, even when a man views it *de profundis*, for the beauty lies within itself, not in the eye of a stricken beholder. Down at the cove the sea is as Spenser saw it:

> . . . the Sunny beams do glaunce and glide
> Upon the trembling wave.

By the light of those beams you understand that utter despair is unnatural because contrary to a healthier part of man's nature. Leopardi preached suicide, yet fled from Naples when a plague broke out. Schopenhauer preached suicide, yet was so terrified of death that he forbade anyone even to mention it. Hardy and Housman grew famous crying that life is a brutish mockery; yet they lived it, and died easily in their beds at a ripe old age. A man who has suffered long and grievously develops a keen eye. He detects the differences between simple agony and sophisticated *angst*. Despite the travail, he finds within himself an urge to live, which he defines as a sense of duty whose fulfilment is its own reward. And, of course, a sense of good humour has righted many a vessel when excessive seas capsized her. Hulks, even, have turned a second turtle, and then sailed away and made a fair landfall.

Nevertheless, you were right to remind me that summer on Exmoor is primarily a means of livelihood for farmers. The Law still requires a village constable to witness the dipping of every flock along his beat; and a very pleasant outing it can be, when the sun shines, the cider flows, and Missus has baked a pasty. Still the sheep must be shorn, their lambs sold, the successors assured. Still the hay is mown and turned and gathered and stacked. Still the hoe clinks between young plants; summer's most excruciating task.

With his cap pushed back from a brick-red forehead, and shirtsleeves tucked above mahogany elbows. a farmhand stoops as he enters the cool tap room: "I said to myseif come twelve o'clock, If I don't rightly get a drap o' liquor, Lord lay me low, I'll die o' solidarity."

Now young Ted appears, his curls swaying from a peaked cap, his fingers slimy with tractor grease: "Give us a coke."

The roses-and-cream old lady decants a curious liquid, bright red: "We've run out o' coke," she says. "But this yere is turruble popular."

The settled man watches from the brim of his beer: "Teddy, my son, I've heard a deal about the perils o' liquor."

"So what?"

"So what do 'ee make o' the chap who had two o' they?"

"Cokes?"

"If that's what you call 'em. Two, he had. And then he walked home. And when he got there his missus said to 'en, 'Arold, your socks is smoking'."

"Smoking? His socks? Why, you'm an old fule."

"That's more than they'll ever say about you, my sonny, 'cause the smoke don't *end* at the socks. It *starts* there."

At Heal and at Ball and along Dick's Path you will look in vain for a strange face. I could, but shall not, cite lanes so secluded that even a July blackbird whistles with alarm when a car goes by. If you wish to join the crowds, that is easy; to escape them is easier still.

One aspect of summer few people ever do take the trouble to savour; and that is the night. Even the moorfolk squander it in a stuffy bar or before a flickering screen. In late summer, when the River Heddon is low and therefore clear, I begin casting soon after midnight, but the fish are merely a diversion, and since I pay little attention to them, I do not feel guilty toward creatures whose fighting spirit lapses with the sun.

On Exmoor we are so attuned to the sound of running water that we interpret it as a part of silence, like the owl, or a sheep, or the sea's sleepless sibilance. When eyes and ears have adapted themselves, many dark aspects of the moor come to light. A shrew crosses the lane, pausing in the middle, to scratch itself. A rabbit lopes through the meadow, neither feeding nor fighting nor mating, but simply out for a walk in the moonlight. Dribblets of scree tinkle 800 feet, and the silent aftermath of their arrival is more dramatic than the sound of their departure. A jay shrieks, making much ado about nothing intelligible to humanity. Sometimes a breeze shimmers the upper aspens. If I move six yards, I may change the acoustic properties, and then the river's predominant bass becomes an assertive treble.

Forestry Commission, near Timberscombe

Between the two arcs of Exmoor I see a light-house flashing.
A ship passes, her port side vivid as a ruby among jet. Is she a
tanker, bound for the Atlantic? Or a tiddler, hurrying to make
Swansea before dawn? Neither: as she glides through the beam of
light, her hull and ensign proclaim a Fishery Protection vessel.
Caught briefly in the glare, her wake lolls like the Psalmist's
white whale: "There go the ships; and there is that leviathan,
whom thou hast made to play therein."

But if I would hear the moor's deepest silence, I make for the
Chains Barrow, its roadless solitude. Even by moonlight those
heights feel eerie. No houses appear, because none exists. No
lights are visible, unless from the sky. This barrow is the loneliest
of all the moor's solitary places. Red deer avoid it; blackbirds
avoid it; sheep graze so seldom that they leave no tracks; even
the rabbits are rare. Black Hill in the Cheshire Pennines is bleak
indeed and boggy; but Chains Barrow is wetter and more weird.
If you know where to look, you will sight a low mound, topped
by an Ordnance Survey plinth, a spire on the roof of the world.
Coming and going thither, I am guided by streams, but having
reached the summit, I hear only the sog of my footsteps through
rushes. On moonless nights it can seem quite alarming to be
confronted by twelve Highland cattle blacker than the sky itself,
each breathing smoke from the darkness. The ponies, by contrast,
are always companionable. Their moor-muffled hooves compose
eine kleine nachtmusik. By day, I find, the mare will not let you
approach her foal too closely; but at night-time mother and child
grow more trusting, and have sometimes followed me, as though
they understood that all creatures dwell somewhat in the dark and
on their own.

In June the nights are so short that you may sometimes forget
to go to bed, or remember to go when it is already too late.
Westward of Prayway Head, and north from Dure Down, there
is a combe so profoundly deep that, once the sun has warmed it,
the steep woods insulate it from above and all around, so that I
have sat there at one o'clock in the morning without feeling
chilled. Bees passed by, and deer like shadows casting shadows.
Somewhere in all that scrubbery a honeysuckle must have
twined itself around a tree, because the scent reached me
whenever a breeze got up. Once I saw a car's headlights
reflected from a cloud, but the car I did not hear, though it
was less than half a mile off; the combe lay so deep that the
4

The fourteenth-century High House, Dunster

noise passed without descending. Immersed like Swinburne in the

> Air, light, and night, hills, winds, and streams,

I had forgotten that Time, too, passes. Looking up, I saw the stars, Meredith's immutable marchers, tracking their own decline:

> Around the ancient track marched rank on rank,
> The army of unalterable law.

Though I walked to the car briskly, dawn overtook me, and was itself pursued by a blackbird greeting the summer day.

VII

THE SOMERSET TOWNS

What is a town? *The Shorter Oxford Dictionary* gives some thirty replies, of which the fourth says: "an assemblage of buildings, public and private, larger than a village, and having more complete and independent local government; applied not only to a 'borough', and a 'city', but also to an 'urban district' and sometimes also to small inhabited places below the rank of an 'urban district' ". In other words, Timberscombe is a town, and so also are Withypool and Winsford. Yet most people will regard all three of them as villages. Nor is the problem solved when *Lorna Doone* refers to "the town of Oare" and "the little town of Brendon", which most people will regard as hamlets. The root of the matter is population. The word *tun* or town was first used to describe a handful of hovel-holders. When that handful grew larger, so also did its town. To King Alfred a Tudor town would have seemed immeasurably large; to Queen Victoria, noticeably small. In the last resort, therefore, a topographer must rely on a blend of history, situation, civic status. Taken *en bloc* the Exmoor towns, both of Somerset and of Devon, may be classified as follows: Barnstaple and Tiverton (municipal boroughs) and Minehead (urban district) are not on the moor, yet they were, and to some extent remain, extra-mural capitals of it. South Molton, a third municipal borough, stands on the edge of the moor, and is commonly accepted as a moorland town. Dulverton, Dunster, Bampton—likewise on the edge—are villages with the presence and the history of towns. Alone of all places within the National Park, Lynton-cum-Lynmouth (an urban district) is a true town albeit small. Such, then, are the candidates here and hereafter presented, without order of precedence: the Somerset towns of Minehead, Dulverton, Dunster; the Devon towns of Barnstaple, Tiverton, South Molton, Lynton-cum-Lynmouth, Bampton. If any Somerset man protest that his own towns have received less space than Devon's, let him reflect that this was proper because the Somerset moor contains only three towns (two of them small), whereas the Devon moor contains five (three of them sizeable). If, moreover, any Devon man protest that I have described Dunster, a summer-crowded Somerset village, as the fairest of all the Exmoor towns, let him consider it possible that I may have been right. If, finally, any man of any county protest that he cannot see the relevance of this *apologia* to what he will call the economic realities of the 1970s, let him recall that only in the built-up parts of Britain has a man's home ceased to be the foundation of all his other loves and a source of friendly rivalry with his neighbour. And now to business.

Minehead lies outside the National Park, and has no connection with mines. Its ancient name was *Mynheafdon*, the *dun* or hill above two rivers, the East and the West Myne. At one time it was second only to Bristol as a harbour of the Severn Sea, but in 1907 Dr. G. W. Wade reported that the harbour "has of recent years abandoned merchandise, and given itself over to the entertainment of visitors . . .". Among that entertainment, you will find a few things worth seeing: first, the hillside church of St. Michael, whose best features are as fine as its view across the sea (a chest in the church bears the arms of Robert Fitzjames, a Tudor vicar—sometime Bishop of London, of Chester, and of Rochester—who built Fulham Palace); second, a statue of Queen Anne, presented by a Swede who became Sir J. Bancks, and in 1696 married a rich widow of the Luttrells (this statue—formerly in the church, now in Wellington Square—was carved by Francis Bird, a protegé of Grinling Gibbons); third, the Plume of Feathers Inn, which survived the fire of 1791; fourth, the remains of a market cross; fifth, the former Court House; sixth, the Almshouse of Robert Quirk (1630), who caused a threat to be carved above the doorway, stating that the place had been built for the poor in perpetuity, "and cursed be that man that shall convert it to any other use"; seventh, the quay called Ichabod. What you will not find is an industry which supplied the stone for Queen Anne's statue, though the industry was thriving when Thomas Gerard mentioned it in his *Particular Description of the County of Somerset* (1633): "Att this place in our tyme a Dutch man hath found out mynes of excellent Alabaster, which they much use for Tombes and Chimney pieces. Its somewhat harder than ye Darbishir Alabaster, but for variety of mixtures and colours it passeth any I dare say of this Kingdome. . . ." Nor will you find what Defoe found:

> The best port, and safest harbour, in all these counties, at least, on this side: No ship so big, but it may come in, and no weather so bad, but the ships are safe when they are in; and they told me, that in the great storm anno 1703, when in all the harbours and rivers in the county, the ships were blown on shore, wreck'd, and lost, they suffered little or no damage in this harbour.

Minehead's mediaeval importance owed much to its lord of the manor, Sir Hugh Luttrell of Dunster Castle, who in 1488 built a quay which, 186 years later, was enlarged into its present shape by another Luttrell. Most of the vessels either fished or plied between Ireland and the Severn Sea, chiefly with cargoes of wool. The great maritime family at Minehead were the Ridlers; of whom John (born 1801) dabbled in ship-building, farming, sea-trading. His timber yard stood near the beach, at the end of Blenheim Road. Until his sons were old enough to leave school, he did all his own clerical work, usually at home and before breakfast. In 1932 one of his descendants, T. K. Ridler, owned a Minehead ketch, the *Orestes*, employed in the coal trade; in 1947 she sailed as a yacht to Mombasa, and was sold three years later for £5,000 or twenty-five times her original price; in 1953 she sank in Tanga harbour.

They keep a good old custom at Minehead, commonly called the May Day Hobby Horse. On May Day Eve and on May Day itself a shipshaped structure, some ten feet long, is paraded from the quay, covered with ribbons and silks, and trailing a cow's tail. This hybrid is said to recall a cow that was washed ashore when a ship sank on May Day Eve, 1722. But the procession is older than that. It may even be a relic of the ship-on-wheels which peasants trundled over their fields in spring, by way of a fertility rite. Tacitus mentioned such a ship in AD 98.

There is one voice that will never again be heard at Minehead nor indeed anywhere else on Exmoor. According to E. T. MacDermot, "in the early spring the forester used to send his men to make proclamation in the neighbouring market towns of the prices at which he would take in sheep, cattle, and 'horse-beats' during the current year. This practice was called 'Crying the moor'. . . ."

Like the National Park, I have never regarded Minehead as a

part of Exmoor. It is too big, too new, too urban. Compared with Countisbury, the coast seems tame; and from being at Heddon's Mouth an undoubted sea, the waters dwindle to an evident estuary. Nevertheless, Minehead succeeded Dunster as an important clearing-house for Exmoor trade; and much of the surrounding countryside tallies with a report that was sent to the Board of Agriculture two centuries ago: "On the rich marsh land near the Bristol Channel, the grazing system prevails. . . . The whole district is full of orchards. . . ."

Our second town, Dulverton, was baptized by two rivers, the Barle and the Exe, which meet at this *tun* beside a *diegla ford* or hidden crossing. Watching the union of those rivers, Lord Tennyson remarked to his son: "An old simile but a good one: Time is like a river, ever past and ever future." Richard Jefferies was more precise: "The brown Barle enjoys his life, and splashes in the sunshine like boys bathing—like them he is sunburnt and brown. . . . He laughs and talks, and sings louder than the wind in the woods."

What a strange thing taste is, how deeply woven among the skeins of conscious and of forgotten memories. Opening Methuen's guidebook of 1907 I find the following: "Dulverton is a primitive and not very prepossessing little place. Its quaintness is quite unpicturesque, and it is generally unworthy of its situation." Since no man ever saw an English country town whose appearance has been enhanced during the past seventy years, I conclude either that beauty is wholly in the eye of the beholder, or that the guidebook (or myself) is mistaken in our interpretation of it. At least the town no longer indulges the sort of progress which F. J. Snell recorded in 1906: "Owing to the constant stream of fashionable visitors from all parts of the world . . . the enterprising inhabitants have lately caused to be installed a system of electric lighting by means of high poles with wire attachments." Fashionable or not, I see Dulverton as a townlike village of charm and interest.

The High Street is scarcely wider than a lane. The small square or market place contains some friendly shops. Beyond it, on a knoll, stands the church, which is modern (1855) but not ugly, having a twelfth-century tower. One minute's walk from the church will take you to the High Street and thence through a courtyard where the *Exmoor Review* is published. Every lover of the moor ought to buy this annual of the Exmoor

Society. Its contributors are for the most part scientists, farmers, shepherds, historians, huntsmen, archaeologists, anglers, craftsmen and poets who either live on the moor or have studied it closely.

Jan Ridd knew Dulverton, and a wild ride he had to get there, over the top to Simonsbath, then over an even higher top to Winsford, and so down to deep Dulverton, the home of Master Huckaback, "An honest hosier and draper, serge and long-cloth warehouseman, at the sign of the Gartered Kitten, in the loyal town of Dulverton. ... And truly, the Dulverton people said that he was the richest man in their town, and could buy up half of the county armigers."

I doubt that even Master Huckaback could have purchased the Sydenhams, who in 1482 acquired by marriage the house and lands at Combe Sydenham, and either held or came to hold other manors in Somerset. In 1568 Sir George Sydenham bought the manor of Dulverton from Francis Babington, a Gentleman of the Privy Chamber; twelve years later he enlarged the manor house, and carved a Latin welcome above its door, saying: "This, George's house, is open permanently, except to ungrateful guests." Sir George's daughter, Elizabeth, must have caused a stir among Dulverton folk when she married one of the richest and most famous men in the kingdom. They will assure you at Dulverton that Elizabeth Sydenham, being then a Maid of Honour, attended the Queen when she received Francis Drake on his return from "The Famous Voyage" in *The Golden Hind*. Accompanied by five pack-horsefuls of Spanish gold and jewels. Drake travelled from Plymouth to Sion House, the Earl of Northumberland's London residence, where the Queen received him in a private audience that lasted for five hours. Having upbraided him for robbing the Spaniards, she accepted their treasure, and went home in a huff.

Some months later, by royal command, Drake received Her Majesty on board his "weather-beaten bark" at Deptford; and there she was graciously pleased to relent, for he had served her faithfully against an enemy. In the face of that enemy, had she not rallied her troops at Tilbury, with a challenge that would affront our own Disunited Nations:

I am come amongst you, as you see, at this time, not for my recreation and disport, but being resolved, in the midst and heat of the battle, to live or die amongst you, to lay down for my God, and for my kingdom, and for my people, all my honour and blood, even in the dust. I know I have the body of a weak and feeble woman, but I have the heart and stomach of a king, and of a king of England too, and think it foul shame that Parma or Spain or any prince of Europe should dare to invade the borders of my realm; to which, rather than any dishonour shall grow by me, I myself will take up arms, I myself will be your general. . . .

So, on this sunny April day, the Queen of England repays a little of her debt to a loyal servant. She will say to him, "Arise, Sir Francis." But, because she is a woman, even Sir Francis must pay the price of her political flirtation with the Duke of Alençon, whose agent is among the guests on board. Therefore, when Drake does kneel, it is not the Queen, but her admirer's agent, who dubs him with a golden sword. All this (they will tell you at Dulverton) was witnessed by the Queen's Maid of Honour, the young and beautiful Elizabeth Sydenham. And Dulverton is probably right.

Three years later, when Lady Drake had died, Sir Francis visited Dulverton, wooing Elizabeth Sydenham, in whose eyes, one might think, he was merely an elderly widower who happened also to be a millionaire. Fame, however, lasts longer than youth. In short, the old salt pleased the young sweet, and a marriage was arranged despite the displeasure of the Sydenhams, for whom neither a knighthood nor a fortune could conceal a lineage. Drake, they pointed out, was the son of a Devon parson; they, the heirs of an ancient heritage.

You may demur when a Somerset man assures you that the parson's son, so far from wooing cap-in-hand, went *sine die* a-sailing, whereupon the lady lost patience, found a suitor, and was about to enter Stogumber church, to marry him, when a ball of fire fell at her feet. "That," she cried, "was a signal from Francis"—a shot, as it were, across her bows (the shot itself, a meteorite, can still be seen at Monksilver). The lady, at all events, hove-to, put-about, and (in our own jargon) called the whole thing off, convinced that Drake would claim her. Sure enough, on the very next tide, he sailed into Plymouth Sound. Again Sir George Sydenham reminded his daughter that, although the fellow may have had a wife in every port, he certainly lacked a coat-of-arms until the Queen granted him "a fess wavy between two stars argent, the arctic and the antarctic". It was of no avail. In the end, therefore, the family acquiesced, though not until they had followed their own ancestors' example of mating Venus with

Mammon. Thus it was, that on the morning of his marriage to Elizabeth Sydenham, Sir Francis Drake handed to trustees a document which empowered them to hold his manors of Yarcombe and Sherford, of Samford Spinney and Buckland Abbey, for the use of "the aforesaid Francis Drake and Lady Elizabeth his wife, and the heirs and assigns of the aforesaid Francis Drake for ever." The Sydenhams were wiser than they knew. Within a few years Drake was dead, and their daughter, soon to become the Countess of Devon, inherited the rich lands of Buckland Abbey.

Of another Dulverton family, the Dykes, we shall learn more hereafter. A humbler, though not less helpful, townsman was Dr. Collyns, whom some of the old folk still remember via hearsay from their grandfathers. Charles Palk Collyns, a Middlesex man, began to practise at Dulverton in 1814. Two years later he married a Miss Anne Moore of Broadclyst near Exeter. His own father, like-wise a doctor, had attended the Earl of Devon at Powderham Castle; so, the son received an introduction to Lord Carnavon of Pixton near Dulverton. But Collyns himself never became a sycophant; he remained a loving physician who took from the rich in order that he might give to the poor. During a severe epidemic of influenza, while other doctors were bleeding people to death, he saved his own patients by nursing them to life. His prowess as a sportsman is still discussed at the Bull Inn. When hounds were disbanded in 1825 he did much to protect the deer from slow death by poachers. He mastered an interim pack until the Devon and Somerset Hounds were formed in 1855. His own stag-hunting book was dedicated to one of the Aclands. By way of more gentle exercise he rode each morning to fetch the family's milk from Perry Farm, a mile up the Barle. No doubt Dr. Collyns held several opinions which all good men now regard as bad; no doubt he felt only a temperate fondness for Muslims, and would have suffered a stroke had one of his illiterate patients presumed to prescribe foreign policy with special reference to the Balkans; no doubt, either, that he was one of a breed which made England what she is now ashamed of having been.

Dr. Collyns died in 1864, at the age of 71, and was buried near the east wall of Dulverton churchyard. The gravestone bears an inscription by his friend, John Kent, a Dulverton lawyer: "He resided for fifty years in this parish, relieving pain, succouring the poor, promoting local improvements, upholding manly pursuits, and actively performing the duties of a loyal English-man."

That tribute recalls another Dulverton man, Sir George Williams, who was born at Ashway Farm in the hills above the town. But his fame spread further than the Doctor's, for he founded the Young Men's Christian Association whose Red Triangle shines like a beacon, often in dark places. The YMCA began as a shield from any kind of inclemency; it continues as a club for every sort of visitor.

Our last Somerset town—the fairest on Exmoor—is Dunster or the *tor* which belonged to a man named *Dunn*, and then, six centuries ago, passed to a family called Lutterell, who still reside there. Hazlitt walked this way, with Coleridge and John Chester; but they by-passed the place because they were making for Lynton: "We had a long day's march," Hazlitt remembered, "and our feet kept time to Coleridge's tongue." Still, they did glance down admiringly: "We passed Dunster on our right, a small town between the brow of a hill and the sea. I remember eyeing it wistfully as it lay below us; contrasted with the woody scene around, it looked as clear, as pure, as embrowned and ideal as any landscape I have seen. . . ." Jan Ridd had already uttered his own Amen: "I never saw a prettier town than Dunster looked that evening. . . ." Alas, Dunster now pays the high cost of living in a place so beautiful that there are times when you cannot see the trees for the trippers. Were the choice mine, I would avoid Dunster, and rely on hearsay or pictures, rather than arrive in high summer. Happily, that choice is not mine. Let us therefore arrive midweek in early May, when the trees wear their new-laundered linen. We see, first, a wide village street, flanked by mediaeval beams, Tudor rafters, Georgian doorways. All is quiet, seemly, real, unruffled. If some ponies have preceded you, their dung may modify your vision of times past. The present is conjugated by a farmer as he gazes at the sky: "Them silly bastards in London is wrong again. If only they'd come down yere, maybe they'd know what sort o' weather we really are having."

"You can say that again. Last time they forecast rain, I spent the next week watering my roses."

The second voice has come from the Yarn Market, a timbered octagonal building, not unlike a small bandstand, which George Luttrell built (*c.* 1609), to confirm Dunster's eminence as a wool town. A Statute of James I refers to "broad cloths called Taunton, Bridgewaters, and Dunsters, made in the western part of Somersetshire ...". Facing the Yarn Market, the 'Luttrell Arms' carries a sign of 1779. Some historians believe that the inn was a residence of the mediaeval Abbots of Cleeve, In Tudor times it was called 'The Ship', which will seem out of place until you remember that Dunster used to be an inland seaport on the River Avill. During the fifteenth century Sir Hugh Luttrell sailed therefrom, in the *Leonard of Dunster*, accompanied by five oxen and two pipes of beer.

Beyond the Luttrell Arms, the street is dominated by a hilltop castle (not to be mistaken for an eighteenth-century folly, the Watch Tower, on a hill at the other end of the town). The true castle, Dunster Castle, is a fourteenth-century building on eleventh-century foundations.

The first legendary lord of Dunster was King Arthur, who is said to have been married and also crowned by Dubricius, the patron saint of Porlock church. Tennyson imagined the scene:

And Lancelot passed away among the flowers
(For then was latter April) and return'd
Among the flowers in May, with Guinevere,
To whom arrived, by Dubric the high saint,
Chief of the church in Britain, and before
The stateliest of her altar-shrines, the King
That morn was married. . . .

Most mediaevalists believe that an Arthurian soldier did rally the British people; some believe that Dunster was his stronghold before he succeeded King Cawdy (or Cadbury).

The first proven lords of Dunster were the Mohuns, one of whom, Reginald, received a papal title, the earldom of Este or Somerset. In 1376, having no male heir, Lady Joan de Mohun sold the castle and lands to Lady Elizabeth Luttrell, daughter of Hugh Courtenay, Earl of Devonshire (the Luttrells still have the receipt for that sale). Lady Luttrell's son—he who sailed with beef and beer—rebuilt the castle and added the gate-house. During the Civil War Thomas Luttrell joined the rebels, but surrendered to the King's men under Colonel Wyndham, who in turn was besieged. In 1645 the Prince of Wales visited the castle, to escape a plague at Bristol. The last of the male Luttrells died in 1737, leaving a daughter who married one of the Fownes of

Nethway, from whom the present Luttrells are descended. So, Dunster Castle has changed hands only once in 1,000 years.

Of the many guests whom the castle has received, two especially stir the imagination. One was regarded as a menace; the other has persisted as a mystery.

The mystery was a giant, six feet and six inches tall, who died in the castle, with fetters on his neck, wrists, and ankles. That is all we know of him. In 1967 Leiutenant-Colonel Walter Luttrell added a footnote, in a letter to Mr. G. B. Wood. After explaining that the skeleton had been discovered by workmen under the floor of the gate-house, Colonel Luttrell continued:

> Under him were and still are a pile of human bones which gave rise to the theory that this pit had originally been used as an oubliette, possibly at the time of the battles between Matilda (whom the de Mohun of the castle at that time vigorously supported) and Stephen. The castle was the scene of several attempted stormings during an unsuccessful siege and it is thought that the defenders probably followed the usual practice of throwing all the bodies of enemy dead into the oubliette. . . . The chained skeleton is thought in all probability to have been a mercenary who would have attracted special attention on account of his height.

The second visitor was William Prynne, author of *Histrio-mastix, The Prayer's Scourge or Actor's Tragedie*, which attacked the stage in general and actresses in particular. William Prynne was born at Painswick, Gloucestershire, in 1600. From Bath Grammar School he went up to Oriel College, Oxford. Having graduated, he was called to the Bar. Despite a puritanical bias, he defied Cromwell's military dictatorship, and was therefore imprisoned at Dunster Castle, where he volunteered to sift the castle records, which, he declared, were in "confused chaos". During his self-appointed task, the prisoner destroyed many valuable documents as "unnecessary paper". Amid the *auto-da-fé* this secular Savanorola must often have marvelled that he was still alive, not because he had defied the rebels, but because he had chided the Queen. The story of that chiding is among the strangest in the annals of the English threatre. We need not here concern ourselves with the difficult problem of censorship. It will do to recall that in Prynne's day the female parts of a play were acted by boys because professional acting was regarded as an unseemly occupation for women. When the Queen invited a company of French actresses to perform at Blackfriars, even the groundlings (as Prynne himself remarked) "hissed, hooted, and pippen-pelted them from the stage". Prynne replied with *Histriomastix*, which the Privy Council answered by cropping his ears, setting him in the pillory, branding his cheeks, fining him a fortune, and imprisoning him for life, or so they assumed. Prynne had certainly been outspoken: "Plain dealing", he declared, "is best." But he was humourless, too, unlike his adversaries. In 1649, for example, he had indignantly to deny the authorship of a new and anonymous broadside, *Mr. Prynne his defence of the Stage-Players or a Retraction of his former book.* The point is, even Dunsterfolk followed this celebrated case, and stood tiptoe to peep at Mr. Prynne.

At the entrance to Dunster Castle the road swerves right, and becomes so narrow that the summer walker must squeeze himself against a wall if he is not to have his toes punctured by tyres. In this narrow thoroughfare stands the so-called Nunnery, a building whose three storeys overhang one another. Whether it ever was a nunnery, I cannot discover; like the 'Luttrell Arms', it may have belonged to Cleeve. During the eighteenth-century it was called High House, and before that, St. Lawrence's Tenement.

A little beyond The Nunnery, stands a church whose spaciousness recalls that Bath Abbey held a priory here. The church, in fact, retains the prior's lodgings, a barn, a monastic choir, and a Norman dovecote that was something more than an ornament because, until 1800, the dove was a protected bird, and the Dunster cote provided 200 young squabs every week, for pigeon pie at the castle and priory. Inside the church a rood screen carves its *sursum corda*, recalling the independence of the laity who had used it as a means of separating themselves from the monks. The three chapels—to the Holy Trinity and to Saints Mary and Lawrence—tell a tale of merchants and of masons working *ad majorem Dei gloriam*. The tower, three years in the making, arose from stones which the townsfolk had themselves supplied and delivered, together with all the necessary tackle, and a promise that they would help to move any stones that were beyond the strength of two or three workmen. The tower itself, a hundred feet high, was designed by one mason (the word 'architect' did not appear until 1563) and built by another (who received 13s. 4d. per foot). Craftsmanship—or the manual skill to mould beautiful objects—is still alive at Dunster, where the

Webbers conduct a thatching business that was founded in 1634. In 1944 Edmund Blunden saluted all such men:

> The scythesman and the thatcher are not dead,
> Or else their ghosts are working with a will;
> Old England's farms are shrewdly husbanded,
> And up from all the hamlets jumps old skill . . .

Within Dunster churchyard you will see the timbered Priest's House, which for several years has been a quiet and pleasant teashop. On a fine May morning, or a mellow September afternoon, I rest and refresh myself there. Through an open door the song of the birds seems to harmonize with the silence of the graves, so that you feel there may be flowers in Heaven, even as Robert Herrick saw that there were flowers on earth:

> In this little Urne is laid
> Prewdence Baldwin (once my maid)
> From whose happy spark here let
> Spring the purple Violet.

Dunster itself is a violet, and a snowdrop, and an aster too, for it blooms when the roses are dead, and the cars have all gone home.

VIII

THE DEVON TOWNS

Although Barnstaple lies a long way from the heart of the moor, and nearly eight miles from the edge of the National Park at Kentisbury, it has for centuries been a commercial magnet, attracting Devon moorfolk. Anciently named Bardanstapol (which some scholars equate with *barda pol* or the post to which a warship was moored), the borough claims to be the oldest in Britain, having received its first charter in AD 930. Six centuries later John Leland arrived in time to record the mediaeval ruins:

> The town of Berdenstaple [he noted] hath been waulled, and the waulle was in compace by estimation half a myle. It is now almost clene faullen. The names of the four gates by the east, west, north and south, yet remain, and manifest tokens of them. There be manifest ruines of a great castelle at the north-west side of the towne, a little beneath the towne bridge, and a place of dungeon yet standeth.

During Cromwell's childhood the ruins were knocked about by a storm, for on 19th December 1601 the town clerk reported "some of the castle walls was blown down". No one suffered harm "saving some ravens were found dead". Thereafter the ruins crumbled. Ninety-seven years later Celia Fiennes mentioned "Barstaple" as a port for "a black stone exceeding hard and glossy like marble very dureable for pavements; this they sent to all parts in tyme of peace and London takes much of it." In 1621 the smugglers had become so active that the Privy Council reduced to three the number of Severn Sea harbours which might lawfully export wool: Bristol, Minehead, Barnstaple. Law-abiding merchants did their Barnstaple business on a so-called bargain stone at the old quay. Nowadays the town is a harbour rather by courtesy than by customs and excise, for a railway bridge barred many ships, and the four quays ceased either to build or to receive the vessels which formerly traded with London, Leith, Liverpool, Bristol and Ireland. That older Barnstaple was described by R. D. Blackmore in *The Maid of Sker*.

Towards the end of the eighteenth-century Daniel Defoe visited Barnstaple: "a large, spacious, well-built town," he announced, whose bridge across the River Taw had been built "by the generous gift of one Stamford, a citizen and merchant of London, who, it seems, was not a native of this place, but by trading here to his gain, had kindness of the town, to offer such a benefaction to them as they enjoy the benefits of to this day". Writing a century earlier, Thomas Westcote hawked a different tale. According to him, the bridge was built—or at any rate financed—by two spinsters who did indeed spin, and taught the craft to children, so that the proceeds of their skill went to pay for the first two piers; the rest of the money being found by beggars specially licensed for that purpose. The bridge itself has sixteen arches, of which thirteen were made during the thirteenth century and three appeared as replacements in 1589. Originally ten feet wide, the bridge was enlarged and then re-enlarged (1834).

Like the harbour, Barnstaple Fair is not what it used to be. The oldest men of Exmoor can remember hearing from their fathers of a fair which outshone all its neighbours. For three days it lasted, and the nights were probably as long as the days. The first day was given to the sale of cattle and sheep; the second, to horse-dealing and a meet of the staghounds; the third, to merry-making.

Barnstaple Grammar School produced two famous men, John Gay and John Jewel. The former was baptized in the parish church on 13th September 1685. Within ten years he found himself an orphan, whereupon his uncle, Thomas Gay, sent him to the Grammar School, and afterwards apprenticed him to a silk mercer in London. The youth, however, would rather wear silk than sell it; so, he returned to Barnstaple, where he employed himself in the business of being idle. In 1708—inspired by Philips' *Cyder*— he wrote a bad poem, *Wine*, which attracted some notice in London, and procured for him a post as domestic steward to the widowed Duchess of Monmouth, who, after eighteen months, dismissed him.

Dean Swift then took up the fallen meteorite and sent him as private secretary to Lord Clarendon, the British Minister in

Hanover. That, too, ended prematurely. In 1736, having resided as the non-paying guest of several poets and peers, Gay composed *The Beggar's Opera*, which created a record by running for sixty-two nights and by proceeding via Bath and Bristol to the Colonies. As literature, the piece is negligible; as a vogue it proved timely. For a single copy of its sequel, *Polly*, the Duchess of Marlborough paid (in modern currency) £3,000. Befriended by the Duke and Duchess of Queensferry—who invested his royalties, and kept the interest under lock and key—Gay died prosperously, and was buried in Westminster Abbey, under his own vapid epitaph:

> Life is a jest, and all things show it;
> I thought so once, and now I know it.

John Jewel was made of sterner stuff. Born at Berrynarbor, overlooking the Severn Sea, he went up from Barnstaple Grammar School to Oxford, where he held the Chair of Divinity. In 1559 he became Bishop of Salisbury. Jewel's masterpiece, *Apologia Ecclesiae Anglicanae* or Defence of the Church of England, was translated into English by Lady Bacon, mother of Francis, first Viscount St. Albans. The book is erudite and outspoken, as, for example, when it arraigns the Bishop of Rome for having anathematized certain beliefs: "He should have commenced his suit rather against the Holy Fathers. For those things did not only proceed from them, but were also appointed by them. ..." Although he spoke out, Jewel spoke courteously, which is why Westcote said of him: "His behaviour was so virtuous that his heartiest adversary ... could not withstanding forbear to yield this testimony in his commendation. ..."

Among the town's buildings are a thirteenth-century parish church; a fourteenth-century Chapel of St. Anne, which became the Free Grammar School; Penrose's Almshouses (1627); Horwood's School (1659) and Almshouses (1674); the merchants' Exchange or Queen Anne's Walk (enlarged in 1708); and the Guildhall (1823). All these—together with some Georgian houses —are rare plums in a destructive duff; for the town's waterfront has been ravaged, almost into Bideford, and the surrounding hills are scarred by offices, factories, housing estates. Every brand of commercial traveller shivers the narrow streets. Time has indeed reversed Defoe's verdict that "the town of Biddiford has flourish'd; and the town of Barnstaple rather declin'd".

5

Dunster church

The next town, South Molton, was formerly *Sudmoltone* (Celtic *moel* or bare hill). The name Molton is relatively modern. In 1746 *The Gentleman's Magazine* published a dialogue "in the Devonshire Dialect and Mode near the Forest of Exmoor", written by a local parson, in which the town is called Moulton. During the reign of King Edward I South Molton was held of the Crown on a tenure of Grand Sergeantry whereby the tenant sent an armed servant to protect the Earl of Gloucester whenever he should go hunting in Gower. In 1334 South Molton stood seventh in a list of nineteen Devon boroughs, being then more important than Tiverton, Honiton, Okehampton, Bideford, Crediton. Having received a charter from Queen Elizabeth I and another from Charles II, the town sent two members to Parliament. In 1970 it supported a mayor, four aldermen and twelve councillors (relics of the twelve burgesses of 1328).

The High Street is divided by an island of shops whereafter it widens to form the Market Place, in which a guildhall and a market house confront the church. The Guildhall is a stone-fronted building (1743) crowned by a comely cupola which, being white, shines like a minaret. The Market House is agreeable Victorian Renaissance (1863). The church peers through an avenue of lime trees, and is topped by a fifteenth-century tower 107 feet high (until 1765 the tower had a spire). A statue at the Guildhall—entitled "Our Great Benefactor"—maintains the memory of Hugh Squiers, who endowed the school (1684) that bore his name; a pleasant building with arched doors and three Gothic windows.

During the nineteenth-century the Congregational chapel sent twenty-seven missionaries to preach the Gospel both at home and abroad; chief among them being Aaron Buzzacott, who began to evangelize in 1827, before a Victorian chapel had replaced the seventeenth-century original. The elder chapel recalls a tale of dissension among dissenters, beginning in 1694, five years after the Toleration Act had granted a degree of freedom to non-Anglicans. An assembly of local dissenters—chiefly Presbyterian layfolk—sat in judgement on every minister both before and during his appointment. The South Molton minister, a Mr. Rutter, proved so unacceptable that his flock complained: "That he doth not give Satisfaction; that they cannot profit by him; that he is not Popular, not Lively; that he doth not rouze them." Perhaps Mr. Rutter had ignored an edict of the assembly discouraging excessively long sermons: "That all future Preachers have a warning given to them to their hour; And that the Clark turn the Glass when the Text is nam'd and take it away as soon as 'tis run out." Mr. Rutter, at all events, sought valour in discretion: "Foreseeing some difficulties that may probably ensue on his going there, he voluntarily quits his interest in the people of South Molton." The people themselves, however, remained hard to please, for another minister protested that they "chose rather to ly at home on the Lords day than to attend on his preaching".

The men of South Molton took part in a famous battle against tyranny. The story opens in 1649 when the rebels have murdered King Charles I; that is, have killed him, without lawful trial, for deeds that were not indictable, but did enjoy the support of many of his subjects. Thereafter, as we have seen, Cromwell became a military dictator. But the English do not care to submit overlong: least of all the West Countrymen. When an ill-advised Roman Catholic tried to intimidate Sir Johnathan Trelawny, the Cornish Bishop of Bath, the West Country arose and was ready to storm the prison where he lay:

> And have they fixed the where and when?
> And shall Trelawny die?
> Here's twenty thousand Cornish men
> Will know the reason why.

Wordsworth set that text to a deeper music when he declared:

> We must be free or die, who speak the tongue
> That Shakespeare spake. . . .

In 1655, therefore, the city of Salisbury is seized by 200 loyalists under the command of Colonel John Penruddock, Lord of the Manor of Compton Chamberlayne, and Colonel Hugh Grove, Lord of the Manor of Zeal (where the new king, now in exile, had sheltered from the rebels). The assault on Salisbury is disciplined. Looting and violence are forbidden. Only the rebel soldiers are to be attacked. From Wiltshire the loyalists move west to Devon, gathering recruits as they go: and there, in the High Street at South Molton, with due ceremony and amid general rejoicing, Cromwell is denounced as a usurper, and the King proclaimed.

That night a large body of Cromwellian cavalry reaches the town, having galloped from Exeter, led by a so-called Colonel,

noted for his brutality. Some of the loyalists run away—the sight
of cavalry is indeed terrifying to labourers who never handled
anything bloodier than a sickle—but the rest stand fast and fight.
Pressed back into the churchyard, they still fight, fiercely and
with desperation because they know that something greater
than their own lives is at stake. At last the inevitable occurs.
By force of numbers they are surrounded and taken to Exeter
Castle. Colonel Penruddock's wife, Arundel, pleads with Cromwell. It is useless. Has he not already exulted in his massacre of
the Irish? Cromwell himself passes sentence obliquely via the
judges. Every loyal officer is beheaded; other ranks are either
hanged, drawn and quartered, or shipped as slaves to Barbados.

Only ignorance or bias will pretend that the Stuart dynasty
was flawless; but not even the most inept of the Stuarts either
desired or attempted to destroy Parliament and to govern solely
by martial law imposed via Major-Generals. The heroism and
heartache of all who defied Cromwell are expressed in the
last letter which Colonel Penruddock wrote to his wife: "The
greatest conflict I have had in this extremity was my parting
from thee; the next encounter is to be with Death, and my
Saviour hath so pulled the sting thereof that I hope to assault it
without fear. Look not towards my grave where my body lies,
but towards heaven, where I hope my soul shall gain a mansion
in my Father's house." In the Colonel's old home they preserve
an account-book wherein Arundel Penruddock had entered the
cost of bringing his body home from Exeter: £7 9s. od. Lord
Clarendon, himself a victim of the rebels spoke for all who died
defending liberty, both there and thereafter: "Whomsoever leads
such a life, needs not care upon how short a warning it may be
taken from him."

In South Molton, they say, began the legend of Mole's Chamber, when Farmer Mole rode homeward from market on a horse
laden with lime. Either because the night was dark, or himself
lit-up, Mole and his mare disappeared in a bog among the wild
heights which now bear his name. There is a ghoulish tradition
that man and beast were unearthed, many years later, having been
preserved by what F. J. Snell called "the antiseptic property of
peat". One thing is certain—Farmer Mole failed to observe the
three forewarnings of our bogs: first, the white bog-flower;
second, the reddish grass; third, the blend of grass and heather.

Meantime the twelve councillors and their aldermen and

mayor reflect with satisfaction that the town is less tipsy than in the years when it contained thirty-four public houses. Cock's *Records of South Molton* (1893) rejoiced in the decline of those thirty-four premises: "There are now twenty-one; and with them we have got rid of the only pawnbroker's shop." In lieu of liquor, said Cock, "we now have a Temperance Hall and Soup Kitchen . . .". But other and more scarlet sins were washed away by soup and tea: "Vice no longer walks unblushingly in our streets and openly tempts the passer by. . . ." Though I have long since ceased to smirk at tragedy, I do smile whenever I envisage South Molton as a fallen woman. The town, after all, is small; its streets, conspicuously public; the air, so bracing that it sweeps those streets clear of anything except puddles. South Molton always has been a breezy *rendez-vous* of moorfolk. As *Lorna Doone* said: "it is a busy place for talking."

Our third town, Tiverton, stood astride a double ford, one on the River Exe, the other on the River Lowman; whence its Saxon name, *Twyfyrde* or the *tun* at two fords. Between 1086 and 1205 the name was spelled variously as Tovretone, Tuiverton, Little Twertona, Teverton, and Tuverton. By whatever name, the place owed its importance to the river-crossings which themselves begat a castle. Throughout most of the Middle Ages the castle belonged to the Courtenays, Earls of Devon, to whom Tiverton looked for its living. As late as the year 1490 the future 'boom town' was still a feudal fief, so insignificant that its tax assessment of 40s. was reduced by half. Thereafter the town arose belatedly, like a phoenix from the middle ages.

When Queen Elizabeth I ascended the throne, Tiverton was among the richest towns in Devon, and continued so until the wool trade declined. Although they bought large quantities of Exmoor fleece, the Tiverton merchants soon sought raw materials beyond their county. Three centuries ago Thomas Westcote noted the arrival of fleece in ships from Wales, and on pack-horses from Cornwall. Between 1702 and 1704 the imports of Irish wool to England were more than doubled; and two-thirds of them arrived at south-western ports. In 1724 Defoe was impressed by Tiverton's prosperity: "Next to Excester," he reported, "this is the greatest manufacturing town in the County, and, of all inland towns, is next to it in wealth." He added a timelessly topical note: "We found the people, here, all fully employ'd and very few, if any, out of work, except such as need not be unemploy'd, but were so from mere sloth and idleness, of which, some will be found every where." A single example will reveal the prosperity of Tiverton and the flexibility of society. In 1764 died John Colwich, a lawyer who became recorder of Exeter; one of his sons was brother-in-law to Sir John Duntze, Member of Parliament for Tiverton; another son married a Miss Burridge (daughter of a Tiverton wool merchant), who became sister-in-law to the wife of a Doctor of Divinity and to the wife of a canon of Exeter Cathedral.

Towards the end of the eighteenth century Tiverton shared the general decline of the wool trade, but was relieved by the arrival of John Heathcoat, son of a Derbyshire farmer, who became a lace manufacturer at Loughborough. When the Luddites destroyed his machines, Heathcoat settled at Tiverton, and opened a lace mill there in 1816, powered by the bobbin machine which he had lately invented. The machine's waterwheel, weighing eighty tons, was hauled from Manchester by sixty horses, an epic of Regency transport—and of craftsmanship also, for the wheel worked seventy-two years without a single breakdown.

The best parts of Tiverton—the old parts—reflect the golden glory of its fleece, and the prosperous piety of its merchants. Look at the church of St. Peter, at its sandstone tower, tall as a Tudor merchant's credit. John Greenaway paid for that church; his statue, his brass and his tomb abide therein. Look at John Greenaway's Almshouse (1529); its cottages were rebuilt, but the chapel remains, and on it an exhortation:

Have grace, ye men, and ever pray
For the souls of John and Joan Greenaway.

Look also at the Waldron Almshouse (c. 1579), the Slee Almshouse (1610), Chilcot School (1611), founded by one of Peter Blundell's nephews. Look next at the Georgian houses in Bampton Street and in Fore Street. Look at Exeleigh, John Heathcoat's Regency villa. But first and last look at Peter Blundell's School, for it is that by which the town will be remembered, not only on Exmoor but also throughout the English-speaking world. Even the mercenary Defoe was amazed: "the beauty of Tiverton" he declared, "is the Free-School, at the east entrance into the town, a noble building ... erected by one Peter Blundell. ..."

Peter Blundell, the son of a poor man, started his career as errand boy for a kersey-maker. By saving a penny here and there, he bought one roll of cloth, and asked a trader to sell it for him in London. From that small beginning his energy and skill ended among riches which he bequeathed to his nephews, having given away a fortune while he lived. He left money to Bridewell and to several other London hospitals; to the City of Exeter ("to be lent to poor artificers"); to Tiverton church ("for poor maiden's marriages"); to Oxford and Cambridge (for the use of needy scholars); and to divers other persons ("carriers, innkeepers, tuckers, and such as had been assistant to him in the way of his trade"). Finally, he practised the preaching of William of Wykham which he delighted to quote: "Though I am not myself a scholar, I will be the means of making more scholars than any scholar in England."

It was on 9th June 1599 that Peter Blundell, wool merchant of Tiverton, made his will, in which he endowed a school for his native town: "In the said school," he decreed, "shall not be taught above the number of 150 scholars at any one time . . . none above eighteen or under six. . . ." The executor of the will was Sir John Popham, Lord Chief Justice of England. Completed in 1604, Blundell's soon became the chief school of the South-west. Its most eminent Old Boy, the author of *Lorna Doone*, sprinkled his gratitude throughout that novel, making the hero, Jan Ridd, an earlier Old Boy, able to construe Tacitus as manfully as he confounded the Doones. The book describes a custom concerning Peter Blundell's initials, which were marked by white pebbles "in the very front of the gate, just without the archway". If the river flooded, and lapped those initials, any pupil was permitted "to rush into the great schoolroom, where a score of masters sat heavily, shouting at the top of his voice 'P.B.' " Hearing him, the entire school hurried out to watch the ablution of their founder's name. Another custom, now obsolete, occurred on Oak Apple Day, when the Upper School was decorated with oak boughs (by courtesy, but not always by consent, of neighbouring farmers). At eleven o'clock, the headmaster being then at his desk, each boy in turn recited a poem of not less than twenty lines; which must have sharpened the headmaster's taste for prose and tarnished his devotion to the Stuarts.

From its foundation until the late nineteenth century the school was classical, and severely so. Archbishop Temple, himself an Old Boy, remembered his set books for the spring of 1838: "Herodotus viii. 133-144 and lx. 1-85. Euripides *Alcestis*, Cicero

Oratio in Catalinam i-iv. and Lucretius i-iii." Holiday tasks justified their self-contradictory name. In 1838 more than one Exmoor youth, gazing perhaps from a farmhouse at Molland, or basking in sunlight at Heddon's Mouth, returned wearily to composing eighteen lines of a Greek ode on *Herculis laudes*, followed by seventy lines of Latin hexameters, in praise of Columbus. *Cujus regio ejus religio*: in Jan Ridd's realm, as in Blackmore's, it was still possible for an educated man to regard science and sums as dust and ashes.

Peter Blundell never saw his school, for he died in 1601, at the age of 80, three years before the first scholars had assembled; but the old building (now private houses) still stands near the bridge across the River Lowman. Its timbers, they say, came from ships of the Armada. An inscription above the doorway recalls "the free grammar school founded at the only cost and charge of Mr. Peter Blundell of this town, sometime a clothier". The new premises, away on the Taunton road, are Victorian (1880–82) but not therefore unpleasing.

As in Barnstaple, so at Tiverton; lorries, offices, factories, super-stores, suburbs. You must arrive either early or late if you would admire those parts of Tiverton that are worth seeing.

Our fourth town, Lynton, is my nearest town. Some people find it a plain place; to others it seems ugly; but none denies the splendour of its setting. When you look down on Lynton, from Barbrook Road, the town appears to lie in a combe beside the sea; but when you look up at it, from Lynmouth harbour, it appears to cling from a cliff above the sea. Lynton's setting is Lynton's name, the *tun* on the *lilynn* or torrent. Strictly speaking, Lynton bestrides two torrents, for the River Lyn has both arms, East and West. With Lynmouth, the town forms an urban district; but hill and harbour remain as they always were, self-consciously separate. Not even Parliament can join what Time and Space have set asunder.

The beginnings of Lynton started very early. At Castle Rock, for example, is a prehistoric pound; and traces of hut circles exist in the Valley of Rocks; but in that valley every man-made object is dwarfed by the rocks themselves, which carve an airy gorge, crowned by impossible castles. In 1806 the population of Lynton was 400; in 1601 it was 403; in 1801 it was 481; in 1961 it was still less than 2,000. Statistically, therefore, the history of Lynton appears to have been placid. The villagers went their own way, unruffled by wars, and not greatly troubled by the rumours thereof. Red Rose and White, Canterbury and Rome, Cavalier and Roundhead—these passed by, on the other side of the moor, or across the water. Pirates may have arrived, and sometimes a Welshman trying to borrow his fare to Barry; but the talk at Lynton was chiefly of sheep, and at Lynmouth of ships (despite Thomas Westcote's opinion of that harbour as "unworthy the name of haven, only a little inlet").

Except during part of the seventeenth century, Lynton lacked a resident squire; throughout most of the eighteenth-century it lacked a resident rector. One inn served both villages. During the nineteenth-century, however, when Napoleon placed an embargo on continental holidays, Lynton was discovered by tourists. In 1807 the first hotel was opened. Three years later a visitor built for himself an eyrie among the cliffs (in 1970 it was the Royal Castle Hotel). Then came a London banker and a Scottish peeress; and after them a man who erected Lee Abbey, which is not an abbey, but a secular residence, part Gothic, part Good Queen Bess, wholly 1850. When the abbey came of age *Murray's Guide-book* spilled some beans: "It is only a melodramatic Abbey." By that time the visitors were unable to do occasionally what the natives still achieve every day, which is to walk from Lyn-mouth to Lynton,; so a lift was built up the face of the cliff, blessed and financed by George Newnes, who got a baronetcy for business. The policeman once told me that in 1908 this railway was enlarged. He may have been right. I feel no strong aversion from the thing. It widens the adventures of the very young and of the very old. But it does not justify the pages of historiography which guidebooks bestow upon it. A worthier candidate is the little museum and its exhibits of Exmoor past and present.

From Lynton came the impetus which built a miniature rail-way north-west across the moor to Barnstaple. The first train departed on 11th May 1898; the last arrived on 29th September 1935. Fifteen years passed before the company paid a dividend, which was ½ per cent. Alas, I never rode on this line, though I often follow the ghosts of its sleepers to Snapper Halt, Parra-combe Halt (alight here for The Haven), and Woody Bay. What a land-and-seascape that railway traversed: Chapman Barrows, the Chains, St. Petrock's church, trout streams, salmon rivers, lanefuls of rhododendrons, and the two Hangmen surging up from the sea. More beautiful than any Bluebell Line,

Exmoor's own railway still serves the imagination, and in leisurely fashion keeps time with Robert Louis Stevenson:

> Faster than fairies, faster than witches,
> Bridges and houses, hedges and ditches;
> And charging along like troops in a battle,
> All through the meadows the horses and cattle . . .

Lynton today is a Victorian-Edwardian town, in August replete, yet never repulsive. True, the Roman Catholic church and convent (1910) are not good to look upon; and a classicist will flinch from the town hall (1898) despite my own fondness for its turreted timbers. The parish church of St. Mary, perching on a knoll above the sea, was well-restored a century ago. The best view of it, from a steep and narrow alley, has been blocked by a telephone kiosk. The church itself contains a memorial to Hugh Wichelhalse of Ley (i.e. Lee), who died on Christmas Eve 1655, and rose again, not only (as we trust) in Heaven, but also in the pages of *Lorna Doone*, where he became Baron de Whichehalse, "a white-haired man, of very noble presence, with friendly blue eyes, and sweet smooth forehead". The Whichehalse family were squires of Lynton. According to tradition, which Blackmore accepted, the first De Whichehalse came from Holland, "where he had been a great nobleman, some hundred and fifty years agone . . . . Being persecuted for his religion, when the Spanish power was everything, he fled to England with all that he could save, and bought large estates in Devonshire." There seems no doubt that the Wichehalse manor house stood on, or very near to, the site of the present Lee Abbey. Jan Ridd certainly knew the way thither: "We rode by way of Brendon town, Illford Bridge, and Babrook, to avoid the great hill above Lynton . . . When we arrived at Ley Manor, we were shown very civilly into the hall, and refreshed with good ale, and collared head, and the back of a Christmas pudding."

Lynton, indeed, is a feature of *Lorna Doone*, for the Valley of Rocks was the winter home of Maple Durham alias Mother Melldrum ("a certain wise woman, well known all over Exmoor", who occupied "a queer old pile of rock . . . called 'The Devil's Cheese-Ring' ".

Lynton's main street contains enough shops to create the substance of a town without destroying the spirit of a village. Among them I divide my custom, so that their welcome is multiplied, and, should a gale blow, I can shelter in any of two bakers, three tobacconists, four grocers. At such moments Lynton recovers an iota of the seclusion which it enjoyed in 1799, when Robert Southey, walking thither with Coleridge from the Quantocks, halted at Porlock, and gazed toward Devon: "This place," he reported, "is in the neighbourhood called 'The End of the World'." Gazing westward to the Devon border, he remarked: "All beyond is inaccessible to carriage or even cart. A sort of sledge is used by the country people. . . ." Time has not marred the coast which Southey followed: "We walked for miles and miles on dark brown heaths . . . with the Welsh hills beyond, and at times descended into little sheltered valleys."

On 16th October 1816 Lynton witnessed the stamina of Exmoor's men and ponies, when Dr. Collyns, having attended several patients before breakfast, rode from Dulverton to a meet of the staghounds at Burridge Wood, whence they chased, their quarry to Lynton. After the kill, Dr. Collyns mounted a second horse, and trotted home twenty-six miles to dinner, which must have been a good one because, on a third horse, he proceeded for another twenty-six miles, to Exeter, arriving there at ten o'clock at night, in time to take his fiancée to a ball.

Down by the sea, Lynmouth harbour supplied the district with several necessities. Here came two small smacks, *John and William* (1858) and *Argo* (1869), carrying coal that was winched by hand, basket after basket, into carts whose ways were one-in-four. Here, too, came Shelley, living stylishly in a rented house and composing revolutionary pamphlets which he launched in bottles on the Severn Sea, hoping that they would be read by beachcombers at Barry or Porlock, as they very probably were, but with disappointed blasphemy because, instead of decanting a bank note, the comber found this:

> Vessels of heavenly medicine! may the breeze
> Auspicious waft your dark green forms to shore. . . .

In 1952 Shelley's cottage was swept away, and many other houses beside, by 300 million gallons of rain that fell on the Chains within five hours. Despite its absence, Shelley's Cottage remains the name of a Lynmouth hotel.

A second absent friend is the herring fleet which Thomas Westcote described, saying that Lynmouth was a place which, in these last times, God hath plentifully stored with herrings (the king of fishes), which, shunning their ancient places of repair in Ireland, come hither abundantly in shoals, offering themselves (as I may say) to the fishers' nets, who soon resorted hither with divers merchants and so, for five or six years, continued to the great benefit and good of the country, until the parson taxed the poor fishermen for extraordinary unusual tithes, and then (as the inhabitants report) the fish suddenly clean left the coast. . . .

The inhabitants, no doubt, fell into a fallacious *post hoc ergo propter hoc*. Even so, the fish continued erratic. From 1747 until 1787 they scarcely supplied a living to the boats; but in 1811, while the people were celebrating Christmas Day at church, so great a shoal was sighted that the congregation dispersed forthwith, and had only to catch the fish as they entered the weirs. The vagaries of fish were explained by Jan Ridd's Lynmouth friend, Mr. Watcombe, a seafarer: "This old Will Watcombe (who dwelt by the water) said that our strange winter arose from a thing he called the 'Gulf Stream' rushing up channel suddenly. He said it was hot water, almost fit for a man to shave with, and it threw all our cold water out, and ruined the fish and the spawning-time. . . ." Jan Ridd's brother-in-law Jeremy Stickles, arrived to "see the levying of poundage in the little haven of Lynmouth . . . which was now become a place of resort for the folk whom we call smugglers, that is to say, who land their goods without regard to King's revenue, as by law established".

Except during August, Lynmouth is likeable. Not even the car-parkers can impair the majesty of its setting at the foot of cliffs. Southey ranked it high indeed: "the finest spot, except Cintra and Arrabida, that I ever saw".

Toward our fifth and last town, Bampton, I feel an especial fondness, though the place itself cannot vie with the beauty of Dunster, nor the history of Tiverton, nor the commerce of Barnstaple. Why, then, do I favour it? My reasons are simple and brief. During the reign of George II a Devon parson, the Reverend Bartholomew Davey, MA, of Blundell's and Balliol, begat a son who, like the father, was named Bartholomew, and from Blundell's went up to Balliol, but with this difference, that he proceeded thence to King's College, Cambridge, so acquiring both a light and a dark degree. In due season, after a properly perspicacious glance at the neighbouring gentry, he married an heiress, Jane, one of the Govetts of Tiverton. In 1785 he was appointed vicar of Bampton, and served there until his death, half a century later. On account of his longevity, he was—and still is—known as Old Bart Davey, whom his flock esteemed because he tended them as a good shepherd ought, and kept a fine cellar, and rode to hounds. This Exmoor parson was my great-great-grandfather.

Bampton is a place that can be simultaneously by-passed and entered. If, for example, you are bound for Taunton, your road will miss the best part of the town, a street of Georgian houses, curving slightly, like the High at Oxford, which enhances the vista by foreshortening it with an aura of surprise. These houses were built for the lawyers and doctors who waxed with the farmers and merchants. No doubt a retired yeoman lived there, next door to three spinsters from a manor house.

Bampton church is large, having a spacious churchyard and vicarage. The west tower is thirteenth century; the chancel, fourteenth; the nave, fifteenth; the pulpit and wagon-roofs, sixteenth. According to my great-great-grandfather, the memorials to Sir John Bourchier and the Earl of Bath used to stand in the chancel, but were removed and then used to line the wall. On 9th July 1536 Sir John Bourchier's will stated that he wished to be buried alongside his father in Bampton church. A century later, two other men achieved a similar union: "the body of Arthur, sone of John Bowbeare of this town, yeoman, who departed this life 17 day of December Anno Do, 1675" and "ye body of John, sone of John Bowbeare of this town, yeoman, who departed this life the 12 day of May Anno Domi 1676". Old Bart Davey's church still keeps the twin yew trees that greeted him when he arrived for his induction two hundred years ago. Each is girt with a circular stone seat, and both have received arboreal dentistry. They may have been planted during the reign of Richard III. Nearby, some village stocks suggest an old way of paying debts incurred by new delinquents.

In 1086 Bampton formed part of a royal hundred-manor, held by Walter of Douai (a mercenary in the Conqueror's army) whose second wife bore him a son, Robert. Not long afterwards Walter fell ill, and was carried to Glastonbury Abbey, where he asked to be clothed as a monk, not because he wished to take his vows, but because any man in monk's habit received free treatment at the infirmary, and prayers for his soul if the infirmary failed to heal the body. Walter's request was granted. On the very next morning, however, the patient's condition had so improved that his servants—fearing lest their kindly master might indeed become a monk—removed the habit, restored his fine clothes, and whisked him away, giving grave offence to the brethren. When at last Walter did die, he avoided Glastonbury, and was buried at St. Peter's church in Bath.

The new lord of Bampton, Robert, likewise offended the Church. The *Gesta Stephani* described him as a drunkard (*vorax vini*). Having defied King Stephen, he was commanded to admit a royal garrison into Bampton Castle. He refused, and the castle was besieged in his absence. However, it reverted to the family when Robert's daughter, Juliana, took as her second husband Warin de la Haule, on whom it had been bestowed. Juliana's son by her first husband ultimately inherited the Honour of Bampton, but no trace of his castle remains. Some people will tell you that it was destroyed by an earthquake, which seems unlikely despite the diary of a Colyton man, William Yonge, who reported:

> There were (1607) earthquakes felt in divers parts of this realm, and, namely, at Barnstaple, Tiverton, and Devonshire; also I heard it by one at Bampton . . . there was a little lake which ran by the space of certain hours, the water whereof was as blue as azure. . . . It was seen and testified by many who were eye-witnesses, and reported to me by Mr. Twistred, who dwelleth in the same parish, and felt the earthquake.

There is a little railway station at Bampton, in ruins; musing as it were upon the green grave of a metal heyday. It was an offshoot from the Exe Valley Line, which had reached Tiverton in 1848, when railways were carrying the industrial revolution into the heart of rural England. Hitherto the Bampton folk had regarded Exeter as distant, and London an Ultima Thule. Now those two cities could be reached within a few hours, at any rate by well-to-do explorers. But, of course, the branch lines did not earn their living from tourists; they relied on the farmfrau who went shopping at Tiverton, on the seedsman who went selling at Barnstaple, and on the merchandise moving to and fro—a prize bull from Dunster, book-shelves for the vicarage, all the tinware and perishables that roads no longer carted. When the last steam train ended its final journey, a coloured chapter was closed, and the plain one began; more efficient (whatever that may mean), more expensive, incomparably less leisurely and companionable. Here, at the Bamptons of Britain, Hodge and his wife awaited the Puffing Billy that should whirl them at thirty miles an hour through Arcady to Avalon. The grandchildren of men for whom a turnpike and the posting-house had brought news of the world, themselves spread that news—better fed, better clothed, better housed—with their serge suit, their black bonnet, their wickerwork pilgrim-basket. All of them laboured harder than our own tractors; many endured painful ailments that have long since slipped into the limbo of medical history; some died in workhouses. Yet while the sun still shone, and the birds could sing, they stood on Bampton platform, more truly gay and more profoundly thrilled by a half-day in Taunton than are the heirs who now queue for the next plane to Paris. I know, for I saw; and, having seen, I give thanks and turn away because a dehydrated diesel is monotonous to hear and not worth looking at.

Bampton has long been the centre for another and more truly native form of transport. Let us now therefore praise famous manes, those shaggy sidewhiskers of the Exmoor ponies that are bought and sold at Bampton Fair, a rubric among moorland red-letter days.

Bampton Fair claims to be the oldest in Devon. Its predecessor may have flourished long before Henry III granted to the priest and his successors a licence to do business in the chapel of St. Luke (which then stood at the north-east end of the church) on St. Luke's Day, 18th October, and for two days thereafter. This fair or market was a favourite *dies non* of Sabine Baring-Gould, who rode thither from his squarsonage at Lew Trenchard on Dartmoor. Even a Londoner, he said, would be impressed by what he saw: "Such a sight will remain in his memory, and when he gets back to town, he will have something to talk about." Baring-Gould died in 1924, not far short of his century. The fair, therefore, changed somewhat during his lifetime. In 1903 F. J. Snell, who had lived awhile at Bampton, was already bewailing its new look: "Gone is the ruined forge, with its moss-grown roof, that not so long ago adjoined the bridge. . . . Gone, too, are certain thatched cottages on the hill where buyers and sellers mostly did congregate." Gone indeed; and I, who never saw them, mourn their passing; but in their place I greet the lavatories, ambulances, pensions, and other beneficent newcomers which the smith at his ruined forge neither knew nor imagined.

Yet the Frenchman was right after all: *plus ça change, plus c'est la même chose.* The smith would still recognize Bampton Fair. Though many of them arrive by lorry, instead of careering across the moor, the ponies are much as usual. Though the farmer no longer stinks, and nowadays worries more about the Bomb that has yet to fall than about the price of wheat that used to slump, he also is much the same. Recognizable, too, under their rouge and jodhpurs, are the Colonel's lady and the postman's daughter, surprising—or perhaps not surprising—each other by the eloquence of their exhortations: "Come up, there, you son of an old shop steward!" These equine asides are interrupted by one or two public benefactors who, at financial loss to themselves (or so they affirm), will sell you a roll of linoleum or two pairs of pyjamas. Bampton Fair, however, is not a canned cacophony. Instead, you will enjoy a less dated music, the hawkers whom Christina Rossetti heard:

> Come buy, come buy:
> Apples and quinces,
> Lemons and oranges,
> Plump unpecked cherries,
> Melons and raspberries,
> Bloom-down-cheeked peaches,

Up in Westmorland, at Brough, they hold a similar though less spectacular sale of their own fell ponies, and at about the same season, whence the phrase 'Brough weather' which describes every kind of weather, from blue skies to a streetful of floods. Bampton, too, paints several self-portraits. I have heard the auctioneers bawling through shirt-sleeved sweat; and I have seen the ponies arriving so caked in mud that they might have passed for outsize St. Bernards, or some indigenous invertebrate hitherto unknown among palaeozoologists.

But ponies are not the only products, for Bampton Fair encourages the farmers to do some unofficial business in cattle and sheep. Bampton, indeed, had its own breed of sheep; and in 1772 Arthur Young received a description of it, which he published in the *Annals of Agriculture*: "The best breed in Devon, existing in the neighbourhood from time immemorial." Some thirty years later, Vancouver's *General View of Agriculture in Devon* repeated the praise: "The sheep most approved in the division of Tiverton are the Bampton notts." They seem to have resembled the

They also served: a Tiverton curio

Leicester, being white-faced, though longer in the leg. Their fleece could weigh twelve pounds. After shearing, they were driven sixty miles to Bristol. But their days were numbered. In 1855 the *Royal Agricultural Journal* said: "Like most of the old indigenous breeds of the county, the Bampton has been replaced by the improved breeds." Five years later Professor Tanner noted that "the improved Bampton rams" had been crossed with Exmoors "with the best possible success".

Ponies, however, are the principal guests at Bampton Fair; and we, their hosts, are chiefly moorfolk because few visitors are abroad so late in the year. Enjoying ourselves by enjoying one another's company, we maintain an old Exmoor custom, and, in the words of W. B. Yeats,

> . . . we find hearteners among men
> That ride upon horses.

Throughout most of the other 364 days Bampton returns to business as usual, which means farming, of all open-air routines the calmest and most agreeable.

6

Lynmouth Harbour

IX

THE PEOPLE

In his essay on Exmoor—a vague and vapid piece—Charles
Kinglsey remarked: "There is no better way of giving a living
picture of a whole county than by taking some one feature of it
as a guide, and bringing all other observations into harmony
with that original key." Before following Kingsley's good advice,
let us consider some generalities. For example, many sorts of
people live on Exmoor, and most of them either tend the land or
supply its farmfolk. Neither the climate nor the contours invite a
pensioner to settle here; more than 200 miles defend us against
weekenders from London. We have no dominant landowner—
no Dukes of Atholl or of Northumberland—though a few of the
old families do retain sizeable estates, notably the Aclands and the
Fortescues. Sheep are the principal means of livelihood; with some
cattle and a relatively small acreage of corn in the more sheltered
parts.

Ethnologically we are less dramatic than the Scottish Highlanders and the Welsh mountaineers. I doubt that there are half-
a-dozen Celtic place-names throughout the moor. Of our own
Celtic forebears we have no monuments except some burial
mounds. Many of us are descended from the Dumnonii, a tribe
occupying what is now Cornwall, Devon and part of west
Somerset. The name Devonshire first appears in a document
concerning a battle in 851. Two centuries before that the Saxons
had arrived from Dorset, to conquer and cultivate the land as far
as east Devon. The native Celts thereupon retreated onto the
moors, that were not amenable to Saxon husbandry. There,
governed by princes, they transformed twilight into a Celtic
dawn, dappled with Irish missionaries, Irish pirates and the deeds
of King Arthur, who, said Tennyson,

> Drew all their petty princedoms under him,
> Their king and head, and made a realm, and reigned.

Neither Saxon nor Roman left a lasting imprint on the heart of the moor.

The most interesting moorfolk were and still are the ancient landed families, and the farmers and their men. Let us therefore consider one of the former (the Aclands) and two of the latter (Harry and George).

First, then, the Aclands: writing in 1890, Sabine Baring-Gould, himself a Devon squire, mourned the passing of his county's gentry: "the Cornydons, Burnabys, Ellacots of Ellacot, Langfords of Langford, Calmadys, Willoughbys, Incledons—all gone, and not one of their houses remaining intact". The records justify the elegy. Thus, between 1531 and 1620 the heralds made four visitations through Devonshire, examining the claims of all armigerous families. At their final visitation the heralds found fourteen such families whose names began with the letter A; in 1900 only one of those families remained, the Aclands. Their story seems the more remarkable because the family began as an alpha, and survives as an omega.

About 900 years ago a certain Acca held a farm near Barnstaple. When he died the track to his farm was called Acca's Lane; and when the house was enlarged, the entire holding became known as Akkelane. In 1238 the property was leased by the Bishop of Exeter, at a yearly rent of 10s., to a family which, because it held Acca's land, became known as Acland. The earliest houses disappeared long ago, but on their site, in the parish of Landkey, you may see a barton (built by the Aclands c. 1480) which gave the hamlet its present name, Acland Barton. The front of the house is inscribed 1591, denoting a later enlargement. The place had a chapel above its kitchen, with oak-mullioned windows and wagon-roof. A Tudor door, studded with nails, is still in use, as though to extend Richard Church's invitation:

> Look at this ancient house; it has survived
> Three centuries of time, and human history.
> Things have grown old in it. Grandfather clocks
> Have frayed much catgut hauling down the hours,
> Pot-handles have worn smooth, and poker-knobs
> Been polished by palms long folded over breasts
> Now quiet and untroubled in the churchyard.

The several enlargements of their property prove that the Aclands waxed with the centuries, not wholly as farmers, for two Tudor members—Baldwin and his son John—married wealthy women, and the habit grew strong. In 1644 the Aclands received a baronetcy. A century later Sir Thomas Acland married Elizabeth Dyke, a Dulverton heiress. In 1771 their grandson, John Dyke Acland, married Lady Harriet Fox-Strangeways, sister to the Earl of Ilchester; wherefrom hangs a gallant story. Major John Acland was wounded and captured while leading a charge against the American rebels. His wife, who had accompanied him throughout the campaign, at once set out to find him, escorted by the regimental chaplain. Rowing up-river into enemy territory, they were challenged by a sentry, to whom the chaplain stated his mission, asking to see the rebel commander. The sentry refused, threatening to shoot them if they moved. All night the couple crouched in their open boat, thinly-clad, without food. But their courage was rewarded, for when at last the rebel commander did learn of their mission, he received them courteously, and allowed Lady Harriet to nurse her wounded husband. Alas, four years later this blend of chivalry and devotion defeated its own purpose when the Major offended one of his brother officers by praising the humane conduct of the rebels. Words followed, and after the words a duel at Bampton. Neither man was killed, but the Major caught cold in the dawn air and died within a week. His widow built Pixton House, and that was part of the Dykes' Dulverton dowry. Her daughter, Elizabeth, became the Countess of Carnarvon (whence the Carnarvon Arms Hotel on the road from Dulverton to Bampton).

Sir Thomas Dyke Acland (1752–94) was appointed Ranger of Exmoor. His prowess on the hunting field, and his splendour as a host, earned him a nickname, Prince of the West. A later Sir Thomas was up at Oxford with Gladstone, where both men took a double first in Greats. The next baronet, Sir Arthur, became Minister of Education; another, Sir Charles, was High Sheriff of Devonshire. In 1970 the Aclands held two baronetcies (1644 and 1890). Here, then, is an example of public service which, though it never reached the summit, did maintain a high level through many centuries, finding on Exmoor the fame and affection which sustained its achievements in a wider world.

And now we meet Harry and George.

No one knows exactly how old Harry is; but his younger son has a married daughter, so I set Harry himself at about 80. If his hair were black he might pass for 60. Neither wind nor worry has furrowed his cheeks, which resemble a pink apple that creases when you squeeze it. His small farm—worth perhaps £4,000 in 1940—would fetch more than £30,000 in 1970. His wife died some years ago, and now a married daughter looks in twice a week "just to see th'old chap ain't starved hisself, or put paraffin in the tea pot. Ah, and I've known him do that afore now." Harry is conservative, tolerant, steeped unbookishly in many aspects of the life of Exmoor.

At shearing time on Monday afternoon Harry looks tattered and torn. His shock of white hair flops like a pendulous question-mark, giving him the appearance of an Old English sheepdog. He wears a khaki shirt, bleached by many washdays; a pair of dung-drenched dungarees, hitched-up by green-and-violet braces; and black boots bristling with blakeys. Lorna, a border collie, keeps closer than his own shadow. They say that Harry's pipe—short-stemmed, with a metal band—was given to him by a nurse at Amiens in 1917. He must have cleaned it since then, but not often and never effectively because the bowl is so choked that only the tip of his finger-nail can press home the strips of liquorice-like shag. Though it is always in his mouth, the pipe is seldom alight.

At churchtime on Sunday morning you see a very different Harry; serge-suited, felt-hatted, white-shirted, crêpe-soled. Then, at the lychgate after the service, he will preach his own sermon, taking a text that never varies: "Some people say we'm feather-bedded down yere, but they only say it 'cause they'm feather-brained. If one of 'em would give me a fivepenny stamp I'd write to Number Ten, I would, saying Dear Sir, you'm very welcome to come down yere, round about lambing time, just afore midnight if you can manage it, when there's a foot o' snow on the tops, and Dunkery looks like a Halp. The hill subsidy wouldn't seem so big then. Not when you'd saddled up, or got th'old tractor to start, and found your ewes and any lambs if they was still alive . . . and then come 'ome and got up again without going to bed, on account of a bull has wrapped hisself round some barbed wire the lorry dropped, having delivered it three weeks late, which is to say ten days after the price had gone up."

At this point he pauses to strike a fifth match.

"Conservative or Labour, I don't see there's any difference nowadays, 'cept they both want their 'eads knocked together.

Whoever you vote for, beer goes up and the market down. I said to my old woman, only the night afore she passed on, Look, I said, if I was to run my farm the way they run this country . . . if I was to come in, week after week, year by year, and say, things is looking up . . . our losses went down again last month . . . well, I said, you wouldn't always be on at me for a fur coat. The height o' your ambition, I said, would be a crust o' bread."

George is a much younger man, still in his thirties, with a small son. He might have had a farm of his own were it not that he could never overcome his spleen at being born outside a manor house. Wherever he went he caused trouble, and no sane man would employ him. Quite literally he was sent to Coventry, to a factory there. After three months he returned home, a changed— or at any rate a changing—man: "There's only one thing them buggers ever thinks about, and that's how soon they can knock off and draw their bloody wage packet. I'm no bloody Tory, but by Christ them bastards fair made me sick. Mind 'ee, they'm all right, most of 'em, when you talk to 'em alone, but you get 'em together in a bunch and they'll believe any bloody lies the steward tells 'em. They'm that ignorant they don't know nothing 'cept about betting and the telly. 'Tis the work, I suppose, if you can call it work. Indoors all day, pulling the same bloody lever or spraying the same bloody panel. Anyhow, I stuck it three months, and then I said, Christ let's get out of yere."

George's chance came when his father-in-law, a small-holder, fell from a rick, breaking both legs. The returned native took command and worked so well that both men were able to rent more land and then to buy it. George, the capitalist, made a right-about turn: "So I said to 'en, you'm due yere at nine, I said, and off again at five. But I sweat the bloody clock round. All you do, I said, is work and draw your bloody wages, and if I can't pay 'em somebody else will. But me, I said, I got to foot the bill. I got to do the worrying. No bloody dole for me, I said. I'm only a self-employed chap. So if you can't get yere on time, for God's sake say so, and I'll do the job myself."

George meets Harry at the village inn; not every night but once a week, that being Harry's abstemious habit (neither giving nor taking, he makes one pint of cider last throughout the evening). At the village inn I meet Harry and George; not once a week but twice a year, that being my own abstemious habit (I was brought up to regard public houses as private places wherein the cottagers may speak freely, uninhibited by intruders from another world).

I like to arrive during winter, on the sort of night that deters all but the hardiest habitué. Imagine, therefore, a hearth of bright logs whose shadows flit across the low-raftered ceiling. The stone floor gleams. Behind his bar, a grey-wispy landlord rests his chin on his hands, his elbows on the counter, his feet in his slippers. Harry—the only customer—is still trying to light that pipe, but after a few succulent puffs the tobacco resumes its customary state of damp fireproofness. Harry's turn-out for the soirée is midway between Monday shearing and Sunday sermoning; to wit, tweed cap, ratcatcher coat (made-to-measure for three guineas in 1940), and a pair of khaki breeches (Army surplus) with canvas leggings and brown boots.

Reaching slowly for another unavailing match, Harry remarks: "Be no one in tonight."

"Only George," the landlord agrees.

"Ah. Settling down, that fella. Canny, too."

"Oh?"

"Talking about some sheep 'e'd in mind. Herdwicks." Harry moves to his chair by the fire. "I always thought they might do well up yere. Good fleece, good food. Ah, and they'll get a living from the snow itself, or so 'tis said, way up north in the mountains." Out in the rain a motor-cycle crackles and then, like Harry's pipe, subsides. "That'll be George."

It is; oilskinned and gumbooted. For a moment he stands on the threshold, blinking at the firelight while rain makes a puddle on the mat.

"Evening, George," says the landlord.

"God, what a night, eh?" George unsheds his armour. "I said to myself, as I was coming over the top . . . same as usual, thankee . . . 'If I don't get down off of yere', I said, 'the bloody foundations'll cave-in.' I tell 'ee, 'tis blowing a gale-and-a-half." Then he notices Harry: "You? Did 'ee come over the top?"

"Ain't no other way. Not unless I dig a tunnel, and come up from the bottom."

"Did 'ee ride yere?"

"How else?"

"One day that pony o' yours will report 'ee to the Prevention o' Cruelty."

"Leastways her don't get no punctures like that old bike."

"Any twins yet?"

This last question is addressed to a young girl, scarcely of marriageable age, who sometimes helps in the kitchen, and is now on her way home to a nearby farm. She knows that the question was meant for her, because she says at once: "More'n twins. Th'old girl's dropped a threesome."

"Never."

" 'Tis true. Dad said yesterday her was kicking up, so he went out, and there they were. Threes." She wriggles into a plastic macintosh. "Night all. Be good. Cheerbye."

George winks at the landlord: "Harry didn't offer her a lift."

"When you get to my age", says Harry, "you won't want to mix your blessings. One is enough. And there's times when even that seems extravagant."

"I 'ear they 'ad a good run this morning, down 'Awkridge way," the landlord remarks.

"You can say that again." George rolls a cigarette. "They run so bloody far th'Honourable her comes cantering up and shouts 'Which way to Wigan?' "

"Miss Heddon," says Harry, looking hard at George, "always did have a biblical turn o' phrase. Rupert was ploughing a field for her once, and he couldn't get the tractor to tick, so he starts cussing and damning. And her shouts across at 'en, 'If I 'ear any more o' that strong language, I'll knock your bloody 'ead off.' "

" 'Eard about young Tim?"

"Tim?" Harry looks up. "What's he done this time?"

"Piled his van into old Rupert's barn," says George. "Brought the whole place down."

"My, my, that's a stroke o' luck."

"Luck?"

" 'Tis for Rupert. He's been wanting a new barn ever since the lightning sizzled his old one."

George draws a chair beside Harry at the hearth. A long silence sets in. The landlord ends it: "I 'ear the Black Anchor's getting up a new darts team. All women."

"Women?" Harry's toleration frowns. "There ain't no privacy left nowadays. Not for a man, there ain't. Not unless he goes and locks hisself in the doubleyou."

George has been married just long enough not to object.

"How," asks the landlord, "is Ted's daughter these days?"

"Last I heard," says George, "she was getting a divorce."

Harry shakes his head, smiling hopelessly: "I do sometimes wonder," he muses, "what my old woman would have said if I'd come in and announced I was planning a divorce." Again the head shakes. "I'll tell 'ee one thing. I wouldn't 'ave got no supper that night." He gazes at another spent match: "Foxes me why some of 'em ever do bother to get married."

"Never mind," says the landlord, on his way to the kitchen. "One day there'll be divorce on the Free 'Ealth Scheme."

The pause returns. Then George remarks: "You'm the most expensive non-smoker I've ever met."

"Me?"

"That bloody pipe o' yours. I've never seen 'en without 'tis stuffed with dead matches."

"I've 'ad this pipe a long time."

"Strewth, I can see that from yere. And smell it."

"French briar, this." Harry sighs. "Wonder if she's still alive?"

"That nurse? She'll be a big girl if she is."

Again the pause returns, which Harry ends: "How's the new dog shaping?"

"Lassie? Her's coming along real good. 'Fact, a fella up Bampton way offered me thirty quid."

"Did 'ee take it?"

"I've put more'n thirty quid o' man hours into training Lassie. 'Sides, the kid's fond of 'en. 'Course, she's only a kid herself yet, but I reckon another year'll make 'en a real old serpent. By the way, there's a horse running at Pontefract."

Harry smiles: "Have 'ee ever seen a bookmaker cycling to work? No, my sonny, and you never will. Not while there's fools enough to buy 'en a motor car."

" 'Tis only a flutter, dammit."

"I dare say. But if you flutter long enough you'll lose the price of a Red Admiral. You back a Building Society. That's my tip. You won't never find one o' them among the Also Rans."

The landlord enters with an armful of logs. George walks to the bar: "Make it a half this time. I got to start backing a bloody Building Society." He quizzes the counter: "Strewth, you got your decimals up early."

The landlord shrugs his shoulders: "Don't see it'll cause all that difference. They'll just take a quid and cut 'en into little French pieces to make 'em look bigger."

"Next thing," Harry mutters, "there'll be a law against

speaking English." He halts, surprised to find that his pipe is drawing. He takes six puffs before it expires. Then he looks at the landlord: "You'm old enough to remember."

"Remember what?"

"That day we all went t'Ilfracombe, to see the warships sail by." Now he looks at George. "We were a nation then. Full o' faults, maybe, but still a nation. What are we now?" Again he is surprised, this time by his own thoughts. "And yet, you know, I remember my old Dad saying 'zactly the same to me. 'You youngsters,' he said, 'you don't know what a day's work is.' ""

Still sore from his recent conversion to reality, George shakes his head: "The pendulum's swung too far, old fella, and now it's knocked us silly." He takes his half-pint. " 'Cause 'tis silly . . . 'tis bloody silly . . . when factory kids ride around in new cars, and fellas on strike take a holiday in Spain. I never did. My Dad never did." He drinks deep. "And I'm bloody certain neither o' you ever did."

And so it goes on, night after night, year in year out; the immemorial wisdom of mankind, the age-old folly and spleen of mankind, leavened with companionship and good humour.

THE PONIES

It was a roistering January morning when I arrived, and still dark. Away on the heights even the stunted grass crouched under a wind blowing north-west from the sea. But in the stables the world was warm and still, lulled by a rhythm of champing jaws and tinkling bridle. Last night's storm having severed the electricity, I slung a hurricane lamp from the rafters.

My pony—or, rather, the farmer's pony—was not a hard-mouthed hack. He carried only the farmer himself, or his daughter, or a privileged visitor. In other words, he was waiting for work, not weary of it. When I patted his haunches, to turn him about in the stall, he breasted the lower door and was eager to be away. I had already mounted when the farmer appeared with a cup of tea.

"Missus says you'll need it. 'Tis fair blowing up there." It was indeed, so we lingered awhile, discussing the best route for a damp day. Then, with a cluck and a heeltap. I moved off, across clattering cobbles, on to the quieter lane, and thence to a muffled moor.

It was light now, with wisps of blue between the grey. Astern, the sea shone palely; ahead, segments of skyline interlocked among treeless arcs. No need to use a switch; it was enough to wait until the pony felt the moor under his feet, and at that very moment to inform him who was steersman on the voyage.

Now if you ride the moor regularly, you can sit back while the armchair rocks you awake; but if, like myself, you ride it irregularly, you must become your own look-out, trying to foresee when the pony may swerve or stumble. But first and last you must grip with the knees and never relax. Mile after mile you go, spurred-on by a wind and the thudding hooves. It is a right royal ride indeed, and Masefield's *Right Royal* caught the very timbre of it:

The wind whirled past him, it hummed in his ears,
Right Royal's excitement had banished his fears,
For his blood was like singing, his stride was like cheers. . . .

Some people used to believe that Exmoor ponies began as a
distinct species of true horse; others, that they became stunted
because of the harsh climate and poor food; others, again, that
they have remained as they were in the beginning (an opinion
shared by Professor Speed of the Edinburgh Veterinary College).
Certainly the Exon Domesday mentions "seven wild horses" in
what is now the parish of Carhampton; and in 1598 the Court of
Chancery heard a dispute concerning some Exmoor "horse-
beasts". It is remarkable that the breed survived at all, for both
commerce and warfare were demanding large and powerful
animals. To King Henry VIII it seemed that the English horse
was "now much decayed and diminished by reason that in the
Forests, chases, moors, and waste grounds, little horses and nags
of small stature and little value were suffered to pasture thereon".
The King therefore approved a Bill for the Breed of Horses,
whose second clause forbade any stallion below fifteen hands to
run on commons or moors. Horses below that height were to be
confiscated, and the rest to be rounded-up once a year in September, so that they could be slaughtered if they seemed unlikely to
develop into a "serviceable animal". We can only guess the
blend of courage and cunning whereby Exmoor continued to
breed its wild ponies.

More than a century after Henry VIII had died, Celia Fiennes
remarked on the ponies, which were still being employed as
pack-horses: "sometymes I met with half a score of horses
thus loaded, they are indeed little horses, their Canelles as
they call them . . .". The transport suited the terrain; witness
Charles Vancouver's *General View of the Agriculture of the County
of Devon* (1813), which carried a note about the roads:

As there are but few wheeled carriages to pass along them, the
channel for the water, and the path for the pack-horse, are equally
in the middle of the way . . . which is altogether occupied by
an assembly of such large and loose stones only, as the force of
the descending torrents have not been able to sweep away or
remove.

The ponies were taken for granted and passed over without
remark. Even in 1798 the reports to the Board of Agriculture

made no reference to them. Yet, as a later chapter shall show, one pony has its own memorial in an Exmoor church.

In 1818 at least 400 ponies roamed the moor, but were soon sold by auction, except for twenty that Sir Thomas Acland took to one of his farms, Old Ashway, near Winsford Hill, which F. J. Snell, writing in 1906, described as "This free and joyous expanse . . . the native heath of Sir Thomas Acland's wild Exmoor ponies, which, in their shaggy deshabille may at times be seen grazing on the rough sward, or scampering playfully over moss and ling." So, having outlived a Tudor monarch, the breed was reprieved by a Georgian baronet.

Sir Thomas himself combined business with pleasure by exporting some of the ponies, wherefrom hangs a tale of smuggling and homesickness. One of the Acland servants, John Rawle, was instructed—or, more precisely, was invited—to take a pair of ponies to the Duke of Baden across the Channel. *En route* a foal was born, which might have caused trouble because Rawle's permit was for two ponies only. However, although he could neither read nor write, Rawle outwitted the *douaniers* by smuggling the foal in a bale of hay. Foreign parts held no great attraction for this Exmoor man, who, having delivered his three charges, took thirty-nine winks, and then started for home before dawn.

Today the breed is supervised by the Exmoor Pony Society. A registered pure bred pony has to fulfil four conditions: first, its sire and dam must be entered in the society's stud book; second, the pony itself must be sound; third, it must be approved by two of the society's inspectors; fourth, it must be branded with the society's star and herd number on the near shoulder and with an individual number on the near pin. The society keeps also a register of first-cross ponies. Among the outstanding ponies of recent years I remember especially Robert Arden (1960) who took first prize at every show he visited, including the Exford Foal Class and the Ponies of Britain. During the 1960s an Exmoor pony won the Danish driving marathon; in Canada the breed is supervised by a branch of the Exmoor Pony Society.

Not every pony on the moor is an Exmoor pony. Some are conspicuously hybrid; others—even more glaring—have been crossed with Shetlands to produce midgets for very young children. How, then, can the layman recognize a pure bred Exmoor? First, I would say, by its muzzle, which is the colour of oatmeal;

then by its eyes, which are slightly hooded, like a hawk's; finally, by its short and pointed ears, whose inside is as mealy as the muzzle. The colours are bay, or brown, or dun; but no pony may show a 'blaze' or white marking. The shoulders are set back (whence the sure feet); the chest is deep and wide; the coat lacks a winter bloom, but in summer becomes hard and glossy. The maximum height for a mature stallion is twelve hands and three inches; the mares may be one inch shorter (the height of a horse is measured at the withers, along a line falling just behind the fore-leg; a hand being four-and-a-half inches). The foals—we call them suckers—weather their first year in a woolly undercoat, topped by long hairs which serve as a macintosh. The Exmoor, of course, is not the only native British pony. There are still some pure-bred specimens of the Dartmoor, New Forest, Welsh, Shetland, Highland and Fell ponies. All have kept their small stature, unlike the thoroughbred horse, which is said to have grown one inch taller every twenty-five years since 1700.

An army textbook of 1918 described the merits of an Exmoor pony: "A combination of the best points of the Hunter with the style and finish of the Hackney produces a class of weight-carrying pony which is always saleable." The commercial value of our ponies is proven by the October sale at Bampton; their endurance is self-evident to anyone who has followed the moorland packs. Our forefathers rode further and harder than we do, but there is no reason to suppose that a modern Exmoor pony would fall short of his Victorian sires. A typical day's run was recorded in the journal of Lord Ebrington for 4th September 1857:

> Found a single hind under Tomshill. Went away over Pinford Bog to the Lynton road across the Chains by Exe Head to Mole's Chamber, turned to the right over Showlsbarrow Castle by Challacombe to the Bray Covers. Beat up the water, and after crossing the next range of covers (Bratton) was finally taken in a small stream at Stoke Rivers, about four miles from Barnstaple. Only four or five at the end.

Of those four or five, two or three probably rode an Exmoor pony, and many of the others certainly rode one; yet their chase had taken them far across the moor; and at the end of the day, as at the start, some of the ponies made a twenty-mile journey.

My own journey, being more leisurely, taught me again what J. M. Synge meant when he said:

I knew the stars, the flowers, and the birds,
The grey and wintry sides of many glens,
And did but half remember human words,
In converse with the mountains, moors, and fens.

In most other parts of England it is difficult to lose sight of
man's handiwork. Farms, hedges, roads, trees, churches, pylons,
ploughland—all become your fellow-travellers. But the heart of
the moor leaves you alone. Nor need you spend all day finding
yourself. By tacking and putting-about you may within one
square mile achieve the kind of liberty which many fail to grasp
though they journeyed 600 miles seeking it. Bereft of your
telephone, your television, your car, your nationalized identity
number, your Dear Sirs, your insurance policy—even, if you are
wise, your wristwatch—naked, I say, you feel the unchanging
wind of reality. And you can see it, too, bleaching the bones of a
fox, flicking a dead crow's feather. City streets are cleansed of
such evidence, but on the moor you perceive whence you have
come and whither you must go. And yet you smile because,
although you feel no urge to fly to the moon, you do exult in
your ability not only to ride a horse but also—insofar as you ride
him well—to become as a horse . . . supple, strong, carefree, and
with no more fear than is required to live another day and to
sleep a tranquil night.

Any fool can drive a machine, if he is clever enough; but deep
indeed is the wisdom whose hands will calm an animal, and whose
silence speaks the language of the birds. That wisdom is being
thrown away; has been thrown away. Men launch a liner or
destroy a city by pressing the button; but the sun is no longer their
clock, nor a star their compass. The bank manager says that men
have grown rich by the loss; but a doctor, having examined their
livers and their hearts, disagrees. Either because he does not
possess, or has abused, a measure of choice, industrial man
imposes on himself a rigid either-or. He must either live like
an animal or behave like a robot. It seems never to occur
to him that the best of both those worlds may lie within his
reach.

When you have reined at last, after chasing the skyline, your
pony seems glad to amble, as though he too is possessed by the
beauty of things so old that, as de la Mare confessed, we cannot
trace their lineage:

Very old are the woods:
And the buds that break
Out of the brier's boughs,
When March winds wake,
So old with their beauty are—
Oh, no man knows
Through what wild centuries
Roves back the rose.

Now the silence of the heather gives way to the clopping lane and a clattering courtyard. Whinnied home by stable mates, the pony makes for his stall.

"Did 'ee have a good ride?" The farmer is there already, with fodder and a bucket of water. "I wish I'd been with 'ee. All I done . . . whoa up, there . . . all I done is fill-in a bookful o' written questions. Next thing . . . no, you'm not going to have that water yet . . . next thing, we'll be having to write to London, t'ask if we can milk our cow 'cause the milkman's on strike. Anyway, you'm hungry no doubt? Well, the missus has summat ready."

She had indeed; and while it was being served I relaxed by a beech-and-peat fire. The farmhouse breakfast was manna from Exmoor. If anyone thinks otherwise, let him digest the evidence of Llewelyn Powys, a Dorset man and proud of it, who likewise was not sent hungry away: "A deep dish of Devonshire cream, and a loaf of brown bread, with lightly boiled eggs, were set before us on a lamp-lit, tea-laid table in a room smelling of the peat fire glowing red on the open hearth. . . ."

The drive home (degenerate times) was a bliss of slow-gear dawdling while I reflected how little the motorists can learn of a land which the horseman rides by heart. Once in the saddle, he recognizes the swamps and the rock-falls, even as shepherds name their anonymous sheep. His saddle overlooks hedges and banks; his nostrils detect all manner of vagrant scents; and instead of submitting the lonely progress to a machine, he shares it companionably with a creature whose senses supplement his own.

Georgian houses, Bampton

XI

AUTUMN

The two arcs of Exmoor are a brown study open to the air. The bracken on them glows like a chestnut in the fire of a sea-blue sky. Even the leaden scree responds to the sun, and sheep wander as though they were mushrooms that sprang up every ten seconds. The river has been so rinsed by wind and rain that it glistens as never before since April. Walking beside it, I follow a leaf while it falls from the calendar into the water and then like a ship goes down to the sea. Sometimes the leaf finds a fairway with a following wind. Sometimes it veers close-hauled on minnowing tacks. Sometimes it enters a Sargasso of fleece and grass and the hulks of other leaves. There I write it off as a total loss . . . until it breaks free and overtakes me, full-sail in mid-stream, swirling among rapids on the brink of a waterfall. Again I lose sight of it; again it sweeps alongside, grazing a pebble, stunned by a rock, yet recovering and proceeding. If I am patient as well as watchful, I may observe the leaf as it joins the sea. At first the waves repulse it, but presently one eddy recedes, and then another and after it a third, bearing the leaf with them, stately as King Arthur's funeral barge which Sir Bedivere saw:

> Down that long water opening to the deep
> Somewhere far off, pass on and on, and go
> From less to less and vanish into light.

Every part of Britain receives two autumns, but on Exmoor the differences between them are heightened by climate and altitude. The first autumn is summer writ mellow. Heather blends with broom. Discarding an August brilliance, the sky softens to a pastel shade; and instead of sailing across it, with their bellies tautened by a breeze, the white clouds ride at anchor. On a warm September afternoon the haze leads you to suppose that they are swaling the moor. Gardens outshine their own youth, as though

7

The medieval yew trees, Bampton church

June had awakened from the dream which Robert Bridges told:

> Deep in the glen's bosom
> Summer slept in the fire
> Of the odorous gorse blossom
> And hot scent of the briar.

After walking all morning through heather, you strike a lane, and suddenly the roses and asters and dahlias write Welcome on the retina, to which the woods reply, proffering a posey of berries. At the Haven the last day of September can outbid the warmest of May. Peering up at the arcs, I find it hard to believe that summer has passed away.

The visitors dwindle to a few hardy perennials, elderly like the year itself. To meet the best of them is both a pleasure and a privilege, for their news of less fortunate places sharpens one's vision of the whole. Gazing wistfully at the sea, they say: "This time yesterday we were in London," or "Tomorrow we'll be in Manchester." There is no answer to that heart-cry of a drab and sometimes sickening routine. Those of us who escaped from it, perhaps by pawning our financial security, glance briefly at the sleek car, and would not have it at that price. One novelty we never shall get used to, and that is the townsman's naïve astonishment at things which to us are a part of the natural order: the awakening each morning to beautiful surroundings and a reveille of bird-song . . . the attar of wood-smoke, the lilt of dialect . . . the daily tang and texture of the sea . . . a way home that is not upon pavements nor in buses and trains, but up steep lanes, through quiet woods, beside blue waters . . . and at the end of the day, when we bid the world goodnight, the assurance of the stars and the companionship of little streams whose lullaby confirms the boon of stillness. But the heart of the moor does not notice the visitors, neither coming nor going; it knows only such change as the seasons always have rung: the silent blackbird supplanted by chorister robins; the red deer's cold-weather coat; furrows where corn was; and the cobwebs that Andrew Young noticed:

> . . . drooped heavy and hoar
> As though with wool they had been knit . . .

In villages away from a main road, life ticks the same tock as in July. Parracombe, indeed, will seem busier on Christmas Eve than on Whit Monday; and at Heal three always have composed a crowd. The sea, too, looks much as it did during August, though a shade slower in getting up, and more inclined to retire early. Yet at teatime the sun takes on the vigour of a hale old man; the cove becomes as warm as in May; its wavelets as blue; the gulls as playful. At sundown the slates on Simonsbath church shimmer like rectangular guineas; and if you hasten to the bridge, you will discover where those coins are minted, for the Barle itself is molten gold. One swift glance from Hawkridge or from Arlington detects no change of season. If you overlook a yellowing leaf here and there, the month might be June, or July, or August. In November I have seen a foxglove flowering near Martinhoe church.

But with the end of October a second autumn appears, and its arrival was described in seamanly fashion by Quiller-Couch: "There arrives a day," he wrote, "when the wind in the mainsail suddenly takes a winter force." That is what most people mean by autumn, and what they most dread. *Autumnis gravis* Horace called it, "dreaded autumn". Passing a graveyard of gardens at Timberscombe, I catch an echo from W. H. Davies:

> Is this old Autumn standing here,
> Where wind-blown fruits decay,
> Dressed up in limp bedraggled flowers
> That summer cast away?

Squelching through mud beside an invisible Pinkworthy, I catch another echo, from Robert Burton: "Of all seasons of the year, autumn is the most melancholy." Yet the same writer, and in the same book, reached the heart of the matter: "If there be a hell upon earth, it is to be found in a melancholy man's heart." Doubtful of Heaven, unable even to imagine it, and forgetful that death may be its gateway, we project onto autumn the fear which it arouses in us. For me the falling leaf tolls. I am the aging acres.

In gentle country the second autumn remains gently mournful. But on Exmoor, rugged and untamed, the mood grows masterful. After many days of rain, the moor seeps and is soggy. The footpath to Culbone has become impassable unless you are willing to ooze calf-deep in mud. Nor need you reach the Chains in order to court danger. Within fifty yards of the road from Challacombe to Simonsbath there are bogs that would engulf a sheep. Like Wenlock Edge, Dunkery Hill is in trouble when October meets November. And the trouble grows more tumultuous as you approach the sea. Whipped by a gale, the breakers snarl, baring their fangs while they attack the cove. Far out to sea the white horses follow their leader through grey furrows. Small ships plunge. Even a laden tanker dips and then shies upward from the spray.

But we are accustomed to such things. We relish them, and exult in their contemporaries, for this is the season of fairs and shows; a time for hunting, shooting and the taking of whatever fish or game are in their season. Incense arises from chimneys; and some of us could say whether the logs were beech, or cherry, or oak. Such are the pleasures which James Thomson had in mind as he enjoyed himself

> While autumn, nodding o'er the yellow plain,
> Comes jovial on.

You cannot learn Exmoor via a correspondence course. You must live there, not for a week or so nor a month or two, but over the years and throughout the seasons. Anything less than that, perceives less than the whole. Books will dig up the past, and holidays dibble the present, but it is only Gilbert White's "stationary men" who come full-circle to fruition. I can be absent for a fortnight, and then collect the threads unbroken; but whenever I return after more than three weeks, I find the threads beyond repair. So it is with autumn; unless I watch them day by day, the leaves elude me and are dead and buried without an obituary.

Autumn's second arrival creates a paradox. Standing above the Haven, overlooking the sea, the woods, the river, the bracken, I am one with Sir Walter Scott among his ain folk:

> Land of brown heaths and shaggy wood,
> Land of the mountains and the flood,
> Land of my sires!

Here, you would think, is autumn stripped of tinsel, bare to the bone. The very air is autumn, keen from a cold and cleansing sieve. Not for one instant could you mistake it for late summer or early winter. This is autumn *par excellence*, the autumn of autumn.

Yet the sharpest contrasts are found not upon the heights, but in the towns and along the roads that link them. Barnstaple becomes audible, having ceased somewhat to shout. At South Molton it is the same. Dunster, Dulverton, Bampton, Minehead; all return as it were to the fold, and you are invited to share the companionable solitude. Says the Porlock tobacconist: "I couldn't live August twelve times a year." Says the Minehead butcher: "I'm in no hurry, midear. Tisn't summer now. I've time to talk as well as speak." Says the Combe Martin grocer: "I wonder why some of 'em bother to come down yere. They only sit in the car all day, or lounge around the pubs, or go grousing 'cause there's no cinema." Says the farmer's cream tea wife: "I don't want to sound uncharitable, mind. They've a right to their holiday, same as anyone else. But Lord, Lord, am I glad to see their backsides."

By courtesy of those backsides, I can drive to Barnstaple, the better part of twenty miles, without meeting above five break-fast-time vehicles. I can walk the six steep miles to Combe Martin without meeting any vehicle at all until I reach the garage there. And on the finest coast road in Britain, between Porlock and Lynmouth, I can hear a car one mile before I see it. Dunkery becomes my own property; I wander there all day without sighting another November traveller. Malmsmead, that commercial mêlée, resumes its ancient status as a house on its own by a bridge. Porlock Weir falls so silent that I have entered the inn expressly to discover whether it were still occupied. Even Dunster is pleasant, for that too belongs to the people who dwell thereabouts.

From its hill in a seaside combe the Haven enjoys the mildest weather on the North Devon Coast; but if I climb either of its two arcs, I encounter the wildest weather. Not Dunkery itself so shrieks and shudders when a gale bruises it. For the dirtiest weather I visit the Somerset Moor, with Mole's Chamber and the Chains as its vortex. There the rain falls as it never does fall at the Haven. There a mist will linger while the cove wraps itself in shreds of sunshine. There come the blizzards; there the ice and the mist and the raw edge of invisible dawns; the whole of Thomson's inclement quartet:

> Hail, rain, and snow, and bitter-breathing frost.

Those variations become most noticeable near the sea. I have left the Haven in sunlight, have climbed 500 yards into a land mist, re-entered sunlight, and emerged therefrom into a sea mist beyond Caffins; but having reached Lynmouth, I found the harbour lapped by a blue sea, and Countisbury Hill swathed in a grey fog 300 yards from the jetty. I know of one elderly couple— November visitors to a moorland farm—who daily telephone their near-neighbours for a weather report. Where the sun shines, thither they seek it; and when none is to be found, they walk waterproofed by their own serenity. Yet it would be wrong to imply that our autumns are less mellow than elsewhere. November's Martinmas will mimic spring, and from our heavy rainfall we reap a harvest greener than in any other county south of Westmorland. At the foot of the track to Trentishoe there is a cottage where roses greet December, and the marigolds see a new year in.

The rough therefore braces the smooth, and is softened by it. Monday may bring such mist that the two arcs disappear as though by some calamity. Tuesday returns them, etched against a willow-pattern sky. Wednesday bends the buds on next year's hydrangea. Thursday coaxes the robin to sing a song of sunpence. Friday comes cold. Saturday shines again. And Sunday calls the faithful through the mud.

Amid all those alterations the moor's metabolism proceeds unhurried. Day by day I watch a calf plumping in the meadow alongside Joyce's cottage atop the hill; day by day the Highland cattle prosper by the Chains. Every night adds meat and fleece to the ewes on Withypool Common; every night deepens the strength of sleeping sap which, when it does wake, will arise indeed, not only summoning up remembrance of things past, but also raising the past itself, onto a green throne, decked with blossom.

All this is known to the stream beyond my window, or would seem to be known, for the stream sings on, ever the same yet always with a new song, as though Blake's miracle were repeated, whereby the water was changed into music:

> And I made a rural pen,
> And I stain'd the water clear,
> And I wrote my happy songs
> Every child may joy to hear.

Watching it between the high banks, and striving to parse its syntax, I regard the stream as a poet who combines the practice of Blake with the precept of Ruskin: "Originality in poetry does not depend on invention of new measures . . . A man who has the gift, will take up any style . . . and make everything that he does in it look as fresh as if every thought of it had just come down from heaven."

XII

THE SOMERSET VILLAGES

There are scores of villages within the National Park, and many
hamlets or clusters of cottage and farm. Beyond the park, along
its perimeter, many hamlets and villages either overlook the moor
or have in some other way become associated with it. But this,
after all, is a portrait, not a panorama. Therefore we shall go the
rounds or, as the mediaeval foresters would have said, make a
perambulation; visiting the places which, in my opinion, occupy
the upper storey of a long list. Our perambulation starts from
the north-east, continues along the coast to the Devon border
near Oare, bears south through the heart of the moor, and thence
swings north again. In other words, the villages will appear in
topographical order, as follows: Watchet, Porlock, Oare, Simonsbath, Exford, Withypool, Winsford, Hawkridge, Timberscombe,
Selworthy. *En route* we shall glance at some of the others, Stoke
Pero and Luccombe among them.

Lorna Doone's mother, you remember, was buried at Watchet,
but the place itself has a less tenuous link with Exmoor because
the little harbour fetched and carried a great deal of moorland
trade. Small ships still call there, chiefly to supply a factory.
The quay remains agreeably unspoiled; and from it, in 1798,
Coleridge launched his *Ancient Mariner*:

> The ship was sheered, the harbour cleared,
> And merrily did we drop
> Below the kirk, below the hill,
> Below the lighthouse top.

But Watchet did not pass therefrom into an ocean of prose. On
the contrary, it helped to perpetuate poetry, in the person of an
old seaman, John Short, who died in 1933, at the age of 95. By
happy chance Cecil Sharp came to Watchet, collecting the remains of English folk songs. Although Short was already very

old, he remembered and sang fifty-seven songs, which Sharp copied and afterwards published—forty-three of them—in his *English Folk Chanteys*. How sad, that a nation should turn from its heritage of song-and-dance, to follow alien leaders through a spurious Wild West, a waggling jungle, a Tin-Pan Alley. This national loss was recorded by an earlier collector, Sabine Baring-Gould, whose *Songs of the West* included an old minstrel's nostalgia:

> I reckon the days is departed
> When folks 'ud 'a listened to me;
> I feels like as one broken-hearted,
> A-thinking o' what used to be.
> And I dun' know as much is amended
> Than was in them merry old times,
> When, wi' pipes and good ale, folks attended
> To me and my purty old rhymes,
> To me and my purty old rhymes.

Each generation must create its own "purty old rhymes", yet one says again, how sad that England seldom sings its own songs, and never composes any.

Watchet church is dedicated to Decuman, one of those myriad Celts whose deeds caused Cardinal Newman to remark that some *Lives of the Saints* revealed "all, and more than all, that is known about them". Decuman, they say, arrived from Wales on a raft, succoured by his shipmate, a cow. Having been washed ashore at Watchet, he resided there until the natives beheaded him while he was praying. His statue may be seen in a niche on the south face of the church. Inside the church several brasses recall the Wyndham family, one of whom received a command from Charles I via "the ranger of our Forest of Exmore", stating "Our will and pleasure is that you deliver unto the berer hereof one fatt stagg of this season and for soe dooing this shall be your sifficient warrant. . . ." It was a Colonel Wyndham who held Dunster Castle when the Prince of Wales escaped thither from a Bristol plague. Some years later, when the Prince had become king, and was escaping into exile, Colonel Wyndham sheltered him at his Dorset home near Sherborne. For two weeks, disguised as a servant, the young King cooked his own meals, hiding in a secret room. After the Restoration, Wyndham stood in high favour at Court. Pepys once used the Colonel's influence to obtain a berth on board the Fleet at Erith: "So I presently on board, and got under sail, and had a good bedd by the shift, of Wyndham's."

In 1963 a newly-formed Watchet Shipping and Trading Company revived the failing harbour; seven years later the quays were exporting scrap metal, and importing chipboard, fertilizers, timber. Plans for the future, costing 3 million sterling, suggest that old Watchet will grow young and ugly.

What does one say of the next village, the *Portloc* or enclosure by a harbour? Whitewashed and thatched, and dominated by the most famous hill in England, Porlock is a place to be avoided during summer. I have sat for thirteen minutes in the narrow street while charabancs and lorries extricated themselves from the sort of mechanized mêlée which posterity will regard either with astonishment that it could ever have occurred, or with amazement that anyone could ever have regarded it as unseemly.

Set back a little from this summer pandemonium, the thirteenth century church with a wooden spire is dedicated to St. Dubricius, who is said to have crowned King Arthur. One of the rectors of Porlock was Stephen Hales (1677–1761), Vice-President of the Society of Arts (in recognition of his eminence as a philosopher) and a Fellow of the Royal Society (for his work on plant and animal physiology). Sir Francis Darwin said of him: "In first opening the way to a correct appreciation of blood-pressure Hales' work may rank second to Harvey's in founding our modern science of physiology."

Pleased by his cordial reception during a storm, Robert Southey wrote a bad sonnet at the Ship Inn, beginning:

> Porlock! I shall forget thee not,
> Here by the unwelcome summer rain confined;
> But often shall hereafter call to mind
> How here, a patient prisoner, 'twas my lot . . .

et cetera. Poor Southey; he had a large family, and, as he put it, only "one inkstand" to support them; a fact which Wordsworth acknowledged but without excusing its effect upon poetry. "Wordsworth", said De Quincey, "disliked in Southey the want of depth . . . of philosophic abstraction." However, the two poets shared the antipathy: "Southey disliked in Wordsworth the air of dogmatism."

But the most important person from Porlock was a man who merely walked through it, Samuel Taylor Coleridge, poet, philosopher, talker, drug-addict. In 1795, unhappily married, with one small son, Coleridge was given a cottage and a plot of land at Nether Stowey, by one of his patrons, Thomas Poole. There the dream-druggist indulged the same sort of fantasy that had lured him into enlisting as a cavalry trooper, alias Silas Tompkins: "I hope to live on it," he wrote, "with a pig or two, for I would rather be a self-maintaining gardener than a Milton" ... two roles which he was congenitally incapable of filling. Three years later, Coleridge went walking alone across Exmoor, and rested at a farm near Porlock, where he took drugs, and fell into deep sleep, from which he awoke with a vision. As we shall presently learn, another Exmoor traveller had a comparable experience, without drugs. Coleridge, at all events, reached for a notebook, and began to describe his dream:

> In Xanadu did Kubla Khan
> A stately pleasure-dome decree:
> Where Alph, the sacred river, ran
> Through caverns measureless to man
> Down to a sunless sea.

And so the imagery surged in spate from a drugged imagination:

> A damsel with a dulcimer
> In a vision once I saw:
> It was an Abyssinian maid,
> And on her dulcimer she played.

When Coleridge had written nearly fifty lines, a head peered round the door: "There's a person from Porlock to see you."

"What?"

"From Porlock. Says he's on business."

"Business? Porlock? But I'm in the middle of.... Oh, very well."

Scholars have analysed Coleridge's dream, discovering in it the skeins of other men's books; but no one knows what really happened when the person from Porlock at last withdrew, leaving Coleridge free to finish his poem. Alas, he never did finish it, because he never could. Having written another ten lines, he wrote no more. The vision had faded, the dulcimer was dumb. Glancing at the unfinished page, the drug-addict may have seen that its last words foretold their own finale:

> For he on honey-dew hath fed,
> And drunk the milk of Paradise.

So, a person from Porlock put the village on the map, associating it forever with "Kubla Khan: Or, a Vision in a Dream", which Coleridge described as "A Fragment"; and such it is, hovering like a moth near the peak of Parnassus.

Another drugged poet, Francis Thompson, said of himself: "Look for me in the nurseries of Heaven." Perhaps he met Coleridge there, expounding German metaphysics to an audience who listened, as they had so often listened on earth, with rapt uncomprehension. Such a meeting would seem just, for much may be forgiven the man who said:

> He prayeth best, who loveth best
> All things both great and small;
> For the dear God who loveth us,
> He made and loveth all.

A seaside lane leads from Porlock to the Weir, a haven for pleasure craft, with a beach and an old inn, and woods high above.

The road to our next village has already been described by Hazlitt. It is a switchback, having the Severn Sea and the Welsh hills on one side, and the moor on the other. Far below lie Oare and its water; *Are* being a Celtic river-name, identical with Ayr in Scotland. Jan Ridd spoke of "the little town of Oare", but the place was never more than a village, and is now a hamlet with a church standing so far apart and so high up that one wonders whether the very old folk ever managed to reach it, unless by bier. "My excellent grandfather," said R. D. Blackmore, "was parson of Oare and Combe Martin together . . . he never lived at Oare . . . but rode across the moors to give them a sermon every other Sunday. And when he became too old for that my uncle used to do it for him." Parson Blackmore sowed a rich harvest when he scattered the seed of Exmoor hearsay onto his grandson's fertile imagination; and the child afterwards acknowledged that *Lorna Doone* owed much to those legends, "some of which came from my grandfather (rector of Oare) *circa* 1790". The church contains a bust of R. D. Blackmore, benign as a whiskered Mr. Pickwick who has taken to sheep-farming. An inscription says:

> Insight and humour and the rhythmic roll
> Of antique lore his fertile fancies swayed.

In 1768 a Mary Ley married a John Red or Ridd at Oare church. Thirteen years later the manor was bequeathed by Nicholas

Snow to his youngest son, John, who, when he died without issue, left it to his nephew, Nicholas (in *Lorna Doone* the family wears an *e* after its name). One of the late-Victorian Snows kept a pack of foxhounds at Oare Manor, the famous 'Stars of the West'. Oare church has acquired a chancel since the day when Jan and Lorna were married there "with the help of Parson Bowden and the good wishes of two counties". As the ring was slipped around the bride's finger, "a shot rang out through the church."

Many people visit Oare, seeking Jan Ridd's home beside Badgworthy Water. This stream (we call it Badgery) was not named after an especially plentiful spate of badgers; Bag is very likely a corruption of the name of the man who owned it, the *worth* or place. In Norfolk, for example, there is a Bagthorpe that belonged to Bakki; in Wiltshire, a Bagshot that belonged to Beocc; in Leicestershire, a Bagworth that belonged to Bacga. The whole region is a babble of brooks—Lancombe, East Lyn, West Lyn. "Each of these", said Southey, "flows through a combe, rolling over huge stones like a long waterfall. . . ." *Lorna Doone* is steeped in Bagworthy Water. The stream itself ambles among woods, and then enters a wild solitude which Jan Ridd explored when he was a child. "It was a frightful thing . . . to venture, where no grown man durst, up the Bagworthy water." Yet the child did venture: "I thought of what my father had been, and how he told me a hundred times, never to be a coward." On, then, he went, saying to himself, "now if my father looks, he shall see that I obey him". Sometimes the boy caught a trout, and shouted with triumph: "But in answer to my shouts, there never was any sound at all, except of a rocky echo, or a scared bird hustling away . . . and the covert grew darker above me, until I thought that the fishes might have a good chance of eating me, instead of my eating the fishes." The rest is known throughout Exmoor and all over the world, for the son had indeed learned courage of the father, and when at last an excess of it landed him into such trouble that he nearly died, he recovered consciousness in the presence of "a little girl kneeling at my side, rubbing my forehead tenderly, with a dock-leaf and a handkerchief". Jan Ridd had met Lorna Doone.

A lane from Oare dives into Brendon Bottom, climbs to Oare manor house, and there joins the road to Simonsbath, over the roof of the moor. After three or four miles the solitude softens a little, and the road swoops down to Simonsbath, a hamlet that long ago abdicated as the capital of Exmoor. A guidebook of 1914 does not even mention the place. *Lorna Doone* names it only once, as the haunt of a witch whom Jan Ridd consulted, "a wise old woman of Simonsbath". Richard Jefferies reported what a villager had told him about the name of the place:

There is a pool at Simons Bath . . . in which is a small whirlpool. The stream in it does not seem of much strength; but the eddy is sufficient to carry a dog down. A long time since a man thought he could swim through the whirlpool. . . . He made the attempt, was sucked down and drowned, and hence the spot has been since known as Simons Bath. So runs the tradition in the neighbourhood, varied in details by different narrators. . . .

Bleak as the hill on which it stands, Simonsbath church was built in 1856, when squire and parson agreed that it "be named and called the parish church of Exmoor; and the said Forest shall be called by the name of The Forest of Exmoor". The first incumbent, Reverend W. H. Thornton, claimed to have ridden forty-two miles in five hours.

Below the church, at the end of a footpath, a cottage served as shop-cum-post office until 1969. Lower yet, the Exmoor Forest Hotel is relatively modern. The original inn took over Boevey's house. A shepherd assured me that in his grandfather's day the publican was forbidden to sell beer because Sir Fred Knight detested the stuff. Port, however, he approved, so he subsidized it at 3d. per glass.

The only other dwellings are Simonsbath House, which was sold in lots in 1969; a house on the hill along the Brendon road; and a few farm cottages. In 1719 the rent of Simonsbath Farm was about 2s. per acre.

Opposite the hotel a path enters a wood and then follows the Barle. For a mile or so it follows the map as well, but thereafter goes its own elusive ways. Five times I have followed that path, and always I ended on a skyline of swampy rocks overlooking a derelict cottage. It took me three years to discover that the only walkable path crosses the Barle via a bridge, and then re-crosses it without a bridge. The pleasantest part of Simonsbath lies alongside the stone bridge, where trees emphasize a bare skyline. Near the bridge a timber waterboard marks the level of the Barle, for, as Leland observed, "the water in summer most commonly runneth flat upon stones easy to be passed over, but when the rains come and storms of winter it rageth and is deep." From the bridge a road climbs nearly 1,500 feet, into a land uninhabited except by one or two isolated farms such as Horsen, standing at the end of two miles of cul-de-sac. Near the summit of this climb a cairn bears an inscription: "John William Fortescue, Historian of the British Army."

According to Holinshed the Fortescues (or Strong Shields) acquired that name when one of them protected William the Conqueror at the Battle of Hastings. During the later Middle Ages they came to Exmoor from East Somerset, where they held the manor of Croscombe. In 1299 a Fortescue was created Baron Clinton; in 1746 Lord Clinton became Earl Clinton; in 1965 the mediaeval barony of Clinton was called out of abeyance for the Trefusis family. The historian himself—the Hon. Sir John Fortescue, fifth son of the third Earl—was scholar and honorary Fellow of Trinity College, Cambridge. In 1905 he became Librarian at Windsor Castle, receiving a KCVO when he retired in 1926. I still have the copy of *The Writing of History* which my father gave to me when I was a child. Fortescue's major work was his *History of the British Army*, but at Simonsbath, where he spent much time, he is known rather for his *Records of Stag-Hunting on Exmoor*, which appeared in 1887. I was lucky enough to buy a first edition for a few shillings. The last quarter of the book will seem tedious to non-hunters. Kingsley poked gentle fun at all such narratives: "Found at A cover, held away at a slapping pace for B Barn, then turned down the C Water for a mile . . . and made for D Hill, but being headed, went by E Woods to F where he was run into after a gallant chase of G hours and H miles." The earlier chapters, however, are less specialized. For example, by pointing out that heather grows on Dunkery Hill, Fortescue challenged the theory that heather is found only on land that has been cultivated. His description of wild life on Dunkery is a mournful litany of loss during the past eighty years: "There are still rare birds and beasts to be seen there . . . polecats are also found . . . the Montagu's harrier is occasionally seen; a snowy owl was shot some few years back, and only two years ago a pelican was found walking in the North Forest." Fortescue added a military footnote to the owl's obituary: "The natives attributed his presence to the cannonading at Tel-el-Kebir!" Ravens, however, still haunt Exmoor; and in 1969 they seized several lambs from a Devon flock.

One must not overlook the foxhounds, kennelled a mile or two west of Simonsbath. There were more packs of British foxhounds in 1970 than in 1870; but as late as 1835 there were only 101 packs of English foxhounds, compared with 138 packs of harriers. Exmoor has four packs of foxhounds: West Somerset, Dulverton East, Dulverton West and Exmoor (heirs of the 'Stars of the West'). To these may be added the Minehead which, despite its green coats and the sub-title Harriers, chases the fox. The only beagling occurs when a visiting pack arrives.

Leland disliked the road from Simonsbath to Exford. He called it "a four miles all by Forest". However, he did approve the "store and breeding of young cattle" on the heights around. Exford itself has supplanted Simonsbath as the unofficial capital of the Somerset Moor. Out of season it becomes a pleasant place, but in summer the several cross-roads are louder than wasps and more dangerous. The village centre is a green, flanked by some small shops and an hotel. On all sides the hills rise up and are pastoral, watered by the Exe, which Celia Fiennes admired succinctly: "The river X is a fine streame. . . ."

Exford church was dedicated to the Celtic Saint Salvin, and rededicated to St. Mary Magdalene. In its hilltop graveyard lies Robert Baker, who gave many alms to Exford and also to his native Hawkridge. A memorial states: "He was born of honest parents, and by hard labour, increased his substance, which he readily bestowed on all occasions for the honour of God and in support of the needy."

The church has another tale to tell, starting in 1858 when St. Audries church, near Watchet, was demolished, leaving behind a fifteenth-century screen. Having lain in a barn for some twenty years, the screen was offered to Williton church, which declined. After another interval in the barn, it was accepted by the South Kensington Museum, but never displayed, because of the cost of re-assembling it. The museum tried to find a Somerset church whose measurements tallied with the screen's. After long search, Exford was chosen. The parishioners paid, in modern currency, several thousand pounds for the screen. The choir stalls were presented by Queen's College, Cambridge. A church path leads to a cottage that used to be a farm, and before that a priest's home or Prescott, which is what the villagers still call it. Certainly the parish had a resident priest eight centuries ago. The non-conformist chapel contains two stained-glass windows by

The prevailing wind
Christmas Day near Simonsbath

Burne-Jones. They were bequeathed by a Mr. Cyril Scott (who spent sometime at Exford during the 1940s) in memory of two friends, neither of whom had any associations with the village.

Lorna Doone mentions Exford several times. You may remember John Fry's story: "I wore over to Exeford in the marning . . . as I coom down the hill, I zeed a saight of volks astapping of the ro-udwai. . . . Rakon there were dree score on 'em. . . . 'Wutt be up now?' I says to Bill the Blacksmith, 'be the King acoomin?' " In 1532 one of Bill the Blacksmith's predecessors left a legacy that helped to build the south aisle of Exford church; in 1969 one of Bill's successors retired, having worked at Exford forge above thirty years.

There used to be a distillery in the village, though Exmoor's *vin de pays* was cider, a commodity that impressed Defoe: "They have so vast a quantity of fruit, and so much cyder made, that they have sent ten, or twenty thousand hogsheads of it in a year to London, and at a very reasonable rate." A century earlier, Miss Fiennes had not been impressed:

> In most parts of Sommer-setshire it is very fruitful for orchards, plenty of apples and peares, but they are not curious in their planting the best sort of fruits, which is a great pitty; being so soone produced, and such quantetyes, they are likewise careless as when they make cider, they press all sorts of apples together, else they might have as good cider as in any other parts, even as good as the Herriffordshire.

However, Miss Fiennes saw something that was visible on one or two Exmoor farms in 1970: "They pound their apples then lay fresh straw on the press, and on that a good lay of pulp of the apples, then turne in the ends of the straw over it all, and lay fresh straw, then more apples up to the top." John Philips wrote a long poem in blank verse, *Cyder*, in which he took a too-optimistic view of the prospects, declaring that cider

> Shall please all tastes, and triumph o'er the Vine. . . .

Until the middle of the nineteenth century Exford held a revel on 22nd July, the feast of St. Mary Magdalene. The chief attraction was wrestling, a sport which the English have exiled to Cornwall and Westmorland, preferring to watch professional prize-fighters who draw blood. In Jan Ridd's day, however, the Devon wrestlers rated themselves the equals of Cornishmen.

The penultimate chapter of *Lorna Doone* shows the hero

8

Fortescue Memorial, near Simonsbath

vanquishing the villain by means of a grip. Although Carver
Doone had tried to murder Jan's bride at the altar, Jan proved
himself a chivalrous enemy: "I offered him first chance. I stretched
forth my left hand, as I do to a weak antagonist. . . ." But Carver
—a cheat as well as a bully—played so foul that Jan was forced
to take him "by the throat, which is not allowed in wrestling . . .".
And then Jan gripped: "Beneath the iron of my strength—for
God that day was with me—I had him helpless in two minutes . . ."
Nor was it Jan's fault that, in the end, an Exmoor bog claimed
Carver despite the victor's mercy: "Carver Doone, thou art
beaten: own it, and thank God for it; and go thy way, and
repent thyself."

From Exford to Withypool is scarcely four miles, but the
journey takes more than an hour because the walker is all the
while glancing right and left at the heights and the combes.
Four lanes meet at Withypool, and one track. The name of the
village means 'willow-lined pool', a reference to the Barle that
flows under a bridge between grassy banks. In 1907 a guidebook
said of Withypool: "It is one of the lonely outposts of civilization
on Exmoor." There was no bad news from the BBC in those
years, no morning paper (unless yesterday's arrived with the
postman), not even a car to be seen; yet they survived, and begat
us who now suffer all those things and many more besides. But
Withypool remains remote. Everywhere the moor rings the sky,
1,000 feet above the sea. At Brightbarrows the contours reach
1,400 feet, and at Wamsbarrows more than 1,400. Our grandfathers heard a strange tale about Wamsbarrows, which some of
them believed. Once a year a midnight chariot was seen on the
summit, careering a ghostly course. No one knew why the vision
appeared, though Richard Jefferies traced its ancestry: "This idea,"
he wrote, "may be an unconscious memory of prehistoric times,
when sacrifices were made in the precincts of tumuli. They were
considered sacred, and the feeling seems to have lingered on down
to the present day." I doubt that anyone now experiences it.
Passing similiar barrows, on his native Wiltshire Downs, Siegfried
Sassoon saluted their secrets:

> These barrows of the century-darkened dead—
> Memorials of oblivion, these turfed tombs
> Of muttering ancestries whose fists, once red,
> Now burn for me beyond mysterious glooms. . . .

Withypool is a small, steep, and pleasant village, of no importance except to people who admire such places; yet it was once a notable outpost with a pound for forest stock. Near the church (restored almost beyond recognition), you will notice a shelter and a seat that were erected in memory of a local girl, Claire Norton, who was killed by a car.

So far as I remember, *Lorna Doone* mentions Withypool only once and only by way of signposting the narrative. However, something exciting happened a mile or two west of the village, at the ancient five-arched Landacre Bridge, when Jeremy Stickles rode that way:

He had only a single trooper with him, [said Jan Ridd], a man not of the militia, but of the King's army, whom Jeremy had brought from Exeter. As these two descended towards Landacre Bridge, they observed that both the Kensford Water, and the river Barle, were pouring down in mighty floods . . . so great indeed was the torrent that only the parapets of the bridge could be seen above the water, the ride on either side being covered and very deep on the hither side.

The trooper was already halfway across when a shot rang out. His misadventure is worth reading.

There was an old man hereabouts whose father grew his own tobacco, which will seem eccentric until you remember that Somerset and Devon were once the chief tobacco-growing regions of Britain. Devon, indeed, claims to have bred the pioneer smokers, Sir Francis Drake and Sir Walter Raleigh; but long before either of them could have introduced it, tobacco was mentioned as a familiar English plant, in a book by Matthias de 'l'Obel, whose eminence as a botanist is perpetuated by lobelias. Although Raleigh's own books mention tobacco only once, in the *Discoverie of the Large and Rich and Beautiful Empire of Guiana*, he did make smoking so fashionable that some of the Court ladies took to a clay pipe. King James I wrote a pamphlet against smoking, *A Counterblaste to Tobacco*, but when the weed became a source of import duties he diverted his counterblast: "James, by the Grace of God etc., to our right Trusty and right Wellbeloved Cousin and Counsellor, Thomas, Earl of Dorset, our High Treasurer of England, greeting. . . ." The rest was an order to shut-down the home producers. When they refused to be shut down, the army was sent to destroy every tobacco plant in the West Country, and when the army returned to London, the growers raised new plants. In 1632 Charles I expressed surprise that, "after so many commands of His Majesty, and by his royal father of blessed memory, any men would have presumed to have planted or maintained any English tobacco". In the end, the West Country growers were allowed to grow tobacco under licence. Devon headed the list with 163 licences; Yorkshire came second, with ninety-seven; Rutland had only four. But some growers forgot to apply for a licence; a fact which Pepys confirmed in 1667:

"My cozen, Kate Joyce, tells me how the Life-Guard which we thought a little while since was sent down into the country about some insurrection, was sent . . . to spoil the tobacco there, which it seems the people do still plant contrary to law." In 1674 *The True English Interest* reported that Devon and Somerset contained thousands of tobacco plantations. In 1752 Christopher Smart sang their praises:

> . . . I'm an English pipe,
> Deemed worthy of each Briton's gripe,
> Who, with my cloud-compelling aid,
> Help our plantations and our trade,
> And am, when sober and when mellow,
> An upright, downright, honest fellow.

The lane from Withypool climbs due east towards Winsford, past Comer's Cross, nearly 1,200 feet above the Severn Sea, with Winn Brook half a mile to the south, and Bye Common to the north, higher even than Comer's Cross. There a blend of pasture and heathland overlooks lanes and farm-tracks whose banks of earth and stone, topped by a hedge, were raised centuries ago, partly to protect crops from climate, partly to defend stock against foxes and wild boars. Unlike many other regions of Britain, Exmoor retains its hedgerows. In 1969 the Nature Conservancy estimated that 8,000 acres of hedgerows were being uprooted throughout Britain every year, and that by the end of the century some fifty species of common shrubs and wild flowers will have become extinct in counties where hedges are destroyed in the name of "scientific farming". Mammon's scorched earth policy was lately counter-attacked, notably by parts of industrial Staffordshire, where the hedges have been replanted, with results that surprised the inhabitants, who, for the first time in ten years, saw bluebells growing there, foxgloves, oxlips, cowslips, primroses, all set to music by birds that were happy to be home again.

Winsford Hill, a mile or so west of the village, stands 1,404 feet above the sea. There roamed the ponies which Sir Thomas Acland saved from the auctioneer's hammer; and not only saved but also strengthened because another landowner, Mr. Knight, happened one evening to find himself sitting next to Sir Joseph Banks, the naturalist, at a dinner party in Belgravia. The talk turning upon ponies, Sir Joseph cited the prowess of the Dongola or Arab stallion, a giant of sixteen hands. Before the end of dinner, Mr. Knight and the Lords Hadley, Morton, and Dundas had subscribed several thousand guineas towards the cost of importing Arab horses to England. Two stallions and three mares reached Exmoor. After several years' trial and error, the Exmoor breed was improved without loss of its character.

There is on Winsford Hill a Stone, sometimes called the Caractus Stone because its faded inscription may be rendered as *Caracti Nepus* or Nephew of Caractus. Some say that the stone refers to St. Caranctus, a contemporary of King Arthur; others, that it refers to Caractacus, King of the Silures, who was captured and sent to Rome as a prisoner in AD 51. No one knows whether the words carved when the stone was raised, or whether they were added centuries afterwards. E. A. Freeman, historian of the Norman Conquest, was so moved by the stone, and by others of its kind on the moor, that he composed a *Requiescant* in the manner of Sir Thomas Browne: "Here upon this desolate spot, which perhaps never experienced the labours of industrious husbandman . . . the eye of reflection . . . sees a number of simple sepulchres of departed souls their names have long been buried with their persons in the dust of oblivion, and their memorials have perished with their mouldering ruins." Hazlitt said the same thing, less directly and more succinctly: "If history is a grave study, poetry may be said to be graver; its materials lie deeper, and are spread wider."

Winsford can properly be called an enchanting place, dominated by the church on a knoll. One of the tombstones (1896) recalls a commercial traveller, Thomas Tame, officially styled the Hawker of the Dunster Book Hawking Society. This venture was not a mobile library whereat the public might eat an author's bread-and-butter without paying him for it; the society was a travelling bookshop, a horse-and-cart concern; and in 1863 it sold more than 3,000 volumes to the moorfolk.

The hub of Winsford is the Royal Oak, shaded by trees that are indeed regal. I have seen a drawing of the bar, attributed to Thomas Sibson *c.* 1837, wherein the top-hatted tipplers and other clay-pipe customers are warmed by a log fire whose smoke cures six flitches of bacon on the rafters. The village green is watered by a stream; the stream is spanned by seven narrow footbridges; the post office is a cottage; and Court Farm recalls Tom Faggas of *Lorna Doone* with an inscription: "Thomas Fugass, 1674."

Ernest Bevin was born at Winsford, but thereafter lapsed into politics. His first home, opposite the Wesleyan chapel, bears a plaque. Exmoor lost a steady farm worker in Bevin. He did try his hand at it, but soon turned to a wider field, being impelled to help the millions of other manual workers who in those years gave too much in return for too little. In 1937 he became chairman of the General Congress of the Trades Union Council; in 1940, Minister of Labour, a post which suited his temperament and his talents; in 1945, Foreign Secretary, a post which emphasized his generosity, and exposed his stupidity, as when he said to Stalin: "Let us open up the world. Let light and knowledge come in." Stalin smiled and with one finger answered his own question: "How many legions has Bevin?"

Winsford is one of the few Exmoor villages that do not seem to be on a moor, because its green hills hide the heathy hinterland. The population at the last census was 362; which repeats a topical question: shall small villages survive, or must they sink beneath housing estates?

There is a National Park footpath from Winsford to Hawkridge, starting at the Punchbowl, a mile south-west of the village. From the highest point of that path, you can see the Welsh hills, and Brown Willy in Cornwall.

Hawkridge reminds you that many mistakes await the placenamer who fails to study the history of each name. I must have entered the Lakeland village of Hawkshead a dozen times before it occurred to me that the name might, after all, *not* refer to hawks, even although those birds do favour a wild habitat; and my second thoughts were justified, for in the year 1222 the village had been called *Haukesset*, the Old Scandinavian equivalent of Hauk's sheiling or the pasture belonging to a Viking pirate called

Hauk. But no Vikings conquered Exmoor, so I was not surprised to find that Hawkridge's mediaeval name was Haweckrig or Hawk ridge. Certainly the hamlet climbs high enough to please any hawk. It is, in fact, a place of immense quietude, overlooking wooded combes and the River Barle. The mediaeval Swainmote met at Hawkridge, in the forenoon of Friday during Pentecost; but in the afternoon, for reasons unknown to us, the Swainmote adjourned to Withypool, there to conduct its business.

The weather-worn church of St. Giles has a Norman door and font. Nearby, you will admire an example of what modern architecture can achieve when it really does try to design a house that blends with the countryside. In 1833 the parson was Joseph Jekyll, a Blundell's man and lifelong friend of Jack Russell. The hamlet's other buildings can be counted on ten fingers.

Hawkridge is known to stag-hunters as the home and burial place of Ernest Bawden, a servant of the Devon and Somerset; craftsmen know it as the home of the Lockes, who have been carpenters for 160 years. The land hereabouts is not so lush as the Luccombe countryside, but it lies farther from traffic, and is therefore twice-blessed. Whenever I come to Hawkridge, I see and hear an especially rich array of those things which Wordsworth heard and saw in Lakeland:

> . . . the earth
> And common face of Nature spake to me
> Rememberable things. . . .

Now we must travel north, with only a glance at many endearing places: little Exton and its stripling river; Wheddon Cross and those twelve memorable miles, almost uninhabited, that climb eastward to Brendon Hill and the perimeter of the National Park; Timberscombe, a valley of timber indeed, with thatched cottages whose occupants exclaim, "We're worth ten of Hawkridge, and a dozen of anywhere else." Hearing them, we halt and are glad that we did so, because the peace is deep, and the church has a Queen Anne spire, shaped like a pyramid; glad, too, because we climb the woods, gazing westward at Stoke Pero, the *stoc* or place that in 1243 was held by William de Pyrhou. Although Stoke Pero Hill hides half out of sight, I have learned it by heart, and can therefore recite its alphabet, which contains (a) one farmhouse and (b) one church. All around, the curves of Exmoor etch themselves as though Durer had done it

for them. At Stoke Pero you stand with Traherne, only a step
from the roof of the moor:

> The Earth, the Seas, the Light, the lofty Skies,
> The Sun and Stars are mine: if these I prize.

A plaque at the gate says that the church is the loneliest and
highest on Exmoor, 1,013 feet above a sea which can be glimpsed
from the meadows. The church itself was decently rebuilt during
the last century. Candles take the place of an electric lighting
that never arrived; the timber roof is handsome. As you enter,
you will notice a small memorial on the left of the door: "Be
Thou praised my Lord with all Thy Creatures. In the year 1897,
when this church was restored, Zulu, a donkey, walked twice
a day from Parson Street, Porlock, bearing all the oak used in
the roof." G. K. Chesterton's donkey made one memorable
journey and for ever after defied the taunts of men:

> Fools! For I also had my hour;
> One far fierce hour and sweet:
> There was a shout before my ears,
> And palms before my feet.

But Zulu's triumph lasted many months. Observing that the
donkeyman lacks a memorial you may change a singular into the
plural by adding: "Well done, ye good and faithful servants."

Being by this time happily lost, uncertain whether we are on
the heights of Stoke Pero, or among the woods of Timberscombe
. . . being, as I say, all at sea in a world of green, we seek the
Pole Star, or, if the sun shines, we find a signpost, and so proceed,
uphill and down, through zany lanes and beside lyrical streams,
into the hamlet of Selworthy, the *worth* or place with a *siele* or
coppice of sallows.

Selworthy is not at home to visitors during the summer season,
being preoccupied with cars and cream teas. At all other times it
is both welcomed and welcoming; a laneful of steeply thatched
houses climbing to the white church on a wooded knoll. In 1052
the lady of the manor was Eadgyth, sister to King Harold. The
south aisle of the church was rebuilt in 1490; the Norman font
has a timber case; the copy of Bishop Jewel's *Apology* was printed
in 1609; the tithe-barn is as old as the south aisle. In 1817 the
rector ordered six new chimney-pots: "Carriage for same from
Barnstaple on three horses, 25 miles by Exmoor, 15s." Selworthy

people looked to the great house of Holnicote, seat of the Dykes and then of their successors-by-marriage, the Aclands. In 1794 the house was destroyed by a fire which consumed 300 pounds of family plate. They say that the squire, Sir Thomas Acland, mourned more the thirty stags' heads which had been scalped during the previous eight years. The church register records his death: "Sir Thomas Dyke Acland went to London the 4th of May 1794; was taken ill in the way thither: and on the 17th day of the same month, abt 6 o'clock in the evening, died. . . ."

The charm and beauty of Selworthy console us for our reluctant by-passing of other Exmoor villages: Brompton Regis, for example, the King's manor, where broom grows; still unspoiled except beyond its steepest summit. Three centuries ago a girl of 19 was buried at Brompton:

> She died young, and so oft tis seen
> The fruit God loves He's pleased to pluck it green.

Luccombe next, where wooded ways confirm those philologists who believe that this was *lufu cumb* or lover's combe; venerable cottages, sandstone bridges over the brook, and the memory of a vicar, the Reverend Henry Byam, who with his four sons fought for King Charles I, went into exile with King Charles II, and in 1660 returned with him.

Wootton Courtenay follows—the place in the woods, whose manor was held by John de Courtney 800 years ago; a mediaeval church, a sheen of thatch, a maze of lanes, a life of quietness.

Now come Withycombe's steep lanes and beyond them, atop a hill, the loneliest house on the Somerset moor—Higher Dumbledeer—accessible via half a mile of tractor ruts.

Our *Nunc dimittis* shall be sung by Cleeve Abbey, a Cistercian ruin near a *clife* or hill, perhaps the moor's noblest ancient monument, so sited that on Thursday the monks had only to tickle the stream for Friday. Not to find a Cistercian monastery on Exmoor would have been surprising indeed, because the order sought always a remote home, usually on high ground, where the brethren could exercise their skill as the finest sheep-farmers in Christendom or out of it. Although they played a full part as creators and conservers of scholarship, the Cistercians relished an active life in the open air, believing that the man who went muck-spreading on a moor might live as piously as the eremite who never left his cell: *laborare est orare.*

As we have already noticed, a good-natured rivalry exists between the Devon and the Somerset moor. When one side is praised, the other reads between the lines, ready to pounce upon overpraise. My own allegiance lies with Devon, yet truth itself presents Somerset as a county *sui generis* and therefore beyond compare. Somerset men may love it more than I, but I doubt that they admire it more.

XIII

THE DEVON VILLAGES

How aptly our fathers named Brendon, a *brunhill* or broom-covered hill; not to be confused with the Brendon Hills, away to the east, whose mediaeval name meant 'brown hills'. A broom-covered hill, then; but Brendon lies at the foot of it, beside the East Lyn and a packhorse bridge. Brendon only just achieves villageship; one row of cottages less, and it would seem no more than a licensed hamlet whose remote church—rebuilt (1738) and restored (1828)—was dedicated to St. Brendan. They say that material for the rebuilding came from Cheriton, near Brendon Two Gates, the site of some prehistoric stones. Brendon's two gates—now replaced by a cattle grid—were double gates, so designed that one of them was always shut by the wind.

News of the world did sometimes reach Brendon, even in Jan Ridd's day: "When I was down at the blacksmith's forge by Brendon town, where the Lynn-stream runs so close that he dips his horse-shoes in it . . . while we were talking of the hay-crop. and of a great sheep-stealer, round the corner came a man upon a pie-bald horse . . . shouting with great glory 'Monmouth, and the Protestant faith! Monmouth, and no Popery! . . .' "

In 1905 the *Daily Chronicle* published a letter from a reader who had copied-down the Doone legends as he heard them from an old man at the Brendon inn, and had then told them to a friend, who used some of them in a story, *The Doones of Exmoor*, which appeared in a magazine, *Leisure Hour*. "Moreover," said the reader, "I had a letter from Mr. R. D. Blackmore, soon after his immortal work (*Lorna Doone*) was issued, wherein he acknowledged that it was the accidental glancing at the poor stuff in the *Leisure Hour* that gave him the clue for the weaving of the romance, and caused him to study the details on the spot."

Two miles west of Brendon, the East Lyn flows among woods to join the Farley Brook at Watersmeet, a National Trust property. At any time between October and June you can walk all day among those woods, hearing only the birds and the brooks and sometimes a sheep. If the wind is in the south, or brings a nip from the east, you may notice clouds overhead—and smell them, too, for at certain times the farmers burn the heather. A statute of William and Mary tried to control that ancient practice: "To burn on any waste, between Candlemas and Midsummer, any grig, ling, heath and furze, goss or fern, is punishable by whipping and confinement in the house of correction." In 1789 Gilbert White reported from Hampshire: "The pleas for these burnings is, that, when the old coat of heath etc. is consumed, young will sprout up, and afford much tender brouze for cattle. . . ." But he added a warning: "Where there is large old furze, the fire, following the roots, consumes the very ground; so that for hundreds of acres nothing is to be seen but smother and desolation, the whole circuit round looking like the cinders of a volcano; and, the soil being quite exhausted, no traces of vegetation are to be found for years." If you have ever seen a moorland fire run amok, you will believe the traveller who told Gilbert White that he once smelled such a fire twenty-five miles away.

We meanwhile must go two miles away, back to Somerset, up the coast road again, which remained unfit for wheeled traffic until the 1850s. When at last the surface was improved, Lynton's three hoteliers welcomed the arrival of visitors whom the old road had deterred. A watch was kept through telescopes, so that horsemen might be sent to solicit customers.

At County Gate the road passes from Somerset into Devon. Legend says that Devon was named after Debun, a Trojan hero who accompanied Brutus to Britain. Having arrived, Debun slew a giant, and was rewarded by sharing the South-west with a fellow-Trojan, Corineus. As Spenser's *Faerie Queen* put it:

> Corineus held that province utmost west,
> And Dubon's share was that is Devonshire.

Certainly the county was called Defnum in 894; but philologists regard that name as a variant of Defnas, the Celtic word for Dumnonii or the aborigines. Somerset's name is less legendary, being a corruption of *saete* or the people of *somer tun* or the place that was occupied only during summer. Michael Drayton stated that the Somerset emblem was "a virgin bathing in a stream", which is partly confirmed by a nineteenth-century jingle:

> Zummerzet vor zeen'ry vair,
> Of water, wood, and land.

But a Cumbrian may not agree with:

> Zummerzet where volk do speak
> Zo volk can understand.

Having stepped into and out of Somerset, we reach the amphibious parish of Countisbury, the *Cynuit* or hill, 1,000 feet above the sea. Countisbury is so small that a midnight stranger might pass through without noticing it. There are a cottage or two, the top of a church tower, and the Blue Ball Inn, at which point it was considered safe to slip two of the six horses that had hauled the coach from Lynmouth, one-in-four below. The coach plied until 1922.

The church of St. John the Evangelist, at the end of a track near the edge of a cliff, is comparatively modern (nave 1796, tower 1835), but the wind and the sea have so bruised it that, at first sight, you exclaim, "Old." The dedication is indeed old; Lynmouth still lies within the ecclesiastical parish of Countisbury.

A path beside the church enters a cottage garden, and then romps away, like a dog off the lead, over the top and (unless you are careful) so deep down to the bottom that your widow will break the news to her orphan:

> Full fathom five thy father lies,
> Of his bones are coral made.

If you are bold enough to follow the path, even when it has become a slither of scree, you will sight the white roof of the Foreland light-house far below, which at certain times is open to the public. My own first arrival, long ago, occurred at an uncertain time; but a chance phrase told the keeper that we had both served awhile.

"In big ships, Sir, or small?"

"The smallest possible."

"Small or not, you'm welcome to have a look round."

Nearly fifteen miles the light shines; tons of shimmering metal so finely machined and so adroitly poised that a fingertip sends it spinning.

"But even today, even with all their fancy gear, they still get 'emselves into trouble. There's one light-ship, up Bristol way, and whenever her crew sights an American, they yell 'Lower the boats! There's another bloody Yankee on the way.' "

"You mean they steer on her beam?"

"Some of 'em *hits* her beam. Her t'other sort. 'Tis true. I've seen the dents."

When a gale crashes in from the north-west, it is a fine thing to watch it from this light-house, and feel it, too, thudding the rocks. Then you will share tales that sound old indeed, though the speaker is under 60 and took part in the events; tales of tall ships overhauling a full-speed steamer, and of a brig whose four-man crew included a woman: "And Lord cuss me if that girl couldn't swear."

High, wide and handsome is Foreland Point. Northward lie the Welsh hills, hiding-and-seeking among the weather, sometimes clear, sometimes invisible. To the south, Exmoor dips deeply and then climbs to its thrones at Parracombe and the Chains. Just below the Blue Ball, a path dives among woods toward Watersmeet. But no path at all will take you to Countisbury's next port-of-call, Desolate, one of the few houses that are named on the Ordnance map. Formerly a farm, it stands in a combe on the edge of the cliff, at the end of a mile-long track. When even the gulls have grounded themselves, you can sit snugly in the garden while a gale whistles overhead. W. L. Page .said of Desolate: "Woods dark with foliage, and warm, sheltered nooks, certainly belie its name."

At Countisbury our coastwise journey ends, though we do re-enter Lynton *en route* for Parracombe, my nearest village, a steep hour's walk from The Haven, uphill and down, along a bent lane between high woods beside the River Heddon. In old times Parracombe was a port-of-call for the travellers who stamped it with their trademark, *peddera cumb* or the valley of pedlars. The last pedlar I saw there, shortly before writing these words, carried no pack, and would have died of unnatural causes had he tried to walk from the village to the Chains. Instead, he got his kingsize car across the tide, at a point where the street becomes too narrow for large lorries. In the end, five farmhands hoisted the remains of his rear bumper, and away he went, at the firm's expense. When quietness had returned, the eldest of the farmhands shook his head at the grocer: " 'Tis the same every time he comes yere. I say to him, why don't 'ee leave the thing upill a bit, where the road's wider? 'Tis only a hundred yards walk. Walk? he says. I can't walk. I'm a busy man." The greybeard looked across at me: "He may be busy, but he ain't no man. Not if he earns his living selling women's linjerry. Cor damn me, I'd rather go and trim a bloody 'aystack."

Parracombe contains two churches, two parts (the higher is called Church Town) and four shops. Although the village is small, a stranger can lose himself among its lanes and *culs-de-sac*. The inn, 'The Fox and Goose', stands at the bottom of the lower village, beside a stream that once drove the old mill. Fifty years ago the village publican was H. R. Blackmore, second cousin of the novelist. Beyond the inn, one large vehicle may graze itself against the kind of Exmoor street that astonished Richard Jefferies: "foot passengers huddle up in doorways to avoid the touch of the wheels, and the windows of houses are protected by iron bars like cages lest the splash-boards should crack the glass." Having swerved to avoid the stores-cum-post office, the street gives up the struggle and resumes its natural state as a steep lane.

The new church (1878) stands on a knoll which appears to dominate the village, until you notice that the knoll is dominated by another, on which the old church stands—or, rather, totters —with a terse signboard stating that it is "dangerous". In 1878 this church was condemned to be demolished, but secured a reprieve by public subscription (the rescuers included William Morris, who was soon to restore the Thames-side church at Inglesham). In 1970 none of the villagers knew whether the church would collapse, or be demolished; many did not care. Its dedication could scarcely have been homelier nor more illustrious, for St. Petroc is believed to have built here one of the very earliest of all Devon churches. Most scholars agree that Petroc himself was the son of a Welsh princeling; that he studied at an Irish monastery; and that he reached Cornwall via the River Camel. Petrocstow was named after him, and so was Padstow whose Abbey retrieved the Bodmin Gospels, the only Cornish monastic book that had survived the Dark Ages. When the monks moved from Padstow to Bodmin, to escape Danish pirates, they took their Gospels with them.

St. Petroc's is chiefly of the thirteenth century. The tympanum was painted (1758) with the Ten Commandments, Creed,

Lord's Prayer, and Royal Arms. The pulpit has (or had) a sounding board, and a desk apiece for the reader and the clerk. Some of the pews were Tudor; others, the box variety, were eighteenth century. Because the interior was never restored, it enables you to see what a village church looked like at the beginning of the nineteenth century. The entire setting is memorable; a steep lane from the inn; an Exmoor skyline where that lane becomes a path; and, at the far end of the path, the relics of Parracombe Church Town, with the priest's house alongside the church, and a farm and a cottage or two half-hidden among trees.

I often think that this knoll would make a splendid cricket pitch if the ground were levelled. But Devon thought otherwise, for it never fielded a first-class eleven, and was evidently not among the regions which Pitt had in mind when he introduced his Defence Act of 1803, limiting to six miles the distance which a volunteer need walk from his home to the parade ground: "The distance I propose," said the premier, "is not more than the sturdy English peasantry are in the habit of going when led to a cricket match. . . ." When Sir Russel Bencraft tried to form a national cricket league, with three divisions and a system of annual relegation, Devon joined the objectors who quashed the idea. Perhaps it feared that the roads would impede cricket practice. Thus, when George Parr led the first All England XI through Devonshire the coach-and-four got bogged one night in a lane, and when the cricketers knocked at the door of a cottage, seeking help, a head appeared from the window, followed by a shot-gun: "I'm deaf as an adder, my sonnies, but don't 'ee come no nearer or I'll show 'ee how straight I can see."

Having descended from St. Petroc's church, and observed the village unfolding around the hillsides, you understand that Parracombe has been preserved by its steep and narrow lanes. A mound beyond the village was the site of Holwell, a Norman castle. Few people know that Parracombe is the place where the Blackmores—and therefore *Lorna Doone*—were conceived. That, however, belongs to a later chapter.

Now from the pedlars' combe our way leads via Blackmoor Gate to Martin's combe or Combe Martin, a seaside village wedged between hills. Charles Kingsley was only half right when he described Combe Martin as a "mile-long mansty". The main street is two miles long, and becomes uglier as it grows narrower.

The village green, Exford

Here and there an old house stands out, or is sandwiched between modernity; but the rest resembles a well-washed mining village. In high summer the street writhes like a crocodile of cars plying to and from Ilfracombe.

Halfway down the street, facing a lane to Trentishoe and Heddon's Mouth, stands an inn, formerly called 'The King's Arms', now known as 'The Pack of Cards'. One of the Leys built it. The fifty-two windows, which I have never counted, are said to commemorate the pack of cards which gave Squire Ley such a fair deal that he won a fortune with it.

The best building at Combe Martin is the church of St. Peter ad Vincula. Nobly it stands, nearly one hundred feet high, defended from the traffic by a field. Those who rest here include a daughter of the manor, Judith Hancock (*obiit* 1634); and Mary Norman (*obiit* 1901), who was R. D. Blackmore's nursemaid and foster-mother when he visited his uncle and his grandfather; of whom the former was married here (1840) and the latter inducted as rector (1833). Mary Norman must have been related to Aggie Norman, who died in 1860, at the age of 83, having spent much time alone among the Valley of Rocks, in a hut that was built by her husband. No doubt Blackmore co-opted the hermitage as part of Mother Meldrum's story.

In 1569 the rector of Combe Martin was Richard Tremayne, a member of a Cornish family that had settled in Devon in 1366. He became treasurer of Exeter Cathedral in 1560, and (if the Earl of Bedford had prevailed) would have become its bishop; but the Queen declined to prefer a cleric who wished to abolish surplices, saints' days, and what he called "curious singing and playing of the organs".

The village's earliest name, Combe, was appropriately simple. In 1086 the manor was held by a Norman, William of Falais, and thereafter by the man who added his name to it, Robert, son of Martin of Tours. In 1264 the right to hold a fair and market was confirmed by the King. In 1630 or thenabouts the villagers acquired a new revel, the Hunting of the Earl of Rone, whose effigy was dragged through the street, accompanied by a donkey and a hobby horse. The so-called earl is said to have been the leader of some unlikeable Irish pirates who dwelt among the combes nearby. His lordship was last hunted in 1837, when the magistrates outlawed him and his tipsy trundlers. The modern villagers—and especially the shopkeepers—are as friendly as those

9

Porlock Weir

at Lynton; which is why I sometimes buy my off-peak-bits-and-pieces in their village. There is, however, no trace of a trade which Westcote described three centuries ago: "The town is not rich; yet the people are industrious and painful; their greatest trade and profit is the making of shoemakers' threads, by spinning whereof they maintain themselves, furnishing therewith the most part of the shire."

The history of Combe Martin was largely that of its lead and silver mines, which forms a later chapter; its grandeur lies wholly in the setting, a green combe dominated by two cliffs, more than 1,000 feet above the spray. Kingsley explained to his friend, Claude, why the cliffs were named Great and Little Hangman: "Some sheep-stealer, they say, clambering over a wall with his booty slung around his neck, was literally hung by the poor brute's struggles, and found days after on the mountain-side, a blackened corpse on one side of the wall, with the sheep on the other, and the ravens. . . ." And not only the ravens: between Combe Martin and Heddon's Mouth you will see buzzards, too, gliding at eighty miles an hour, swooping with a vision eight times sharper than our own.

From Combe Martin we return towards Blackmoor Gate, but bear right before reaching it, along the Barnstaple road and then along a lane to Arlington, which began life as the *tun* of *Aelt*hriff's people, and is now a hamlet hidden among trees and a stillness that seeps like sunshine through the pores. Here is one of the very few stately homes on Exmoor, Arlington Court, designed in 1820 by Thomas Lee, a Barnstaple man, formerly apprenticed to Sir John Soane. Despite its Doric porch, the exterior of the Court is simple, almost plain; but the interior resembles a palaceful of treasures: rare pewter and silver down the centuries; clothes worn by the family during the early nineteenth century; some Old Masters; and a water colour by William Blake, which was discovered during the 1950s on top of a cupboard in one of the maids' bedrooms. Arlington Court belongs to the National Trust.

The church of St. James was decently rebuilt in 1846; its west tower, some fifty years later, from a copy of the buttressed original. There are memorials to a rector who served for sixty years, to his son (a naval officer) and to a lady who died in 1791. All bear the same surname, Chichester.

The Chichester family is among the oldest on Exmoor. One

mediaeval member held land at Marwood, north-west of Barnstaple, including the farmhouse called Wescott Barton. To historians the most eminent member of the family was Arthur, first Baron Chichester of Belfast, Lord Deputy of Ireland, who pioneered the Pale by urging King James I to grant "to every man of note or good dessert so much (land) as he can stock conveniently and manure by himself and his tenants and followers for five years to come . . .". Lord Chichester meanwhile undertook to "bring in civil people of England and Scotland at his Majesty's pleasure, with condition to build castles or storehouses upon their lands". This Exmoor imperialist fulfilled a hard task wisely. When, for example, his lieutenants urged him to build a jail, he replied that they were better employed creating a town because "the habitations of this people are so wild and transitory as there is not one fixed village in all this county". The land must have been primitive indeed if its dwellings could seem so uncouth to an Exmoor man of the seventeenth century. Lord Chichester summed it up in a despatch. Ireland, he said, "was as inaccessible to strangers as the Kingdom of China".

The Chichester barony soon became a viscounty. In 1646 Thomas Stucley, a member of another ancient Devon family, confessed that there was "a Statute of £1,000 acknowledged by his father unto lord viscount Chichester yet unsatisfied . . .". In short, the Chichesters had been helping the Stucleys to recover from the cost of their allegiance to the King.

A seventeenth-century Chichester, Sir John, was Master of a pack of staghounds; and when they were disbanded, in 1827, Sir Francis hunted the stag with foxhounds. When even the foxhounds were disbanded, poachers nearly exterminated the entire herd of deer. Not the least renowned member of the family is that Francis Chichester who, having sailed alone around the world, was knighted by Her Majesty Queen Elizabeth II.

Now from Arlington we do reach Blackmoor Gate, passing through Challacombe, the *celdecomba* or Cold Valley, whose best parts are down-and-up-again to the church and barton. And so past Friendship Farm to a lane on the left, which probes the wild highlands of Farmer Mole's Chamber. They re-made this road during the 1960s, and a motorist will thank them for it, but some of the natives prefer the old one and its grass down the middle. And so again by devious ways to Molland, the land on a *moel* or bare hill, a remote hamlet and therefore friendly.

Molland hill smiles across at other hills, and looks down benignly at the green combes below. Among the earliest lords, said Westcote, "I find Sir William Bottreaux in the time of King John." Here is the finest small church on the Devon Moor, though you would not think so by looking at the weather-worn exterior. Like St. Petroc's at Parracombe, Molland church escaped Victorian restoration. You will admire the wagon-roof, the box pews and a three-decker pulpit whose sounding-board supports a trumpeting angel (did the congregation, listening yet again to the same sermon, pray that the trumpeter might sound "Sing unto the Lord a new song"?). Painted vividly in 1808, The Ten Commandments and the Royal Arms offer an illuminated version of Fear God, honour the King. The west tower is the work of the same fourteenth-century mason who built those at Stoke Rivers and Lapford. The only famous vicar of Molland was infamous, the fox-and-deer hunting John Froude, whom Blackmore depicted as Parson Chowne in The Maid of Sker.

The rest of Molland—perhaps a dozen cottages—clusters around the London Inn, a name which neither the Mollanders nor myself can explain. Did one of the publicans come from London? Did he for some zany reason hope to go to London? Or was Molland, as we say, on the way to London? The inn itself is snug, low-ceilinged, Devonshire. I cannot say the same of its miniature zoo; nor, I think, can the cottagers who must listen perpetually to the opinions of its inmates (birds, chiefly), led by a loquacious parrot.

In 1803 James Quartly of Molland became a man in authority, for during that year, as in 1940, England stood alone against a foreign tyrant who had already enslaved a large part of Europe. The precautions against Napoleon's imminent invasion were, after their fashion, as efficient as those against Hitler. The whole of southern England was surveyed by a miniature Domesday Book which recorded the number and occupation of inhabitants, and several other relevant details. If Napoleon did invade, cattle were to be driven away, standing crops burned, and everything else destroyed that might aid the enemy. In certain places only men of military age were allowed to remain; the rest were to be moved or, as we said in 1940, evacuated. That is why the follow-ing despatch was sent to James Quartly: "On receiving orders for the removal of Stock, you are to direct Edw. Cockram, William Cockram, James Brewer, and William Dovel . . . to proceed with the Stock to Molland Town . . . there to put themselves under the direction of Mr. Henry Quartly . . . and afterwards to obey his commands." Having directed Edw. Cockram and cronies to carry provisions "for a few days", the despatch continued:

Mr. James Quartly, Mr. John Palfreman, and Mr. George Forst. You are to remain in your Parish and act as you shall receive orders from the General Officer or Deputy Lieutenant of your Division. If the enemy should approach very near before you can receive orders to do so, you are to destroy the Hay and corn and the cattle of all descriptions, particularly the Horses not retained for public service . . . and you are to assure all those, whose property is thus destroyed that they will be repaid for their losses. . . .

The Quartlys were Exmoor yeoman. At the beginning of the seventeenth century two brothers, James and Henry Quartly, rented land in Molland parish, paying £2 yearly for one of the Bartons, where they prospered as graziers. In his *General View* of North Devon farming (1813), Vancouver remarked: "The soil here, from the coolness of its bottom, is generally considered more favourable to the culture of grass than of corn." By the beginning of the eighteenth century the Quartly Red Cattle were winning first prize whenever they were shown at Smithfield. Artists came from many parts of Britain to paint them. Even the King's painter came, a certain H. B. Chalon. They say that the first wheeled vehicle ever seen on the moor was ordered by a Quartly who lived at Withypool during the middle of the last century. In other words, many an Exmoor man, still very much alive, must have heard of that arrival, from the lips of his grandfather who had seen it. The Molland Quartlys were cousins to R. D. Blackmore's uncle, the Reverend Richard Blackmore, vicar of Charles. Richard, in fact, married one of those cousins; and his nephew set Molland on the map of *Lorna Doone,* wherein Tom Faggus greets Jan Ridd "with some very good news to tell. . . . He had taken up purchase from his old friend Sir Roger Bassett of a nice bit of land . . . in the parish of Molland. . . ." A nice bit of land indeed: was it, I wonder, along that uphill-and-down-combe lane to Bottreaux Mill? Wherever it lay, the land overlooked both the pastoral and the heathery moor, seeing that each was good.

From Tom Faggus's "nice bit of land" we steer westward

through a labyrinth of narrow lanes, past Twitchen, Gotcombe, and Millbrook; observing (since we are in no hurry) their down-to-earth baptisms, for Millbrook is a trickle from the River Mole; Gotcombe is the sort of place where goats did graze; and Twitchen is still *twicen* or the fork of a road . . . so many forks that only the oldest acquaintance can learn them all by heart. Even today I carry a map lest I am misled by the happy dearth of signposts. Meanwhile we draw near to North Molton.

Sometimes you will pass a Wesleyan chapel in these parts, alone by the wayside; and sometimes it is a chapel no longer. Anyone reaching Exmoor from Cornwall must notice that the chapels have dwindled. John Wesley, who visited Cornwall thirty-two times, is still regarded there as the father of the people. In Wesley's day some of the old Cornishfolk still spoke their own language; in earlier days even their bishop left them alone, fearing the roads and the robbers. Cornwall inclined 'agin' the Establishment. Devon, by contrast, stood more firmly by its Englishry. Only twice did it receive Wesley with warmth: when he was entertained to luncheon by Bishop Ross and again by the vicar of Charles Church in Plymouth. At Tiverton the mayor tried to turn him away, saying that the people already had four places of worship: "and if they won't go to Heaven by one or other of those ways, by God they shan't go to Heaven at all while I am mayor of Tiverton". Eighty years elapsed between Wesley's last visit to North Molton and the building of its first dissenting chapel. Wesley himself lived and died as a priest of the Church of England, a high Tory, a respector of respectable persons. Many of his followers, however, were farmhands and small shopkeepers who wielded their religion as political goad with which to bait the Establishment. Not a few of them became frankly subversive, and some were unscrupulous in other ways: notably one Nutt, the so-called Pope of South Molton, who undertook to shrive sinners at a penny per week. When Wesley came to North Molton in 1762, he was surprised by the smallness of the congregation. It seems that a landowner had threatened to evict everyone of his tenants who did not disavow Wesleyanism.

Jan Ridd dismissed North Molton as "a rough rude place at the end of Exmoor . . .". But Faggus himself would have mocked the ignorance of any man who classified it as a village. Like Molland, it bestrides a *moel*, though the hill is considerably less bare than in 1086, when Domesday mentioned *Nortmoltone*.

During the nineteenth century, however, the glory departed to *Sudmoltone*. You must hurry if you would see the relics of North Molton's glory, for the village lies just beyond the National Park, and is therefore *in partibus infidelium*, an outpost of Mammon-land. Already its western parts suffer an erysipelas or bungaloid fungus; and you can be certain that house agents and acre-owners are conspiring against the rest.

The main street is steep. Midway up it a 'Miners Arms' recalls gold rushes that came to very little. Some of the houses are old and therefore handsome. Having climbed itself, the street rests awhile in a small square, dominated by the church of All Saints, which has a three-stage tower and, as at Molland, a pulpit sounding-box with trumpeting angel. The monuments include one to Sir Aymas Bamfylde, 1626. Documents spell the name variously as Bampfylde, Bamfield, Bamfeild, Baumfield; today we would say Beanfield. The Bamfyldes acquired North Molton by marriage during the Middle Ages; their principal seat lay at Poltimore in south Devon, but some of the family resided at Molton; the baronetcy was created in 1641. Sir Thomas Bampfylde became Speaker of the House of Commons; his nephew, Sir Coplestone, was pricked as High Sheriff of Devon. Two lesser members of the family resided awhile in Newgate jail: Francis, for publishing seditious pamphlets, and John, for smashing Joshua's windows (the smasher had wished to marry Sir Joshua Reynolds' niece, but was found wanting). In 1831 the sixth baronet, Sir George, was created Baron Poltimore. At the beginning of the twentieth century the family owned two houses near the church: Court Hall, a Georgian home, and Court House, built in 1553. It is possible that these Courts were named after, or in some other way recalled, North Molton's Courts Leet and Baron, which were held latterly at 'The Poltimore Arms', a lonely wayside inn, some distance from the village. Sixteen local men formed the king's jury, and four spoke for the manor. Their chairman or Portreeve was commonly called the Mayor of North Molton. After the annual debate, a feast was provided by Lord Poltimore.

From North Molton one of several lanes passes Bampfylde Hill, almost 1,000 feet up, and then heads north-west towards Charles, and both are unfit for any motor vehicle that is unwilling to reverse one-in-four downhill while a load of manure or a crateful of pigs breathes heavily against its radiator. On Exmoor we do not consider that we have begun to climb until second gear is engaged. You may therefore assess the way to Charles by reading its signpost, *Very Steep*.

The longer of those lanes is a joy to climb. Even an athlete will pause to inhale the view between gaps in the tall bank. Northward lies Shoulsbarrow Castle, a Celtic fort whose embankments have been eroded to mere humps of grass and rushes. Further yet, the Chains fall twelve inches short of 1,600 feet; and there also the rushes grow, but with good grass between, and on it some Highland cattle, shaggy as a Landseer. Southward all is soft, green, wooded, yet never flat; even the valley at Charles is higher than anywhere in Essex, and twice as high as the steepest Fenland hill.

Scarcely a mile away the village of Bray stands on its own hill. Sir Walter Scott went to Bray, to a farmhouse there, which appears in *Kenilworth*: "The ancient seat of Lidcote Hall . . . adjoined the extensive forest of Exmoor, plentifully stocked with game. . . ." Abbottsford lies a long way from Exmoor, and it may seem strange that Scott's imagination should have travelled hundreds of miles in search of a setting. Certainly he loathed London ("incredibly tiresome", he told Morritt), but England he loved, and the West of England especially, having spent some of the happiest days of his life there, for which he said a good grace briefly: "Delightful England."

By this time the lane has become a leisurely slope, and never so leisurely as in April, when primroses outshine the sun. Only in the west will you see such greetings, and only on Exmoor do they grow so high. The lane has a green parting down the middle, and when you walk on it you deepen the stillness of bird-song, sheep-bleat, and breeze. Suddenly, on the left, a large sign appears, bearing the word Charles. How fantastical, that a population of twelve should be compelled to cause such a waste of their own and other men's money. Travellers who do know Charles, know also when they have arrived there. Travellers who do not know Charles, have already been told *how* to arrive there. It is as though a book were to contain not only a list of contents but also a list of the contents of the list of contents.

It is difficult to visualize Charles as 'a rocky palace'; yet that seems to be the correct etymology, back to a pair of old Cornish words, *carn lies*, which became Carmes, then Charnes, then Charles. We shall never know the identity of the princeling who held court here, lording it over a wild land, from what is now a hamlet with no shop, no inn, no pavement, no nothing-at-all except its church, three houses and (in 1970) a family that occupied part of a ruined farm. Of the Celtic palace there is neither trace nor shadow of trace. The fanfares and the fine ladies lie with the venison and the bright swords, all rusted by the dew of Time.

I may have been wrong in crediting Charles with twelve people. There could be as many as fifteen. During the 1940s there may have been thirty, for in those years the row of crumbling cottages was occupied. I visit Charles every month or so, and have done for several years; but only once did I see an inhabitant, a child playing in the grass beside the church. Often I have been tempted to quote Walter de la Mare:

"Is there anybody there?" cried the traveller.

Yet the hamlet never seems lifeless nor dispirited. On the contrary, I find it a cheerful place despite those derelict cottages.

As in many other Exmoor villages, the church dominates from a knoll. Its tower and outer walls are old; the rest is chiefly late Victorian; but in this land and at that height a building soon loses its youthful appearance. Charles church and rectory formed a seed-bed wherein *Lorna Doone* germinated. The first Blackmore to live there was John, born in 1764, who received what is in every sense a classical West Country education at Blundell's and at Exeter College, Oxford. Having been ordained, he served as curate at High Bray, where he married, and begat two sons, John and Richard. Finding that the curacy hardly fulfilled his desire to serve, and believing that Charles would soon need a new rector, Blackmore bought its advowson. But someone had blundered. Fifty years passed before the living fell vacant, and by that time John Blackmore was too old to take it, having already spent an arduous life as rector of Oare and of Combe Martin, which he held until his death at the age of 78. When Charles did come on the clerical market, the patron gave it to his second son, Richard, uncle of R. D. Blackmore. The novelist certainly stayed at Charles rectory. By all accounts he spent a large part of many school holidays there. So, the author of *Lorna Doone* climbed the lane to Charles, first as a child and then as a man, reliving the legends that would one day bring fame to himself and to the land of his fathers.

It was in this scattered parish that I first watched the making of

clowtyd, the old name for clotted cream. Celia Fiennes watched
it, too: "they scald their creame and milk in most parts of these
countrys," she wrote, "and soe its a sort of clouted creame as we
call it, with a little sugar, and soe put on the top of apple pye. . . ."
Even in print it looks delicious. An Exmoor farmwife in 1970
follows much the same recipe as her predecessors in 1570. First
she pours the milk into a shallow pan, and then lets it cool for
twelve hours. Next, she sets the pan on the kitchen range, taking
care not to jog it, and there heats it slowly but without boiling.
When the cream has risen to the surface, she scalds it, returns the
pan to the dairy and lets it stand for another twelve hours. Next
day the cream is removed with a slice, and the whey goes to pigs
or young cattle. But neither the recipe nor the herd holds the
secret of Devonshire cream; that belongs to our herbage, a harvest
of geology and climate. During the 1960s the government outlawed the hawking of any old cream as Devonshire Cream. All
cream bearing that name must now contain a specific fat-content.
But you can't keep a bad businessman down. He still sells Cornish
Cream Toffee which, when you examine the package, is seen to
have been Made in London.

And now, as the time comes to conclude our tour of Devon
villages, I find that I have not the heart to pass over un-named
those fair and faithful friends who by their presence lit the hours
that were lampless, and thereafter, in Wordsworth's phrase,
"added sunshine to daylight, by making the happy happier". Let
us collect some of them into a posey: Rose Ash or the hamlet
with a great ash tree, which in 1198 belonged not to a woman,
Rose, but to a man, Ralph, whose name has been transexed.
Here, gazing north towards Anstey Barrows, you share a vision
with Richard Jefferies: "On the distant hills the only break in the
slow curve of their outline is caused by an occasional tumulus."
Having gazed, you turn toward a church where the Southcomb
family served as rectors in unbroken succession for 250 years.
And from the church you lope down a hill among woods to
Cuckoo Mill Cottage and the stream, an idyll lovely as its name.

Kentisbury, off the beaten track yet on the park perimeter:
shopless and as totally abstinent as Charles, having a wagon-
roofed church with an old neighbour, a barton of 1674, and
another neighbour also, even older, for its standing stones were
raised from the infancy of man.

Trentishoe or Trenlesho, the hill with a circular top: one

church and three small houses, not quite peering over that top, else they would see the waves below. Inland the hills of wooded water-music fall from sight and then are seen again, pinned to a higher sky. My daily walk, this: a pilgrimage of grace.

These hamlets and their kind are not the illusions of a rose-tinted reverie. Their people sin and suffer, strive and are glad, decline and fall. Yet, as Bridges knew, the love of home abides:

> And through all change the smiles of hope amend
> The weariest face, the same love changed in nought. . . .

XIV

THE DEER

On Exmoor the word 'deer' is a synonym for hunting. And throughout Britain the word 'hunting' arouses strong emotion, similar to that which is evoked by capital punishment and papal infallibility. Now all human thoughts are accompanied by emotion. To say, therefore, that hunting is an emotional topic does not mean that the arguments for it and against are based solely on temperamental bias—unless, of course, you compulsively accept the argument of those biochemists who believe that every argument is compulsive (their own included), being simply a chemical reflex, beyond our control.

Compulsive or not, hunting is a prominent feature of this portrait. Baring-Gould reported that whenever a church bell was rung "in a jingling fashion and with more than usual alarm . . . it was the signal that a fox had been tracked to ground . . . and the bell summoned every man who possessed a pick-axe, or a gun, or a terrier, to hasten to the spot and lend a hand in destroying the noxious animal." Most of the Exmoor hunters are either farmers or members of farming families; followers on foot represent all classes and incomes. A meet of the Devon and Somerset staghounds is the most important secular event on Exmoor. Small children follow, and spinsters who first followed sixty years ago. One-man shopkeepers close their shutters for an hour, just to watch hounds move off. And if you happen to be walking within a mile or so of the chase, blondes in Land-Rovers, and bald-heads on bicycles, will shout, "Have 'ee seen 'em?" These things being so, let us eschew a non-human impartiality, and examine some facts that are often ignored and widely unknown.

Deer are destructive. I have seen a carrot-field trampled into ruins by one stag. I have seen an acre of young trees nibbled to death by one stag. And I have seen one stag reduce a garden to a litterbin. If the number of deer were not controlled, many

Exmoor farmers would be harmed, and some would go bankrupt. But the number is controlled because farmers are willing to be pilfered in return for the right to hunt. If ever that hunting should cease, the deer will be wounded and ultimately exterminated by marksmen who are unwilling to see their crops damaged without compensation.

In 1965 a professional forester, a non-hunting man, told the truth about deer-shooting: "There is," wrote Richard Prior, "a terrible and often unsuspected trail of wounded deer. Many times I have seen relics of these shoots; a doe with her foot shot half away, and walking on the stump; a fawn still living but with his shoulder rotting and maggot-infested." A non-hunting naturalist estimated that in 1970 there were at least 25,000 British deer with gunshot wounds. By comparison, hunting seems merciful. Many people do not know, or have chosen to forget, that hounds kill swiftly: one bite, and the deer is dead.

What of the effect of hunting on hunters? I have chased both foxes and hares, but I never have known a chaser who took pleasure in prolonging the kill. On the contrary, I have seen them despatch their quarry, or call-off hounds. Some of the jolliest days of my life were spent chasing a hare which I never saw, with beagles that disappeared after ten minutes; and in the end the hare escaped. For many people the best part of hunting is its good companionship, the hazardous exercise, some fleeting nature study, and a kingly bath to crown them. That, of course, does not acquit us of the charge of causing suffering. But only ignorance or perversity will arraign the average hunter as a gross sadist.

Foul-mouthed and foolish hunters I have indeed met, though not so many as some newspaper reporters claim to know intimately (and none at all so foolishly foul as some of the acrobatic anti-hunters who wobble on the edge of the Arts). I have met also some fanatics who really would enjoy torturing the chasers. Pacifists tend to use a cowardly form of violence in support of non-violence. They throw stones (and run away) or wound horses (and stay to watch).

Nevertheless, the anti-huntsmen have a case, even although some of them do plead it for reasons of which they are unconscious. Clearly no animal enjoys being hounded to death. Clearly, therefore, it is cruel to chase an animal into exhaustion and terror. Clearly, too, it would be wholly good if man's leonine *ego* were to lie down peaceably with his lamblike *alter*. But the human psyche is not yet a "holy mountain", nor are there any valid reasons for supposing that it will soon become one. Even the Pope has his dreams; and the average laity wears a skin-deep civility. I happen to believe that hunting, as it is now conducted in Britain, does more good than harm to those who relish it. It allows them to exercise certain ineradicable impulses that might otherwise be deflected onto human beings. Think of the anti-hunting trouble-makers in our midst; the Hyde Park Lenin, the sit-down shop steward, the non-tax-paying student, the super-tax-paying playwright who grows rich by chipping his own shoulder. A day with hounds would leave every one of them too tired to commit his public nuisance. In any event, why pick on hunting? Is it not cruel to catch a fish by tearing out its intestines? Is it not cruel to punch prize-fighters into idiocy? Or to go for a walk and thereby squash the beetles? Or to breathe, and eat insects alive? Hunting, one feels, has been attacked because the average townsman continues to regard it as a monopoly of the rich, despite the fact that it remains a pageant which is enjoyed by all classes of countryfolk, many of whom regard the factory worker as Croesus.

All this is basically a matter of ethics; but ethics never was basically a matter of logic. For example, I choose not to chase stags; and my reason for that choice is aesthetic—because, unlike hares and foxes, the stag is a noble-looking beast. To conclude: persons who project their own aggressiveness onto hunters, will continue to do so until a less oblique therapy relieves them of that need; but men whose basic concern really is for the deer will share the astonishment of the non-hunting forester when he wrote: "It seems strange that all the sympathy of the anti-hunters is directed against a few packs of staghounds. Nobody seems to bother about the far larger cause (shooting) of suffering to the stag."

Stags roamed Britain 500,000 years ago. Some of them were giants whose antlers measured thirteen feet from tip to tip. Today their need for a wild and relatively unpeopled habitat confines them chiefly to the Scottish Highlands, Thetford Chase, Ashdown Forest, New Forest and Exmoor. You may see a deer anywhere within the National Park, and sometimes without; but their favourite coverts lie rather toward the centre and the north-east of the moor; notably around Culbone, Horner, Molland,

Simonsbath. The calves are born in June, and twins seem un-
common. Dr. Collyns of Dulverton was precise; he believed that
calves are dropped within a fortnight, from 7th June onward.
After about two months the dappled calf acquires the red winter
coat of adults. During the first few weeks of its life the creature
cannot easily move, and is therefore vulnerable to foxes and other
carnivores. Within three months or so it can fend for itself, but
remains with the hind for a year and perhaps for two, by which
time the male acquires short horns that are shed in the spring,
and regrown during September. Regrowth causes such intense
irritation that the stag rubs his horns against a tree (we call it
'a flaying stock'). In this way many willows and young conifers
are destroyed. During his third year a stag seeks the hinds, and
loud rivalry is heard.

A mature red stag, *Cervus elephans*, is the noblest of Britain's
ancient *fauna*; six feet tall to the top of his antlers. A true king of the
forest carries his head proudly indeed, with a brow antler, a bay,
a trey, and three a'top, forked like a main-royal trident. Because
of his good looks and proud bearing, the stag has received more
praise than any other of our wild creatures. Landseer painted a
splendid portrait of one, lording it over a Scottish glen. Thomas
Bewick, the self-taught Northumbrian genius who observed and
engraved wild creatures, describing the stag's eyes as "particularly beautiful, soft, and sparkling". Gilbert White saw the
red deer as "a beautiful link in the chain of beings". Richard
Jefferies saluted him as "a king". Beatrix Potter—another dedicated naturalist—was enchanted by the calves whose action she
depicted in *Peter Rabbit* fashion, "lippity, lippity, like a rabbit".

Alas, too many of those monarchs end as Charles II ended,
who took "an unconscionable time a-dying". Their teeth decay
before their strength, and, being ruminants, they starve slowly
through the final winter of their discontent. But while they live,
roaming and roaring and razing, they enhance their homeland
like a sovereign who remains aloof. When Beatrix Potter visited
Exmoor she was not granted an audience: "Unfortunately, we
saw no deer, though a herd of thirty-one had cruised into the
valley the night before, and were living in Horner Woods." My
own closest encounter with a stag occurred on one of the rare
occasions when I had left the dog at home, and was walking a
midnight road near Brendon Two Gates, through wind and mist.
Suddenly I found that I was following a stag, in the middle of the

road. By halting I must have alerted him, for he was away quicker than his own shadow—though I doubt that he indulged more than trot, for at that speed a stag can almost keep pace with a cantering pony. I often wonder which of us was the more surprised.

That brief encounter deepened my dilemma. On the one hand I seemed to overhear the suffering caused by unlucky or indifferent marksmen; on the other, the voice of Llewelyn Powys: "That civil people can still be found willing to hunt to death these proud beasts is to me extraordinary."

The lane to Stoke Pero

XV

THE SEA

Devon is the quarter-deck of England. Sir Francis Drake, Sir Walter Raleigh, Sir Richard Grenville, Sir John Hawkins, Sir Humphrey Gilbert, John Davis, John Oxenham, Stephen Borough: all were Devon men, and two of them learned their seamanship on the Severn Sea. No other British county has a comparable company.

Stephen Borough was born in 1525, at Northam near Bideford, in a house called Borough. He knew the reefs of Lundy as surely as he timed the tide at Heddon's Mouth. He it was—the first Englishman to sail to Russia—who named Cape North, the most northerly in European waters. His ship was a small pinnace, the *Serchthrift*; his number one, William Borough, a younger brother, not yet of age. Their setting-out was memorable, for Sebastian Cabot, then in his eighties, came to bid *bon voyage* to the Arctic explorers. Borough entered the occasion in his log. Cabot, he said, mingled with the crew and with the townsfolk of Bideford, "divers gentlemen and gentlewomen giving to our mariners right liberall rewards ... and the good olde gentleman Master Cabota gave to the poore most liberall alms, wishing them to pray for the good fortune and prosperous success of the *Serchthrift*." A dance was held, at which the veteran Inspector of the English Navy found his sea legs, inspired by "the very joy that he had to see the towardness of our intended discovery ... which (dance) being ended, he and his friends departed most gently, commending us to the governance of Almighty God."

Next day the *Serchthrift* sailed, carrying two casks of sherry from the Queen to Ivan the Terrible. But radio she did not carry, neither engines nor anaesthetics nor bathrooms nor anything at all that an Atomic seaman would recognize as food, or drink, or chart, or sextant, or chronometer. Down the Torridge she went, over the Bar, into the Severn Sea and thence among waves

10

The village inn, Winsford
The lane to Martinhoe

that would one day witness another English convoy, bearing richer gifts to an Ivan more terrible and less thankful.

But Stephen Borough was not content to ply for profit alone. He therefore joined the Queen's Navy as a trainer of seamen and the Chief Pilot of England. So, having learned his craftsmanship on these waters, he led that gallant company whom Masefield hailed:

> "By God and guess," the seaman's proverb was,
> So are paths found, where paths were never made.
> By thought's intensity transcending thought,
> The way is found, the ship to safety brought. . . .

There was no dancing when Sir Richard Grenville sailed in the *Revenge*, with five other vessels, to waylay a *flota* of Spanish treasure ships at the Azores. Having arrived, the small squadron encountered a fleet. Discreetly valorous, five of the English ships ran for safety, but the *Revenge* tried to cut her way through. At first the venture succeeded; Grenville, however, soon came under the lee of the largest Spaniard, the *San Felipe*, whose towering hull took the wind from his sails. Becalmed, he was attacked on every quarter. In theory the *Revenge* ought to have been sunk or seized at once; in fact, she fought from sunset until midnight, one ship against many. Eight hundred hits (they say) shattered the *Revenge*; water in her hold rose taller than a man; of her own men most were dead and none unwounded. Grenville himself lay dying. And still the *Revenge* fought on, for the Queen's ships never had surrendered to Spain. Remembering perhaps the little *Dolphin*, which blew herself up rather than yield at Gibraltar, Grenville ordered his men to follow that proud example, but they begged otherwise, for the sake of their families. So, in the end, the Spaniards boarded her, the only royal galleon which they ever did capture. Grenville died of his wounds, on board the Spanish flag ship. His last words will outlive the fashion that now finds them old-fashioned: "Here die I, Richard Grenville, with a joyful and quiet mind, for that I have ended my life as a true soldier ought to do, that hath fought for his country, his queen, religion, and honour. . . ."

His ship soon followed him, when a gale struck the Spanish fleet, sinking seventy of its warships. The epitaph was composed by another Devon seaman: "So it pleased them," wrote Sir Walter Raleigh, "to honour the burial of that renowned ship, the

Revenge, not suffering her to perish alone, for the great honour she achieved in her life-time."

Nelson, too, knew the Severn Sea, having spent some time at Bristol, as guest of his kinsfolk, the Tobins. That was in 1788, during the doldrums of his career, when the Admiralty had beached him. Watching the ships sailing westward to the Atlantic, the newly-married lieutenant confessed to Captain Locker: "I begin to think that I am fonder of the sea than ever." By bracing him against frustration, the Severn Sea preserved him for the fame which his father shared: "The height of glory to which your professional judgement, united with a proper degree of bravery, guarded by Providence, has raised you . . . few sons, my dear child, attain to, and fewer fathers live to see."

These waters continue to serve. During the 1939 war an officer of the Severn Division of the Royal Naval Volunteer Reserve was appointed Director of Combined Operations Signals School; and in 1956 the same officer became the first Volunteer Reservist to attain Flag rank, as Commodore F. T. Pollinger, CBE, VRD, DI, RNVR. One year later a history of the RNVR spoke the truth when it said: "Only those who are whole heartedly patriotic would make the sacrifice in time, and the effort that is called for by the RNVR today." Politicians scuttled the RNVR, but could not make it touch the bottom. The wavy gold lace of that famous institution is still worn by officers of the Sea Cadet Corps. And wise men still acknowledge the signal which their Lordships of the Admiralty made in 1661: "It is with His Majesty's Navies, Ships of War, and forces by sea, under the good Providence and Protection of God, that the Wealth, Safety, and Strength of this Kingdom is so much concerned."

William Harrison's *The Description of England*, which appeared in 1587, contains a succinct survey of ships: "The Navy of England may be divided into three sorts, of which the one serveth for wars, the other for burden, and the third for fishermen which get their living by fishing on the sea." Few men, if any at all, now catch a livelihood from this sea. They look rather to the visitors who hire boats. Of the trading ships some were coastal craft plying between the Severn harbours from Chepstow and Gatcombe to Lynmouth and Swansea; others, the larger vessels, sailed around the globe. But largeness is relative; for example, until the last century most of the world's commerce was carried by ships of less than 600 tons, and most of those ships were home-made. Every Exmoor harbour had its shipyard, employing carpenters, blacksmiths, cordwainers, sail-makers. From Watchet to Barnstaple a mast-head was as indigenous as the church, the manor, the mill.

One of the spiriteliest Victorian veterans was the *Haldon* of Barnstaple, a seventy-ton ketch, launched in 1893. Having traded in Scottish waters, she was bought by the Slades of Appledore, a famous North Devon family, who converted her as a three-masted schooner. In 1939, while unloading in Ireland, *Haldon* received a signal: "*Haldon* requisitioned by HM Government for balloon barrage purposes. Proceed to Appledore for inspection." In the event, she was not accepted.

Summer visitors regard the Severn Sea as placid, but *Haldon*'s last Devon skipper, W. J. Slade, admitted that even a seaman may come adrift between Barry and Porlock. One of his voyages, he said, "taught me a lesson I had yet to learn and that was that I could get into serious trouble even in the Bristol Channel". It happened like this: approaching Swansea through heavy rain, *Haldon* lost sight of Mumbles Head; her auxiliary engine failed; she would neither stay nor wear. "I could see nothing," her skipper reported, "so I set the mainsail again to try to drive her down on the port tack. Then we saw the buoy off Swansea pier close to leeward. I yelled, 'Lower the mainsail!' " The order came too late. As a desperate venture, Slade struck his ship against a mud bank, where he repaired the engine: "We got in dock that evening and I never felt more relieved." In 1948 *Haldon* was sold to a continental firm; in 1956 she still earned her keep, as a converted motor vessel, trading in Icelandic waters.

Another veteran, the *Result* of Barnstaple, led both a charmed and a challenging life. Launched in 1893, this three-masted topsail schooner was brought by a group of seamen at Braunton, a village on a creek of the River Taw (according to White's *Directory of Devon 1850*, the place contained half-a-dozen master mariners). Up to Bristol, down to Falmouth, across to Antwerp, timber, bricks, cattle, corn—the tradition was centuries old. In 1917, however, *Result* created a precedent by becoming HMS *Q23*, one of those apparently defenceless sailing ships with which the Admiralty tackled the German submarines. Commanded by Lieutenant (afterwards Rear-Admiral) P. J. Mack, she carried a crew of twenty-four—chiefly fishermen—and had three twelve-

pounder guns to reinforce a brace of torpedo tubes. Wearing
Dutch colours, she engaged a German submarine off the Dogger
Bank. The submarine escaped, but her captain and three ratings
were killed by *Result*'s gunfire. A few weeks later she engaged
another and larger German submarine which would certainly
have sunk her if Commodore Tyrwhitt's destroyers had not
arrived unexpectedly on patrol. The *Result* and her men belong
to a breed whom Joseph Conrad praised in his essay on the Patrol
Service: "In their early days some of them had but a single rifle
on board to meet the three four-inch guns of German destoyers.
Unable to put up a fight and without speed to get away, they
made a sacrifice of their lives every time they went out for a
turn of duty. . . ." During the 1960s the *Result* was trading as a
ketch.

Are any other sailing ships still working the Severn Sea? It is
difficult to answer that question; but in 1969 a lighthouseman
told me that he had lately sighted the *Kathleen* under full sail. One
assumes that *Kathleen*'s profits keep pace with the cost of living.
In 1908, for example, the ketch *Yeo* of Barnstaple gave her
skipper a wage of £3 weekly, with which he had to pay his
crew and to buy their food. Even so, he saved enough money
to become part-owner of the ship.

Visitors to Exmoor are sometimes perplexed because, having
noticed a dozen vessels in as many minutes, they return next day
to an empty sea. This uneven flow is due largely to the tides,
which move so fiercely that shipping prefers to go with rather than
against them. During the last war I saw sizeable merchantmen
riding at anchor when an adverse tide outran their own maximum of twelve knots. However, an assiduous look-out will
usually sight some kind of vessel. She may be a tanker, out from
Avonmouth; or a diminutive errand-girl, entering Watchet;
or a fishery protection vessel, her White Ensign singing to the
breeze.

There was a time when that Ensign would have been hailed
with joy by Severn sailors, for I doubt that any of their harbours
escaped the attention of pirates, either directly by assault or
indirectly through the loss of ships and men. The pirates' base was
Lundy Island, a speck or rock, north-west of Ilfracombe, whose
name is Old Norse, *lundi* or puffin. In clear weather the island
seems so near that Thomas Westcote wrote: "It is but four hours
sailing from hence with a good wind: let us view it." During

the eleventh and twelfth centuries Lundy belonged to the de Marisco family, who ruled there as petty kings, often defying the true king. In 1242 William de Marisco was hanged for piracy. Three centuries later Lord Saye and Sele—alias 'Old Subtlety'—more or less stole the island from its rightful owners, the Grevilles. His lordship was remembered by Celia Fiennes when she explored the coast as far as Hartland Point: "I discerned the Poynte very plain," she wrote, "and just by I saw the Isle of Lundy which formerly belonged to my Grandfather William Lord Viscount Say and Sele which does abound with fish and rabbets and all sortes of fowles. . . ." Miss Fiennes might have added "and all sorts of pirates". There was Captain Salkeld, leader of a gang of buccaneers; Admiral Nutt, another non-naval personage, who also led some brigands; a Frenchman named Pronville; and a crew of Moors from Barbary.

The pirates were followed by the smugglers, notably during the war against Napoleon, when the Royal Navy blockaded all trade to and from a large part of the Continent. The subtlest Exmoor smuggler was also the most flagrant—Thomas Benson, an eighteenth-century Member of Parliament for Barnstaple, who leased Lundy from Lord Gower, and then used it as a base for contraband. Having contracted with the Government to transport convicts to America, Benson landed them on Lundy, where they farmed his land and built new houses. He also arranged for ships to catch fire, after they had unloaded their cargo at Lundy, but the losses became so heavy that the insurance companies detected his ruse, whereupon he fled to Portugal, without bothering to invoke the Chiltern Hundreds.

Later owners of Lundy included the Heaven family, one of whom transmitted the first telegraph message from his island: "The kingdom of Heaven rejoiceth." The last private owners were the Harmans. In 1969 the island was acquired by the National Trust. So ended many centuries of private enterprise, and with them the island postage stamps (showing a puffin) and its freedom from licensing laws, Customs dues and several other public inconveniences.

Ships and men, however, are not the only traffic on the Severn Sea, for these waters are warmed by a stream which flows from the Gulf of Mexico, commonly known as the Gulf Stream although, on this side of the ocean, it ought properly to be called the North Atlantic Drift. On that stream several immigrants have reached Britain—Brazil nuts, West Indian seeds and particles of a soapberry tree from Central America. Exotic fish, too, have arrived, so that Barnstaple seamen blinked when they saw the tentacles of *Physalia* or Portuguese man-of-war, and the blue *Velella* whose white sail bloweth where the wind listeth (in 1954 the Plymouth Laboratory reported that *Velella* had been found along the Exmoor coast).

The sea and the land wage an ancient war. Sometimes a victory has seemed complete, as in the years when only the summits of Exmoor showed above the water, their tough sandstone rinsed by spray. At other times—which include our own—the victor retreats so slowly that his reverse is half-concealed. Thus, the Straits of Dover are widening at the rate of nearly a yard a year, and in parts of Norfolk the low coastline recedes at the rate of one foot every month. Yet the sea may lose most at the very moment when it appears to gain most—that is, when a cliff collapses, and deposits its débris over a mud-flat. The British Isles are growing, not shrinking.

The coastline of England and Wales is 2,751 miles long, and much of the Cornish and North Devon sectors are of high and irregular granite cliffs which bespeak prolonged erosion by the sea; or perhaps one should say by the waves, because tide and current are relatively powerless against rock. If I go down to the cove I find pebbles and boulders which, during calm weather, remain unmoved, as in *King Lear*:

> The murmuring surge
> That on the innumerable idle pebbles chafes. . . .

But during a gale the waves will hurl those stones against the base of the cliff, so undercutting it that the blocks are split along their joints, and fall therefrom by force of gravity, offering fresh ammunition to the sea, Keats was too placid when he cited

> The moving waters at their priest-like task
> Of pure ablution round earth's human shores.

I know the coast of Britain passably well, and parts of it intimately, not only from the land but also as one who has sailed the waters and lived thereon through the four seasons. If "infinite variety" be accepted as the yardstick which awards marks, I give second place to the northern climate of the Pentland Firth; my first goes to the Severn Sea. When I am on Exmoor never a day passes, and seldom a night, without I watch those waters; and neither at night nor by day do they wear the same expression for long, unless mist or rain obtrude their own opaqueness on it. You may scan the North Sea, or the Atlantic Ocean, or the English Channel for hours, and yet fail to detect any change in their sunlight or in their chiaroscuro; but for hours the face of the Severn Sea may change its expression every few moments, chiefly because it is a high sea, overlooked on the one side by Exmoor and on the other by Welsh mountains, so that its cloudscapes rise and fall like evanescent Alps.

Neither the clock nor a calendar will safely navigate those moods. Even the Meteorological Office has been known to misinterpret them. Any sea may be calm on Christmas morning, and convulsed on midsummer night; but only an ocean and an estuary and their mountains can so tap the barometer that it backs at dawn, veers with noon, and in twilight moves to midships. Sometimes the Severn Sea is as cruel as Shelley's:

> Treacherous in calm, and terrible in storm . . . .

Sometimes it is shrouded by the mists which prompted Sir Humphrey Gilbert's orders to his captains: "Item, if it shall happen a great fogge to fall, then presently every shippe to beare up with the Admirall, if there be winde; but if it be calme, then every ship to hull, and so to lie at hull till it be cleere." Sometimes the sea becomes as Coleridge saw it when he walked by starlight from the Quantocks:

> The harbour bay was clear as glass,
> So smoothly it was strewn;
> And on the bay the moonlight lay,
> And the shadow of the moon.

On a summer dawn the westward horizon—empty of all land save America—utters an invitation which Keats accepted:

> O ye! who have your eye-balls vex'd and tired,
> Feast them upon the wideness of the sea . . .

Empty at one moment, with the next this fairway shows what V. Sackville-West saw, a frigate or a tanker maybe,

> . . . leaping out from narrow English ease
> She faced the roll of long Atlantic seas. . . .

No other British waters have a comparable coastline; none a

lovelier nor more luxuriant hinterland. Meadows slope like lawns toward the cliff. Over a rump of glistening sheep you sight the sea's blue mantle, reflected from the sky. Ahead, the Welsh peaks shimmer; astern, the heights of Exmoor; all around, a quilt of heather and herbage and woodland. And always the scene is set to music; sometimes in moonlit rhythm with the slow movement of Beethoven's Emperor concerto; sometimes with Wagnerian Valkyrie; more often with a *scherzo* that Aeschylus loved:

The laughter of innumerable waves.

XVI

THE MINES

Matthew Arnold pictured the Phoenicians who sailed in search of British tin:

> To where the Atlantic raves
> Outside the Western Straits, and unbent sails
> There, where down cloudy cliffs, through sheets of foam,
> Shy traffickers, the dark Iberians come.

Those "dark Iberians" or British Celts were indeed shy. Having set their wares on the beach—corn and ornaments, as well as tin—they retired out of sight, to see what kind of bargain-in-kind the strangers would set alongside the British offerings. But mining is older than that. They still take lead from a mine in Attica which was working 600 years before the birth of Christ; and at Rio Tinto the mine works as it did for the merchants of Tyre and Sidon. In 1925, while excavating a hill castle near St. Just in Cornwall, an archaeologist uncovered a lump of smelted metal which the assayers proved to be tin, more than 2,000 years old. Victorian Cornishmen believed that their distant ancestors had mined the tin which became the brasswork in Solomon's Temple. Tudor Cornishmen believed that St. Paul himself not only preached to Cornish miners but also—like a good visitor—bought a lump of tin from the Creegbrowse Mine near St. Day. Joseph of Arimathea, they said, was a tin-worker.

The Exmoor mines must be classified according to their geology. Thus, the so-called Devonian rocks of slate and black shale are rich in uranium and other ores; the limestone belt at Combe Martin yielded silver and lead; other North Devon minerals included coal, copper, gold. We know that the Romans mined on Exmoor and that they improved the road from Exeter to Molland, a famous source of lead. The British Museum has a lump of iron slag, found near Dulverton, containing Roman coins.

In 1086 Domesday Book mentioned four iron-workers or *ferruarii* at North Molton. But the early history of all the Exmoor mines was summarized by William Camden: "of the first fynding and working the silver mines there are no certain records remaynge".

One early record shows that in 1550 a certain Wynston received licence to work "divers mines of iron within the King's Forest of Exmore." Queen Elizabeth I invited German miners to come to England. Some of them went north into Cumberland (Keswick became a centre of the lead pencil trade); others reached Devon (near the Exe valley a hill is still called Eyesen or Eisen). In 1618 the Earl of Pembroke received licence to dig for silver at Bushford. At Molland they struck gold, and Jan Ridd deplored the fact: "Although there are very ancient tales of gold being found on Exmore, in lumps and solid hummocks, and of men who slew one another for it, this deep digging and great labour seemed to me a dangerous and unholy enterprise." At about the same time, Celia Fiennes noted the West Country copper: "the oar is something as the tinn only this looks blackish or rather purple colour and the glistering part is yellow as the other was white; they do not melt it here but ship it off to Bristol. . . ." A heavy price was paid for this industry, "which employs a great many people at work, almost night and day . . . and all every day includeing the Lords day which they are forced to do, to prevent their mines being overflowed with water. . . ." Both the ore and the water were hauled up in buckets "much like the leather buckets they use in London to put out fire . . .".

Toward the end of the eighteenth century Defoe reported a decline: "The county of Devon has been rich in mines of tin and lead, though they seem at present worked out. . . ." Defoe, however, overlooked the Devon copper mining, which reached its zenith when Parliament sanctioned the building of a canal from Tavistock to Morwelham, through the heart of the Dartmoor lodes; but the Devon mines soon began to fail, and today they no longer mar the life of Exmoor. Only the very oldest inhabitants can remember them, and only from the hearsay of their fathers. Nevertheless, the industry existed for thousands of years, and has left its mark throughout the moor. For example, you may remember that when we explored Simonsbath we discovered a footpath which walked off the map, leaving us high and damp on the summit of a treeless ravine beside the Barle, overlooking a ruined cottage. That is the site of the Wheal Eliza Copper Mine (Wheal being the Cornish *hwel* or mine, and Eliza being Queen Elizabeth I). Men had dibbled thereabouts for centuries, but it was not until 1846 that John Knight did business with Russell Riccard (a South Molton lawyer), Richard Sleeman (a Tavistock surgeon), Oliver Matthews (a Molland 'developer') and John Lock (another from South Molton). The quintet belonged to a tribe which Izaak Walton described as "money-getting men, men that spend all their time, first getting, and next, in anxious care to keep it; men that are condemned to be rich, and then always busie or discontented . . . poor-rich-men". The four 'developers' agreed to employ at least six miners on the site and to pay John Knight the sum of 1s. 4d. on every poundsworth of ore that was mined, less the cost of transporting it. When 200 tons of ore had been obtained, the aforesaid were to build six cottages for the miners; but it was forbidden to "kill or molest the Red Deer on the Forest". The potential squalor begat a murder, committed by a man named Burgess, a widower with one daughter, who occupied a cottage near the Wheal Eliza Mine. Burgess objected to his daughter's fiancé, and when she refused to break-off the engagement, he murdered her and then buried the corpse on the moor. Not long afterwards some sheep-stealers arrived, intending to bury their carcass until a suitable buyer had been found. Noticing a shallow grave, they assumed that one of their own kind had lately been at work; and this they told to Burgess, who at once removed the corpse, and threw it down the mine shaft. But when the poachers again examined the grave, they found part of a frock and with it some human hair. The hunt began. Arrested in Wales, Burgess was hanged at Taunton.

Ten years later the *North Devon Journal* announced that "an important lode has been discovered in the working of the Wheal Eliza Copper Mine on Exmoor". Forthwith Frederick Knight bought back the lease (in a friend's name) for £328 17s. 6d. which included the miners' beds, blankets and cutlery. Although the yield was adequate, the cost of transport became excessive. In 1860 the mine closed. But it had been a narrow escape, for the Knights planned to transform the moor into a loud eyesore riddled with roads, railways, arc-lights, housing estates and other higher standards of a living death. Knight, indeed, visited Wales, hoping that the Dowlais Iron Works would help him to destroy the moor. And Dowlais agreed. Nearly 7,000 acres were to be

'developed', and a railway was to be built from Bristol to Simonsbath, with a branch line for Porlock Weir. The Weir itself was
to be swamped by a commercial dock. Nor did the scheme remain
on paper. Gangs of Irish navvies hacked a track from the Mineral
Railway; Porlock Weir screeched with cranes and steam-hammers.
By happy chance—Celia Fiennes would have called it the grace
of God—the 'developers' decided that their receipts would not
cover costs. So, having been snatched from the jaws of prosperity, Exmoor now utters a resounding No to Blake's famous
question:

> And was Jerusalem builded here
> Among these dark Satanic mills?

It is still fashionable to dismiss as 'romantic' anyone who protests
against the erosion of farmland by industry. In 1969 a group of
scientists announced that the fashion must change. If, they said,
industry continues to expand, so much heat will be generated
that, within the next twenty years, the world's ice-caps will melt
and a large part of this planet will disappear under the waves.

The Combe Martin silver mines were thriving when Edward I
licensed 337 miners to migrate thither from the Peak District of
Derbyshire, a region whose mines Celia Fiennes described as
"impregnated with rich Marbles Stones Metals Iron and Copper
and Coal mines in their bowells . . .". Peak, in fact, became a
familiar surname on the Devon Moor. Westcote says that in 1490
the Combe Martin mines "being then both deepe and almost
worn out, ceased". A century later they revived: "In the time of
Queen Elizabeth", says Westcote, "there was found a new lode
on the lands of Richard Roberts, gentleman." A prospector with
mining interests on the Mendips, Sir Bevis or Beauvois Bulmer,
made a fortune from the new lode. By way of gratitude he presented a silver bowl to "Sir Richard Martyn, Knight, Lord Mayor
of London, to continue in the said citie for ever". The bowl still
does continue "in the said citie", though no longer as a bowl,
having been melted down to make three tankards. The original
bowl carried a long inscription, explaining that the silver had
been found

> In place cal'd Comb, wher Martin longe
> Had hydd me in his molde,
> I did no service on the earth,
> Nor no man set me free,

> Till Bulmer by his skill and charge
> Did frame me this to be.

A similar bowl was presented to William Bourchier, Earl of Bath; and that, too, extolled the merits of its donor:

> In Martyn's Combe long lay I hydd,
> Obscured, deprest with grossest soyle,
> Debased much with mixed lead,
> Till Bulmer came; whose skill and toyle
>   *et cetera.*

One surmises that the same hand scrawled both doggerels, and was very likely Bulmer's. Hearing that the cup had been sent to a famous person in London, Exmoor insisted that the person must be the Queen herself; an error which Jan Ridd detected when he recalled "the tales I heard concerning mines in Cornwall, and the silver cup at Combe-Martin, sent to the Queen Elizabeth".

During the Civil Wars the Combe Martin mines were managed for the King by Thomas Bushell, who, via his friendship with Francis Bacon, became Mint Warden and Master for "His Majesty's Mynes Royal in the Principality of Wales". In 1643 Bushell shifted his headquarters to Bristol and thence into North Devon. At the height of the fighting he shipped his precious metals to Lundy Island, and there commanded a garrison which he had equipped at his own cost. Lundy was among the last of the loyal places to surrender. Bushell himself had evidently sought the King's permission to yield, because, on 4th July 1646, he received the royal reply: "Bushel, We have perused your Letter, in which We finde they care to Answer thy trust We at first reposed in thee . . . We do hereby give you leave to use your discretion in it with this Caution, that you do take example from Ourselves, and not be over-credulous of vain promises, which hath made Us great only in our sufferings. . . ." Having himself suffered imprisonment and exile, Bushell returned with the Restoration. At the age of 73 he was still hoping to revive the Exmoor mines and "to pursue Comb-Martyn Mine in Devon".

The mine, however, remained quiescent until 1796, when it became so active that within six years 9,393 tons of ore were sent to Wales. Then the work ceased until 1813, when a second revival sent 208 tons to Bristol in eleven months, but at such heavy cost that work ceased four years later. Various financiers took up the challenge, but none succeeded for long. In 1876 a West

Combmartin Silver-Lead Mine Company began—and soon after-wards stopped—digging near the Little Hangman. In 1900 a cer-tain A. S. Doidge of Callington, in Cornwall, hoped that he was on to a good thing when his agent assured him:

> The above mining property is situated in the Parish of Parracombe, North Devon. One mile from the Railway Station. The Grant is very extensive and contains three or more well known Silver and Lead Lodes. . . . I am fully convinced it is a property of great value, and with judicious management the workings will be very profitable.

Stupid fellows; they did no more about it; so, instead of being arc-lit and arterialized, Parracombe is still a quiet and beautiful village. Long may the moor elude all who would defile it in the name of progress.

Anyone who walks the moor will see for himself what it would have been like if the mines had prospered into the late twentieth century. Their débris extends from Combe Martin to Simonsbath, from Molland to Dulverton, from Swimbridge to North Molton. Fortunately, the litter is hidden among trees or beneath the grass. At Stowford Mine, near North Molton, I found part of a tower and under it an archway to the shaft. Having crawled in, I retreated quickly when several sizeable stones clattered onto my neck. The next day, while walking from the Chains, I crossed the Challacombe road, west of Simonsbath, and there discovered a hole in the rocks near Cornham Farm. Below lay a mine shaft. Someone had set a few planks across the cavity, but an inquisitive child could be lost without trace. Two miles from South Molton, on the Combe Martin road, the shaft of a silver and lead mine, nearly 200 feet deep, was working until the 1870s. In the parish of Dulverton, above Beer Farm, there are some shafts of a derelict copper mine. The wild land of Mole's Chamber contains several shafts, mounds, and slag heaps.

The Exmoor miners led to wretched life, coming and going wherever and whenever the market invited them. Parish registers reveal a race of rootless migrants—from Germany, from Holland, from Sweden, from Cornwall—shunned by the natives whose livelihood they had usurped. Thus, when Richard Slader, the Exmoor poet-tramp, sought temporary employment at North Molton, and was accepted by an immigrant miner named Julieff, he soon afterwards sacked himself, declaring that he never would work for a foreigner.

The loneliest parts of the moor were enlived by inns for the miners; 'The Red Deer' near Exford, 'The Gallon' near Simonsbath, 'The Acland Arms' at Mole's Chamber. Now only the 'Sportsman's Inn' remains, alone on a lane at Sandyway. Although the miners were spared the hazards of coal-mining (the nearest coal pit lay west of Barnstaple), and although they earned more than the farm workers, many of them died prematurely, killed by an unnatural life, out of the sunlight and away from the wind. John Wesley and his brother Charles came down, to help if they could. Each preached to a large crowd beside the river at North Molton. John Wesley preached at Simonsbath also. And the miners and farmfolk of North Molton founded the first Wesleyan chapel in North Devon.

I have seen more than fifty photographs and drawings of the Exmoor mines in action a century ago. One especially—the Bampfylde Copper Mine at North Molton—reveals the shape of things that came and mercifully went. Against the beauty of the moor, you see shacks, brick walls, smoke, and the wheel of an unmerry-go-round. Worst of all, you see miners whose faces are as white as the depths wherein they worked were black. In 1837 Doctor Lanyon made a study of Exmoor miners. Their average life-span, he discovered, was thirty-one years; their working life, sixteen years and eight weeks. The commonest causes of death were heart failure and lung disease. Working in a temperature of 90 degrees Fahrenheit, a miner could lose six pounds' weight between breakfast-time and supper. In 1840 an official report described miner's consumption as so common that the colliery villagers were surprised when a middle-aged miner did not contract it. When Doctor Couch made his own survey, he had no need to examine each miner; it was enough to stand at the pit head: "To see the men arriving at the surface after eight hours' work is a most sickening sight. Thin, haggard, with arms very much lengthened and hanging almost uselessly by their sides, they seem like men worn out rather than tired." In 1847 the Royal Cornwall Polytechnic Society reported: "Of the miners working in a single parish of this county, nineteen in every hundred die a violent death. . . ." But there is no need to emphasize the self-evident. In answer to Blake's other famous question:

> And did those feet in ancient time
> Walk upon England's mountains green?

Selworthy church

the answer is: "Only on Sunday. For the rest of the week they crawled and crouched like moles beneath the surface." The Exmoor mining industry was an early and vivid example of a countryside whose folk were not countryfolk—nor even townsfolk—but inhabited a nether-region, of a kind that in our own day is a rootless desert of identical human-hutches dumped in straight lines beside screeching traffic. That is what Exmoor might have become. Therefore I say again, long may the moor elude all who would defile it in the name of progress.

11

Packhorse Bridge, Brendon

XVII

WINTER

The wind thumped the house, and entered uninvited down the chimney. But the din remained so constant that I felt each thump without hearing it. Sometimes the curtains moved, as though a ghost had passed. When I opened the door, it was slammed by a gale which lifted the mat.

Outside, the path seemed to sway. Clouds raced overhead, black-edged as though in mourning for the universe. Rain slashed sideways, parallel with the ground. Then my cap was ripped off, and I crawled after it up the steep bank behind the Haven, like an old man stooping for the bait which mischievous urchins have tied to a string. Away the cap went, tumbling the snowdrops that had lately flowered, over primroses that soon would flower; and so for another twenty yards into the wood. At last I caught it and jammed it onto my head, and stood staring in amazement at the trees. How could those top-heavy towers heave so violently through such an arc? Two had already fallen; one lay flat, the other lolled against its neighbour; and the roots of each resembled the tentacles of a flailing octopus. Lumps of leaves, weighing a pound apiece, were being flung about like confetti. The red earth ran with its own blood. Above, one gull flapped and flapped, as though straining to reach the Ark, but without ever gaining steerage way. Slowly its rate of striking fell, and at last it careened and was swept astern, swifter than the bubbles in a ship's wake.

Punched by the gale, I stumbled down the path and thence into the lane, where a flood struck my boots with white waves carrying straw, twigs, fleece, pebbles, grit, moss. An empty cigarette packet took off and flew over the hedge. Cascades of rainwater scoured the sides of the inn. All puddles overflowed into a single lake.

The river roared, thirsting for the sea; but whenever I moved more than a few yards from its bank, the roar was lost in the general din. Two boughs struck a midstream rock with such force that they somersaulted salmon-wise. Usually the sides of the ravine were speckled with sheep, but now I saw none; all had sought shelter on lower ground.

I supposed that the uproar never could increase, yet when I came within fifty yards of the sea, I overheard the *crescendo* of waves out-thundering the wind. At thirty yards I tasted the brine; at twenty I was rinsed by it, and could scarcely stand upright. The cove itself was shrouded in spray.

Far out to sea, grey hills broke to become white mountains that collapsed and surged forward and then rose again and then again collapsed and re-arose. Some of them collided in their race to the shore, creating seaquakes of spume, as if from innumerable whales. The turmoil resembled a cavalry charge, each horse hurling itself to death, and falling back, to be trampled by the next. Dimly through the spray I sighted a small tanker, and was half-surprised at not being able to hear the crunch of her bows when she crashed into a trough. This was the weather that sank Sir Patrick Spens:

> I saw the new moon late yestreen
> Wi' the auld moon in her arm;
> And if we gang to sea, master,
> I fear we'll come to harm.

But the assault on the beach seemed a mere sideshow when compared with the cannonade against the cliffs, for each wave unleashed its own scaling ladder, twisting and turning up the walls, and then—before it fell back defeated—transcending itself with one final effort that begat a fountain. Sometimes the waves discovered a cavity and dived into it, and were spewed back, seething like a dragon's breath. Nowhere did the battering cease nor falter.

I began to climb the cliff path, clutching at gorse as I went. When the path veered inland, under the lee of its own brow, the wind abated; but I knew that when the path emerged again, even higher, it must meet the very summit of the gale.

It did. I could not breathe against it. I had to turn my head. Sideways, therefore, I looked down upon England beseiged by inexhaustible squadrons whose lifeblood wove a necklace round the coast.

Then the snow arrived; not flake by flake, but in a phalanx, wetter than rain. Before I could glance from east to west, the world went white and was invisible. But I continued to climb, all the while clutching at whatever shrub or rock offered security. I was astonished to see the snow rising up, as though driven out of the sea and thence against the cliffs into the sky. Visibility was nil, so I turned for home. On that part of the coast two false steps would end in the maelstrom below.

All night it snowed, heavily and without pause, so that men awoke to a world of impassable lanes. You could not even tell where the lanes lay. The moor was a Trappist, sworn to silence.

But now at last the clouds dispersed while a cold sun blinded without warmth. Again I went down to the sea, staring at the white beach. The walk thither had been through fairyland where rocks wore snowy crowns above trees that formed a crystal avenue beside the river.

Ploughs did clear one road, but it remained stripped of its tributaries. All signposts stood like gallows in a shroud. The Haven was marooned. For two days no one came nor went, except the postman, who had trudged from the village four miles away. His arrival so surprised him that thankfulness tripped over its own negatives: "My dear man," he told the inn, "I wouldn't care not never to do that not every day I wouldn't. I ain't never been so far and seen so little. 'Fact, I hadn't gone a two-mile afore I was wondering if the world hadn't ended without bothering to tell me. Then I saw old Reuben's plough, sticking up 'longside the road, and I thought, 'Maybe the world hasn't ended.' But after another half-mile I said to myself, 'But maybe it *has* ended, and Reuben and all the rest with 'en. Maybe there's a new world come to pass—a bit easier than th'old—with ploughs lying around, readymade as you might say, so's folk needn't have the troubling of inventing 'em.' "

He glanced up, reassured by the familiar outlines of the inn; and his assurance was confirmed when the landlord issued an order: "Go into the kitchen, and ask for some tea."

"Well, now, t'wouldn't hardly be polite to say No, would it?"

And away he went, like a genial snowman, trailing his tracks on the carpet.

That afternoon the sun grew colder and then hazy. At dusk the wind died. By nightfall more snow seemed imminent. But at three o'clock next morning I awoke to a *rondo* of rain, pelting and persistent.

Five hours later I thought that spring had arrived, for the storm-cock was silent, and thrushes greeted January with a song.

By noon the rain had rinsed away most of the snow. At four o'clock, having climbed the hill, I found no snow at all until I looked eastward to Countisbury, and even there only the summit was sugared. Across the sea, Wales, too, wore white; but in this part of England the sun shone, glinting the green grass. Sheep returned to graze above the Haven. In the woods where I had lately chased my cap, the only drops of snow were flowers, clustered at the foot of those two fallen trees. So there it was: black days and white days and now this greenscape under a fleecy sky. I thought of the beautiful legend of the halcyon or kingfisher, which, so the Ancients believed, could calm the winter solstice while she hatched her brood and set them floating in their nest upon the water: "Then came the halcyon," wrote Shenstone, "whome the sea obeys. . . ." And not only the sea: the road to Simonsbath, the lane to Lynton, the track to Trentishoe . . . all shone and were calm. The snow had slipped its burden of unwonted silence. Sheep spoke up, querulous after the blizzard. Robins joined the rehearsing thrush. Rooks haunted their old home, as though they had read Shelley:

If Winter comes, can Spring be far behind?

Down by the river a pony slopped and clopped. Waves on the beach were mild lips, nibbling at sunny rocks.

No one had come out to witness the spectacle; those who did see it, glanced sideways from whatever task they were at —shoeing a horse, feeding a herd, or scanning a frigate as she steamed westward into the Atlantic. Exmoor is like that in winter. Some parts are exactly like it throughout the year; Dick's Path, for example; or the lane to Ball, which is a tributary of the lanes to Molland; or those sheepwalks above Exford; or the lane from Dean to Parracombe, which a wise council conserves as unfit for motor vehicles.

Something of this wintry seclusion overspills into our little towns. Thus, the Lynton shops are never so friendly as at toasttime in December; then and there the native knows and is known. And how eerie to visit Dunster at noon in December, with only one Land-Rover in a street so still that you overhear a sparrow pecking the cobbles of the Yarn Market. All tokens of tourism look *démodés*. At Dulverton a 'Vacancies' board creaks on its hinge, irrelevant as a Bible in Piccadilly. At Lynmouth a snack bar sleeps and will not wake till Whitsun. Never a charabanc, never a cream tea; neither jackpot nor litter nor lucky charm; Mammon has retired on the profit of a summer spree.

All around, for many days and starry nights, Exmoor bestrides the summit of an ancient stillness.

XVIII

THE STORY OF LORNA DOONE

Some places live in the books which they created. One thinks of George Crabbe's Aldeburgh in *The Borough*, of Emily Brontë's Haworth in *Wuthering Heights*, of Thomas Hardy's Dorchester in *The Mayor of Casterbridge*, and of R. D. Blackmore's Exmoor in *Lorna Doone*. Such books are steeped in the outward and visible signs of an inward and spiritual place. They heighten our awareness of the countryside which they describe.

Lorna Doone is not a flawless work of art; it is something less austere and more immediately endearing, for it ranks with those two or three other books which may claim to be the best-loved and most widely-read English novel. Every educated person has heard of it, and many have read it, very likely when they were too young either to detect its faults or to assess its merits. In that sense, therefore, the story of *Lorna Doone* needs no re-telling. But there is another story—as it were the story behind the story—the life of the author and the birth of his book. Each is an aspect of Exmoor.

"I was launched into this vale of tears on the 7th of June, 1825, at Longworth in Berkshire." Such was Richard Doddridge Blackmore's account of his nativity as the third son of the Reverend John Blackmore, sometime Fellow of Exeter College, Oxford. The son added a postscript: "Before I was four months old, my mother was taken to a better world. . . ." Seeking a refuge from his grief, the bereaved father returned alone to Devonshire, the land of his own fathers, first at Culmstock, then at Ashford, and finally at Heanton Court, the seat of his late wife's family. R. D. Blackmore meanwhile was tended by an aunt, Mary Knight, who lived at Nottage, a Tudor mansion near Porthcawl in Glamorganshire. When Miss Knight married the rector of Earlsfield, the child accompanied her to that quiet Oxfordshire village.

Having reached an age for schooling, Blackmore joined his father in Devon. A farmer, who died in 1926, remembered the lad as a weekly boarder at South Molton's sixteenth-century grammar school. Later he attended King's School at Bruton in Somerset, and thereafter received the classical West Country education at Blundell's and Exeter College, Oxford.

Time has changed the buildings which Blackmore knew at Blundell's but not the classical education which he wore next his heart, as a touchstone that could sift the meretricious from the meritorious, and the merely modern from the more abiding. Despite some rough handling by bullies, Blackmore loved Blundell's. His books and letters express gratitude for what it had taught him: "The nature and nurture of solid learning," he declared, "were better understood when schools were built from which came Shakespeare, and Bacon, and Raleigh. . . ." Man's quest for knowledge has roamed widely since Blackmore's day, but the insight of Plato and the eloquence of Lucretius can never fall behind the times.

In 1843 Blackmore went up to Exeter College, where he took the Gifford scholarship. Oxford and Blackmore might have been made for each other. Railways were scarce; the roads, white and leisurely; the university, uncorrupted by the fallacy that education has any necessary connection with 'a job'. Blackmore, however, needed a job; though no one knows why he chose the Law. Perhaps he was persuaded thereto by an ancestor who became Solicitor-General. In 1849, at all events, Blackmore was admitted to the Honourable Society of the Middle Temple, but preferred to work under a barrister of the Inner Temple and Chancery Bar. Three years later he was himself called, and thereafter practised as a conveyancer until 1857, when his health refused any longer to suffer an enclosed life: "My medical adviser", he wrote, "said I would have to give up my profession, seek outdoor employment, or die young." Meantime, he had married Miss Lucy Maguire, a Roman Catholic, who submitted to Canterbury. With her he lived happily until she died, thirty-five years later. The marriage being childless, Blackmore consoled himself by loving other men's children. He became godfather to many infants, and was asked to sponsor Noël Coward, but declined because, he said, twelve of his godchildren had died of spinal meningitis, and he was beginning to feel superstitious. When Francis Armstrong, the artist, became a father, he named his daughter Lorna. Writing in 1931, a friend remembered Blackmore as "a most dear and kindly old man".

Soon after his marriage the retired barrister became classics master at Wellesley House School, Twickenham, where he published his first book, *Poems by Melanter*, which was praised by *The Athenaeum* as the work of a man "at least of education and refinement, with much rhythmical skill, if not endowed with poetic genius". Two more poetry books followed and, like the first, were soon forgotten.

Once again his health rebelled against a sedentary life: "Considering for sometime what occupation to follow, I decided to become a gardener and horticulturist." This change was made possible by a legacy from an uncle, the rector of Neath in Glamorganshire. So, Blackmore bought sixteen acres of fertile ground at Bushy Park near Hampton Court; and in 1860 built himself a home, Gomer House, which was demolished in 1938. We have no record of his studies in horticulture, but he was a child of the countryside and may have received help from one of his Twickenham friends, Professor Richard Owen. Like Virgil—whose *Georgics* he translated—the husbandman cursed the climate and the pests:

> Our heavenly Father hath not judged it right
> To leave the road of agriculture light;
> 'Twas he who first made husbandry a plan,
> And care a whetstone for the whit of man. . . .

Nevertheless, the new life suited him so well that he was able to begin his career as a novelist: *Clara Vaughan, Cradock Nowell, The Maid of Sker, Alice Lorraine*—all are good tales told well. "Perhaps taken altogether," he believed, "*Alice Lorraine* is the best." Taken altogether they do indeed justify the verdict of Eden Phillpotts: "He enriched the language with many great works . . . proceeding from his own abundance as an artist and a man." The public, however, still regards him as a one-book author. *Lorna Doone* certainly put Exmoor on the map, and has kept it there, alongside Hardy's Wessex. Blackmore himself came of an Exmoor family. As we have already noted, his grandfather was vicar of Oare and of Combe Martin; his uncle, rector of Charles. Blackmore stayed at all of those places, and from them he roamed the length and breadth of Exmoor.

But the story of *Lorna Doone* has roots far older than the

nineteenth century, for the Blackmores traced their descent from
Tudor times. In 1616 a Walter Blackmore of Martinhoe rented
Bodley Farm. His son, Richard, acquired more land near Parra-
combe. An indenture of 1630 stated:

> John Snt Albon of Alfoxen in the countie of Somerset, Esquire . . .
> doth demise graunte and to farm lett unto . . . Richard Blackmore
> and Jane his wiefe all the third pte of Bodeleigh Berrie contayning
> by estimacion five and twentie acres be it more or less situate
> lyeinge and beinge about Bodleigh Grattens and the north side of
> the same within the parishe of Paracombe.

Thus from yeomanry the family rose to gentility as country
parsons. Other of the novelist's ancestors had achieved an earlier
eminence. For example, Blackmore owed his second Christian
name to Sir John Doddridge, who became Solicitor-General in
1604 and a justice of the King's Bench in 1607. Blackmore knew
that Francis Bacon and Thomas Fuller had praised his knightly
forebear; with his own eyes he had seen Sir John's tomb in the
Lady Chapel of Exeter Cathedral and his portrait in the National
Gallery. Born therefore and bred upon a sense of history, at a
time when England stood at her zenith, Blackmore found nothing
comical in remarking: "the knee of an Englishman goes down to
none except his Maker." He would not have approved the
current value of an Englishman's passport.

It was during the early 1860s that he began researching for
Lorna Doone. In 1865 he was at Lynton, and soon afterwards at
Withypool, Oare, Charles. A Porlock shopkeeper remembered
him with notebook and pencil, copying down whatever he could
learn of local lore from local people. Several Exmoor villages
claim that he stayed in them while he wrote parts of the book.
But his own relatives stated that the book was composed almost
entirely at Twickenham. The writing of it began in 1867 and
ended at six o'clock on the evening of 15th April 1868. Composition proved difficult: "I threw it by in ill content", he confessed, "four or five times, and then went ahead." Chaucer had
shared a comparable discouragement:

> The lyf so short, the craft so long to lerne,
> Th'assay so hard, so sharp the conquering.

Even so, the difficulty of writing must have seemed slight when
compared with the task of publishing. Messrs. May Smith and
Elder, to whom he first offered it, rejected the book, having

taken eight weeks to confirm their stupidity. The next publisher took five months, and then returned the manuscript "so dirty that I must rewrite the beginning". And still the search continued: "It had been rejected by all the best magazines, and the leading publishers, and I felt *nearly* certain that they must be right." This, remember, was not a first book; it was his eighth. With much courage, and not a little grace, Blackmore continued to submit himself to the humiliating heartache: "I brought home the manuscript more than once in sorrow and discomfiture; and at last was fain to accept an offer of nothing for it." Sampson Low, in fact, had accepted the book on niggardly terms, after five weeks of discussion by their experts.

Having appeared, the book disappeared. Blackmore spoke wryly of "the first faint praise of the noble army of critics". All occasions conspired against him: "Of the first 500 copies," he mourned, "only about 300 were sold, and the rest in a batch transported for Colonial fare." The author bore himself more manfully than most of his tribe in similar straits. He had written *ad majorem Dei gloriam*, which is an altruistic way of saying "for his own delight"; and during the next ten years his reward was indeed in Heaven, since on earth it never exceeded 3s. a day.

Blackmore's opinion of *Lorna Doone* remained ambivalent. Long after it had been published he confessed to a friend: "It will always be out of my power to understand why so many people have formed almost an attachment for one of my books, *Lorna Doone*, while they care not to look at any of the others." But another friend received a different verdict: "*Lorna Doone*", wrote George Putnam, "had always been his own favourite."

As with Mary Webb, so with R. D. Blackmore; a chance event tilted the scales when they seemed forever set against success. In 1870 the Princess Louise pleased herself and the world by marrying a Scottish peer, the Marquis of Lorne; and an earlier Lord Lorne, as Jan Ridd remarked, "was some years the elder of his cousin Ensor Doone". Suddenly the book reviewers remembered that Sampson Low had lately issued a cheap edition of the unsuccessful *Lorna Doone*. One reviewer—who read history as negligently as he noticed Blackmore—announced that the novel was about the family of the Princess's husband. Thus, where talent had failed to sow, topicality was quick to reap. Sampson Low assured the author that "the book is going to have a run". And run it did. Solely because of a royal marriage and an ignorant journalist, *Lorna Doone* gathered mass with momentum. Years after the wedding had ceased to be news, a sixpenny edition of 100,000 copies was sold within one week. Yet Blackmore reaped no riches therefrom; his royalties remained constant at less than £1 weekly. Like Joseph Conrad, he consoled himself by remembering that "an artist's richest treasure is in the hearts of men and women". Six years after his death, in 1906, the Yale College Class chose *Lorna Doone* as their favourite novel (*Vanity Fair* having lost the race by nine votes). In 1969, in the preface to a cheap edition, the editor hoisted a straw in the wind of change:

> for modern readers particularly, a little tired perhaps of disillusion-ment and the fictional fashion of matrimony endured rather than enjoyed, the assurance that Lorna became "a more and more loved wife" whose beauty grew year by year "with the growth of good-ness, kindness, and true happiness", will bring its own music and inspiration.

Blackmore's preface to the first edition defined the book's *genre*: "This work", he announced, "is called a Romance, because the incidents, characters, time, and scenery are alike romantic. And in shaping this old Tale, the writer neither dares, nor desires, to claim for it the dignity, nor cumber it with the difficulty, of an historic novel." Yet he affirmed the historicity of the Doones by emphasizing the legends which they evoked: "any son of Exmoor, chancing on this volume, cannot fail to bring to mind the nurse-tales of his childhood—the savage deeds of the outlaw Doones in the depth of Bagworthy Forest, the beauty of the hapless maid brought up in the midst of them, and plain Jan Ridd's Herculean power. . . ."

Did those Doones really exist? We do not know; nor does our ignorance greatly matter, for art and history have each their own Muse, and both are the better for it. But one thing is indisputable: Blackmore did not invent the Doones. Six years before his novel appeared, *The Leisure Hour* had published eight weekly instalments of a tale called The Doones of Exmoor; and even before that, in *Legends of the West Country*, an author stated: "The Doones of Bagworthy were a gang of blood-thirsty robbers who haunted the roads of Exmoor about the reign of Charles I. . . . Many tales are still extant of their daring and ferocity." In 1901 the *West Somerset Press* published an article by a lady who signed it with both a false and a true name—"Ida M. Browne

(Audrie Doon)"—which sought to prove that the Doones were Scottish aristocrats who had fled southward in disgrace. The problem is interesting but not important. If one takes Robin Hood and Hereward the Wake as analogies, it seems reasonable to suppose that their smoke arose from a living flame.

Meanwhile, Blackmore basked in the sun—and sometimes in the shade—of personal fame. Exmoor teemed with pilgrims eager to identify this or that place in the novel. Some readers taxed him with topographical negligence; others, with excessive verisimilitude. Among the former was James F. Muirhead, who, while editing Baedeker's *Handbook to Great Britain*, declared himself "struck by the discrepancy between the actual scenery of the Doone Valley and the description of it in *Lorna Doone*". He questioned Blackmore, and was told: "If I had dreamed that it would ever be more than a book of the moment, the descriptions of scenery—which I know as well as I know my own garden—would have been kept nearer to the fact." Yet how seldom he did stray from the fact, and how slightly. Few Exmoor readers could cite more than a couple of confusions; as when Jan returns from Blundell's, and is told by his servant, John Fry; "us be naigh the Doone track now, two maile from Dunkery Beacon". . . whereas Blackmore's account of their journey proves that John and Jan were at that point considerably more than two miles from Dunkery. Again, you may track every yard of Jan's "Bagworth river" without discovering "the great black pool" that nearly swallowed him. You will fail, also, to find Jan's home, Plover's Barrow Farm. There is at Malmsmead a teashop which likes to be regarded as Jan Ridd's home, but the claim must be rejected because the stream flows visibly within a few yards of the shop, whereas the stream at Plover's Barrow was so hidden that "a man may scarce spy it".

The vagueness of those particular descriptions is balanced by the precision of the general descriptions, notably the snowscape in the famous forty-second chapter, *The Great Winter*, where Jan goes out to find his sheep:

> But behold, there was no flock at all! None, I mean, to be seen anywhere; only at one corner of the field, by the eastern end, where the snow drove in, a great billow, as high as a barn and as broad as a house. This great drift was rolling and curling beneath the violent blast, tufting and combing with rustling swirls, and carved (as in patterns of cornice) where the grooving chisel of the wind

swept round. Ever and again, the tempest snatched little whiffs from the channelled edges, twirled them round, and made them dance over the chine of the monster pile, then let them lie like herring bones, or the seams of sand where the tide had been. And all the while from the smothering sky, more and more fiercely at every blast, came the pelting, pitiless arrows, winged with murky white, and pointed with the barbs of frost.

To the charge of excessive verisimilitude, Blackmore pleaded ignorance and offered apology. When a Mr. Snow complained from Oare that he had been lampooned as Nicholas Snowe, the author responded with a courtesy that was typical of himself and of his generation. He did not know, he said, that a Mr. Snow— nor even a Mr. Snowe—was then living at Oare.

Most people agree that *Lorna Doone* is a fine tale, flawed some-times by prolixity, presented always in the manner of its era. It does not aspire to Tolstoy's analysis of history, nor to George Eliot's dissection of motive, nor to Virginia Wolfe's evocation of mood. Least of all does it aspire to anyone's malice. "Of all human dealings," said Blackmore, "satire is the very lowest, and most mean and common. It is the equivalent in words, to what bullying is in deeds. . . ." Modern insight perceives that *Lorna Doone*'s super-ego looms too large, notably in a preface to the sixth edition, where Blackmore gives thanks because his book "has entered many a happy, pure, and hospitable home". Not that the book itself is mere black and white—all good or all bad; on the contrary, both Lorna and Jan acknowledge their own short-comings. In any event, if it must choose between an inflated super-ego and a compulsive id, mental hygiene will decide that Black-more's struggle toward the light is certainly braver and probably wiser than fiction's present obsession with illiterate trivia and psychopathic violence.

Blackmore's prose may seem over-rich to readers who have been reared on a diet of gruel. Some even of his contemporaries found the music too loud for their own deafness. But Blackmore knew what he was about, for he had been bred upon Rome and Greece, and upon the classic of English classics, the Bible. Neither his ear nor his integrity could accept the lesser cadence, the lazier clause. When a monoglot book reviewer rebuked him for writing hexameters, the stylist replied *de haut en bas*: "I used," he aid, "to write Latin and Greek verses by the thousand, and for any man who talks of 'hexameters' everywhere in *Lorna Doone* to charge me with ignorance of metre and rhythm is a fine proof of daring. There is no hexametrical movement (though plenty of trochaic and iambic too, quite unstriven at in the composition). . . ." To make the point for a second time, Blackmore had sipped the milk and honey of the Bible, that anthology of simplicity, sonorousness, manliness, majesty. Nowhere is this more evident than in the aside with which Jan ends his account of an autumn dawn on Exmoor: "So perhaps shall break upon us that eternal morning, when crag and chasm shall be no more, neither hill and valley, nor great unvintaged ocean; when glory shall not scare happiness, neither happiness envy glory; but all things shall arise and shine in the light of the Father's countenance, because itself is risen."

With its stint of flaws and a treasury of excellence, *Lorna Doone* remains the finest evocation of Exmoor as it was and as it has not yet ceased to be. Jan Ridd, for instance, explains why health abounds on Exmoor: "No Devonshire man, or Somerset either . . . ever thinks of working harder than his Maker meant for him." Many Exmoor folk still follow another piece of Jan's good advice:

twelve o'clock is the real time for a man to have his dinner. Then the sun is at his noon, calling halt to look around, and then the plants and leaves are turning, each with a little leisure time, before the work of the afternoon. Then is the balance of east and west, and then the right and left side of a man are in due proportion, and contribute fairly with harmonious fluids. And the health of this mode of life, and its reclaiming virtue are well set forth in our ancient rhyme,—

Sunrise, breakfast; sun high, dinner;
Sundown, sup; makes a saint of a sinner.

Still, too, at harvest-home the moorfolk echo Jan Ridd's Te Deum:

The corn, oh the corn, and the yellow, mellow corn!
Here's to the corn, with the cups upon the board!
We've been reaping all the day, and we'll reap again the morn,
And fetch it home to mow-yard, and then we'll thank the Lord.

Still at the inn the descendants of Farmer Snowe combine curtness with courtesy, like Jan's friend, who observed to an adversary: "I be plazed to call 'ee a liar." Still at a cottage or farm you will see what Jan saw at Plover's Barrow: "Farmer Snowe sat up in the corner, caring little to hear about anything, but smoking slowly, and nodding backward, like a sheep-dog

dreaming. Mother was in the settle . . . knitting hard, as usual. . . ."
Still in the lane you will meet men and women who share Jan's
opinion of London: "it was not worth seeing, but a very dirty and
hideous place, not at all like Exmoor." *The Cambridge History
of English Literature* hit the mark with a single sentence: "*Lorna
Doone*", it declared, "is redolent of the scents and stained with the
hues which come of the tilling of the soil and the tending of
stock. . . ."

The creator of all this lived to a great age, alone as a childless
widower, plagued by unremitting pain. But he had already
proved that the Lord was his Light. On the threshold of death,
in the grip of disease, he could assure a friend: "Still spirits are
good, and there is plenty to do, and (to some extent) to enjoy."
To the end he remained a gentle man, a country man, a devout
Anglican, a high Tory, in every sense a classic. Like the rebel, such
spirits are a part of true progress.

Blackmore died on 20th January 1900, in his eighty-sixth
year, and was buried beside his wife at Teddington. Four years
later, in Exeter Cathedral, a window and a statue were dedicated
to his memory. Eden Phillpotts paid a just tribute: "His manliness,
insight, glorious humour, were a tonic to the mind, and heartened
a man at every page to purify his own motives, and to ennoble
his ambitions."

There is a postcript to this man of the moor. As we have
seen, he began his career by writing poetry, but soon afterwards
accepted his limitations, though not without hope that he might
one day transcend them and discover both the depth and the
height that were beyond his present ken:

> Shall ever come a fairer hour
> When thou shalt be a spirit-wing,
> To glide unseen, yet glittering,
> And bear immortal power?

Blackmore answered his own question, for on Christmas Eve
1879, long after he had set aside all hope of achieving fame as a
poet, he dreamed a dream, which he described in a letter to the
editor of *The University Magazine*: "Having lately been at the
funeral of a most dear relative, I was there again (in a dream) last
night, and heard the mourners sing the lines enclosed, which
impressed me so that I was able to write them without change of a
word this morning." The editor printed Blackmore's poem,

Near Countisbury

under the initials *R. D. B.* Its title, taken from the thirty-seventh Psalm, was the motto of Blackmore's University: *Dominus Illuminatio Mea,* the Lord is my Light. But *The University Magazine* had only a small circulation, and the poem itself lacked the author's name to commend it. For more than twenty years it lay unremembered, and would surely have remained so, had it not been resurrected by Sir Arthur Quiller-Couch, who was then compiling his *Oxford Book of English Verse.* Quiller-Couch felt so moved by the poem that he chose it to be the last in his anthology. Inexplicably, however, he printed it as 'Anonymous'. Perhaps a friend had sent him a copy of the lines, without adding the initials. As a result, the poem won a renown which the poet lacked.

Nine years later, in 1909, Miss Agnes Cook, daughter of one of Blackmore's friends, wrote to *The Athenaeum,* stating that she possessed the original manuscript of the poem and also Blackmore's letter to the editor. Thereafter the poem ceased to be anonymous; a sad dream had made a happy one come true. Instead of being remembered solely as the author of one prose book, Blackmore did in the end find that "fairer hour" and with it achieve an "immortal power" which Professor Waldo Dunn rated as "one of the most moving and beautiful poems of its kind in the English language". *Dominus Illuminatio Mea* speaks to all who have kept watch by the deathbed of an old and loving friend:

> In the hour of death, after this life's whim,
> When the heart beats low, and the eyes grow dim,
> And pain has exhausted every limb—
> The lover of the Lord shall trust in Him.
>
> When the will has forgotten the lifelong aim,
> And the mind can only disgrace its fame,
> And a man is uncertain of his own name—
> The power of the Lord shall fill this frame.
>
> When the last sigh is heaved, and the last tear shed,
> And the coffin is waiting beside the bed,
> And the widow and child forsake the dead—
> The angel of the Lord shall lift this head.
>
> For even the purest delight may pall,
> The power must fail, and the pride must fall,
> And the love of the dearest friends grow small—
> But the glory of the Lord is all in all.

12

Molland: the lane to Botheans Mill

XIX

THE STORY OF LYNMOUTH LIFEBOAT

The night of 12th January 1899 was so wild that the landlord of
the Anchor Hotel at Porlock Weir decided to shorten his customary stroll. He had already turned for home when, through the
darkness, he sighted a full-rigged vessel, close inshore despite a
whole gale blowing from the west. Next moment a distress flare
went up.

The landlord ran to the post office and sent a telegram to the
Lynmouth lifeboat station. In those years that was the quickest
way of passing a message. His telegram reached Lynmouth at
seven o'clock. In one sense it could scarcely have come at a worse
moment. The lifeboat's second coxswain, G. S. Richards, wrote
a description of the scene: "The sea was sweeping right across
the harbour and over the sea front. The sea-spray was like smoke.
The tide was turning. It was obviously impossible to launch the
boat from the beach in face of such a gale." Nor was that all, for
the landlord's telegram arrived just before the gale smashed the
wires. Lynmouth, in short, was isolated; unable to reply that the
boat could not move. The nearest other lifeboat was so far away
that the stricken ship would have foundered long before a horseman could bring news of her plight. She may have foundered
already.

It was then, at the moment of defeat, that victory was born.
The coxswain conferred with his deputy, and both agreed; they
must drag their boat across the moor, slide her down Porlock
Hill, and then launch her from a less exposed beach. Having
announced his verdict, the coxswain was met with shouts of
protest from the crowd on the quay. It was impossible, they said.
The honorary secretary of the station, the Reverend A. R.
Hockley, raised his hand, and turned to the coxswain: "Go," he
told him, "and do the best you can."

First, then, a messenger hurried uphill to Lynton, asking for twenty horses from a stables there. Next, the boat's signalman led six volunteers up Countisbury Hill, armed with pickaxes and shovels, to widen the narrowest parts of the road, so that the boat might pass. At eight o'clock, within one hour of receiving the signal, the Lynmouth lifeboat began her voyage overland, lashed to a cart, dragged by horses and men and women—chiefly by men and women to start with, because the horses had difficulty in pulling together on a sodden surface.

Somehow they scaled the one-in-four lane to Countisbury, and then came the first disaster. A cart-wheel fell off, its linch-pin loosened by incessant jerking. Again the second coxswain's log set the scene: "We were now at the top of Blue Ball, a very exposed part of Exmoor, 1,000 feet above sea-level." In wild darkness, lit only by oil lamps, they hoisted the boat, replaced the wheel, and went on. By this time the women and the older men were forced to return, drenched and exhausted. Even so, twenty volunteers remained; and help was needed indeed because the road became so narrow that not a hundred shovels could have widened it for the boat to proceed. The second coxswain awaited orders: "Jack Crocombe, the coxswain, said we had come so far, and we were not going to turn back without having a good try for it."

So, they uprooted a gatepost, demolished part of the bank, and hauled their boat from the cart, which some of the horses dragged across the heather. That done, they set timber skids under her, which had to be removed and then replaced every few yards, by the light of lamps that had to be relit every few minutes: "It was a very difficult job. We could only drag the boat a little way and then had to stop while the skids behind were picked up, carried forward, and laid down again in front of her. They were placed about six feet apart. We worked in turns at carrying the skids forward and the road was so narrow that we had a job to pass between the boat and the wall." After a while, however, the road became wider, and they were able to hoist the boat onto the cart again. The strange cortege reached the summit of Porlock Hill.

Now even a modern car, even on a summer day, descends Porlock Hill with extreme caution, dropping to bottom gear for the one-in-four sector. But those men had to slide a lifeboat down, in darkness, through a gale, over a road that was more like a swamp than a highway. They had, in fact, to haul *uphill* at their ropes lest the cart slithered forward, crushing the horses. But they need not have worried; their head carter—one of the twenty volunteers—was Thomas Willis, a veteran horseman: "Old Tom said if we were able to keep the boat from slipping off her carriage he would be able to get round the corners, very dangerous though they were." Tom Willis was right. The cortege reached the foot of Porlock Hill.

Then someone remembered something. "Coxswain," he called, "we won't never git 'en past that wall." He was right. The wall of a cottage jutted into the road, blocking the way. They began to demolish the wall. Aroused and alarmed, an old woman peered from the bedroom window: "Hey, there! You'm all zany mad. Walking in yere, this time o' night, pulling down my wall." The second coxswain remembered the incident:

> She wanted to know what right we had bringing a thing like that at that time of night, knocking down people's walls and waking them up. When we told her that it was a life-boat she was very surprised, as she had never seen one in her life before. We told her that there was a ship in distress off Porlock Weir and we were going to try and rescue the men, so that put things all right with her, and she came along with us.

On, then, toward the sea, and a ship that may have foundered; but not far on, for now a party of men arrive, announcing that the road to the sea has disappeared, breached by the sea itself. The second coxswain recorded their reaction: "We were not going to be beaten after coming so far. Off we set along the higher road and got along fairly well until we came to the Lane Head. . . ." At Lane Head they find the boughs of a huge laburnum tree barring the way. The cart sways and halts. Through loud darkness a voice calls: "Tiffy, come yere a minute."

Tiffy comes, the man with a saw. He looks up at the boughs, and down at the girth. "This'll take a little time," he says, rubbing his hands. While he works, others lasso the tree, ready for its fall. The crackle is heard even above the storm. The cortege proceeds.

It was now six o'clock in the morning. For ten hours they had been heaving and pushing, uprooting gateposts, shovelling earth, sliding skids, demolishing walls, felling trees. Every man was weary, wet, hungry. But not one of them wavered. Having at last found a suitable beach, they launched their boat, wading hip-high through waves. And away she rose, snatched-at by darkness, seeking a ship that might not be there. But at least they had wasted no time: "We launched the boat right away, not even waiting for anything to eat."

After an hour and a half of groping they did find her; and a strange tale she told, cupped hoarsely through hands. She was the *Forrest Hall*, of 1,900 tons, on tow from Bristol to Liverpool, with a crew of fifteen. On the previous night, while battling down the Severn Sea, the line had parted, and the tug that towed her disappeared into the storm. With her own rudder smashed, the *Forrest Hall* had tried to anchor, but the wind was too strong, and she drifted slowly to destruction. There was no food left on board. Every flare had gone. The crew were exhausted.

While all this was being shouted, the lost tug suddenly reappeared, but the lifeboat's work had only begun, for she alone could stand close enough to pass a line from the tug to the *Forrest Hall*. By this time a semi-dawn had broken, and in the light of it the coxswain saw what he already felt, that wind and waves were still too high to allow the ship to return to Bristol. These, remember, were Masefield's men,

> Whose books were Nature's doings, seamen's guides,
> Shallows and depths, sea-currents, sets and tides;
> Rocks breaking and rocks hidden, where the tint
> Upon the water's surface gave the hint. . . .

The second coxswain's log stated: "We got a rope from the tug to the ship and with the help of some of the lifeboat crew who went on board the ship the captain got her anchors up." After more shouting, they decided to make for Barry on the Welsh coast. The tug rang down for Full Ahead. The hulk came into the wind, sullen and sluggish. But a single screw was no match for a Severn Sea. Soon the tug lost way, and the *Forrest Hall* wallowed broadside-on. The outlook was bleak: "As there was no rudder, we could not manage to steer the ship, and we were very near the Nash Sands." After yet more shouting, they agreed to send for a second tug.

A landsman may at this point wonder whether the lifeboat's overland journey really was necessary. It was indeed: first, because it had been asked for; second, because without it a line might never have been passed to the ship, and the ship herself might never have weathered the stormy lull between sighting her own tug and finding another. Meanwhile the lifeboat stood by, not with engines but with oars.

Though he may shout in his cups, no true seaman raises his voice when recounting these occasions. Very likely he will decline to recount them, unless in the course of duty, and then his tale is stripped of everything except the facts. True, he may allow himself a brief *forte* when describing other men's exploits, but of his own he has little to say, and prefers not to mention them. That this is so you may gather from the second coxswain's log: "It was still blowing very hard when we reached Barry which was about six in the evening of Friday, the 13th." He makes no reference to the overland voyage nor to the twelve hours that had been spent in the lifeboat, pulling and tacking. He is content to state a fact plainly: "We had had nothing to eat since the day before." His next sentence touches the heart: "The men at Barry Docks very kindly took charge of the life-boat." No other words can equal those with which that seaman ended his log: "The men at Barry Docks sent us to an hotel, where we were cared for by the Shipwrecked Mariners Society with dry clothes and food. We got back to Lynmouth the following day. A steamer gave us a tow for part of the way."

The story of Lynmouth lifeboat cost £118 7s. 9d., which included the hire of horses and the repair of walls. Toward this the owners of the *Forrest Hall* contributed £75. The thirteen lifeboatmen received each an award of £5; volunteers who had helped to launch the boat shared an award of £27 5s. 6d. A native of Lynmouth, F. H. Fry, presented every member of the lifeboat with a gold watch, and a gold chain thereon for the coxswains.

Service does not solicit a reward, being self-sufficient and instinctive, like the act of breathing. Many men and women continue to serve, in many capacities; and most of them pass unnoticed by the world. The sea holds no monopoly of sacrifice. Yet those lifeboatmen—like their heirs today—do stand out as vivid examples of the man who, in the last resort, will lay down his life, not only for his friend but also for those whom he never met before, and may never see again.

The crew of the Lynmouth lifeboat were: J. Crocombe (coxswain), G. S. Richards (second coxswain), R. Ridler (bowman), J. Ridler, R. Burgess, G. Rawle, J. Ward, W. Jarvis,

C. Crick, B. Pennicott, D. Crocombe, T. Pugsley, W. Richards (aged 16, his first Service). Their monument was carved by John Masefield, Master Mariner and Poet Laureate of England:

O memory praise them, before Death efface.

THE STORY OF JACK RUSSELL

If one sought a single character who reflected the life of Exmoor, a good choice would be Jack Russell, for his days were spent among squires, farmers and other open-air men, to whose interests he added his own experience as parson of a moorland flock.

Much nonsense has been written about Russell. Some people hail him as the splendid disciple of a Master who was *in excelsis* the Master of all Meets; others consign him to the flames because he was himself an MFH. A middle way is so conspicuously the fairway that only bias can account for the number of rival extremists.

John Russell—known everywhere as Jack—was born in 1795 at Dartmouth in Devon, his father being an Anglican priest. During the fifteenth century the word *russel* was used of a kind of woollen fabric, which suggests that the family had been in the wool trade. During the sixteenth century, however, they came to the fore and were advanced by the Tudor dynasty of *nouveaux riches*. Hitching its star to the commercial-Erastian wagon, the family reached London via numerous Devonshire estates; and ultimately begat Bertrand, an anti-metaphysical computer.

Jack Russell himself belonged to a less flamboyant branch of the family. From Plympton Grammar School he proceeded to Blundell's, where he Mastered a pack of hounds (four and a half couple). Confined to fields near his school, the boy who was soon to hunt foxes and stags remained content with Wilfred Scawen Blunt's quarry:

> I love the hunting of the hare
> Better than that of the fox.

Between the meets, he took a closed exhibition to Exeter College, Oxford, which had been founded in 1314 by Walter de Stapledon, Bishop of Exeter, who called it Stapledon Hall. On receiving a charter from Queen Elizabeth I, the hall became Exeter College, and was soon afterwards enlarged and re-endowed by Sir John Petre, Secretary of State, with several scholarships confined to youths from the Scilly Isles, Somerset and Devon. Exeter College produced many eminent Victorians, including J. A. Froude, R. D. Blackmore, William Morris, Sir Edward Burne-Jones, Sir Charles Lyell. Russell graduated *viva voce* according to the custom of his time; but among fox-hunters he had long since ceased to be a novice. Three packs lay within hacking distance of Carfax, and Russell followed them all.

In 1819 he was ordained deacon, and went as curate to Nympton St. George, a near-moorland village, which modernity has rebap-tized as George Nympton; no doubt an even newer modernity will add *and Co. Ltd*. After a short while Russell moved to South Molton to help its vicar, but without extra stipend. His reward, however, was in another kind, for at South Molton he met Penelope, daughter of Admiral Bury, who lived near Swim-bridge. The couple married and went to Iddlesleigh, where the bridegroom served his father as curate. Six years later he received the livings of Swimbridge and of Landkey, whose advowson was held by his wife's cousin. People who dismiss Russell as a fox-hunting, non-residential cleric are confounded by the facts. When he arrived at Swimbridge, the two parishes together held four services a month; soon after he arrived, Swimbridge alone was holding four services a week. Russell's flock was self-helping; it had a shoemaker, a tailor, a tanner, three carpenters, five farriers, six publicans.

At Swimbridge the young vicar Mastered a pack of fox-hounds, with which he hunted a wide area of the moor, and made the disreputable acquaintance of Froude, vicar of Molland. His own sporting tastes led him to choose athletic curates, one of whom, E. W. L. Davies, had coxed the Oxford Boat Race crew in 1836.

The Bishop of Exeter admired Russell's flair for preaching simple sermons to simple souls. Any other kind of sermon lay beyond his scope and, indeed, beyond that of most of his fellow-clerics, for the English Church was only then beginning to awake from its Augustan snooze. Wesley was dead, and had in any event failed to arouse the snorer; Keble and Pusey and Newman were still in their cradles. After the sermon, however, the Bishop took the preacher aside, requiring him to forsake the chase. Russell was unable to concur. He shared the belief of his younger contemporary, Sabine Baring-Gould, the Devon squarson who asked: "Why should not the parson mount his cob and go after the hounds? A more fresh, invigorating sport is not to be found. . . ." Baring-Gould reported a remark which he had overheard from an Exmoor farmer: "Jack Russell, up and down his backbone, he's as good a Christian, as worthy a parson, and as true a gentleman as ever I seed."

One member of Russell's flock disagreed. He started a campaign of slander and libel, claiming that Russell had refused to conduct a burial service because it clashed with a hunting appointment. The accuser then perjured himself, and nearly went to jail, while trying to procure evidence from a neighbour's servant. In the end, Russell sued, but the quarrel was settled out of court. It had been a wretched affair, and in the course of it Russell lost his temper.

But neither preaching nor hunting could contain his energies. He became Provincial Grand Chaplain of a masonic lodge, and honorary governor of the North Devon Infirmary, for which he raised large sums of money. He supported also the Devon Agricultural Association and the North Devon Wool Fair. To most people, however, he is known as a founder-member of the Kennel Club and as a breeder of miniature terriers.

Now an historian discovers and assesses both sides of a problem; but what shall he do when the problem is polygonal? For example, one 'expert' states that the coat of a Jack Russell terrier was "perfectly smooth"; another, that it was "a trifle wiry". A third, gives the terrier's weight as twelve pounds; a fourth, as eighteen. A fifth declares that Russell kept a careful stud book; a sixth, that he bred from any dog or bitch which pleased him. A seventh describes the terrier's eye-patch as "black"; an eighth, as "dark tan". One writer claims that Russell 'invented' the breed. Since Russell terriers are closely associated with Exmoor, their ancestry seems especially relevant. The word 'terrier' is at least five centuries old. Its sire was the mediaeval Latin *terrarius* or dog that goes to earth. The earliest description of a terrier was written *c.* 1570 in Latin by Dr. Keys, who so admired the classics that he Latinized his own name as Caius. Nine times President of the College of Surgeons, the erudite Doctor refounded Gonville Hall as Gonville and Caius College, Cambridge. Toward the end of the sixteenth century his book was translated, under the title *English Dogges*, and in it the ancestor of Jack Russell's breed appears as a pot-holer whose task is to "make afrayde, nyppe and bite the foxe and badger". If the nip fails to kill the quarry, then the terrier must "hayle and pull them perforce out of their lurking angles, darke dongeons and close caues . . .". From time immemorial the Westmorland and Cumberland farmers employed a small brown terrier to unearth the fox. I have one myself, a very well-bred old gentleman. At the Kennel Club he is called a Lakeland Terrier, though that name was almost unheard of until the 1920s, and it was not until 1928 that the breed began to make public appearances outside Lakeland. Up north the older people still remember the years when all such dogs were known as Fell terriers, or Westmorland terriers, or Cumberland terriers. One sporting spinster near Dulverton always refers to her own Jack Russell as an Exmoor terrier.

When and where did Russell start to breed the dogs that bear his name? No one knows, least of all myself who took some pains to study the conflicting evidence. The most likely version goes back to Russell's undergraduate days, when he noticed a Marston milkman's terrier bitch, and decided to mate her with one of his own dogs. I doubt that he would have approved some of the irascible midgets which are now shown under his imprint. Breeders have exterminated courage and brains, setting in their place a stupid neurosis. Look what they have done to the English Cocker spaniel: his elephantine ears unfit him for working; the rococo 'feathers' make it impossible for him to penetrate a thorny cover. Russell, by contrast, bred working dogs, which is to say brave, intelligent, and hardy dogs. And Victorian photographs prove that his own terriers were of middling size, not midgets.

During all this time Russell was increasing his fame as a chaser of stags and foxes. The tales about his courageous stamina are legion. We know, for instance, that he once hacked forty miles to a meet, spent four hours following hounds, and then hacked forty miles home. Even in my own heyday I found that twenty miles was as far as I wished to go, and thirty as far as the horse could comfortably go.

During the 1870s Russell was introduced to the Prince of Wales at Admiralty House, Devonport, where he made a deep impression, and was soon afterwards commanded to renew the acquaintance, this time at Sandringham. Now Sir Francis Drake—another son of a Devon parson—caused some merriment on first opening his mouth at Court: "These yere Dons," he said; and London laughed. Russell spoke the Queen's English—Victoria's English and Elizabeth's English—for he kept the 'thou' and 'thee' which France and Germany still retain. We may picture him, then, as a late and lesser Georgian country gentleman, a farmer who had passed through the civilizing sieve of Blundell's and Oxford. Such a man—forthright, Tory, courteous—could not fail to impress the canny Prince, all the more so because the Prince had surrounded himself with some of the most unlikeable sophisticates of his day. Therefore, on leaving Sandringham, only Russell was surprised when the Prince desired him to return, not by command, but as a guest who had been invited to share the royal Christmas party . . . and to uplift it with a simple sermon. At that party one of the guests was the Bishop of Peterborough, who described the cosmopolite company as "a curious mixture, two Jews (Sir Anthony de Rothschild and his daughter), an ex-Jew (Disraeli), a Roman Catholic (Colonel Huggins), an Italian duchess who is an English woman and her daughter brought up a Roman Catholic and now turning Protestant . . .". Fortunately, the man from Exmoor was ecumenical as well as non-theological. Perhaps he remembered his West Country colleague, Reverend R. S. Hawker, who, when asked by his bishop why he had invited a very mixed gathering of religions and irreligions to dine with him, replied: "My Lord, since they never will meet in Heaven, I thought it well that they should meet on earth."

Both the exalted host and his plain guest acquitted themselves well that Christmas. During dinner one night the Prince remarked with pleasure that Russell was tucking-into a certain dish. For a moment there was silence. Then the old parson confessed with horror: "Sir, I have done what my wife warned me not to do. I have asked for a second helping." Throughout the rest of his visit Russell received by royal command a second helping of his favourite dish. On a later and more formal occasion he was to receive yet another token of regal sensitivity, for when he died, a wreath arrived from the Prince—not an ornately expensive affair, but the sort which Russell would have prized above all others, a posey of wild flowers.

Russell met the Prince again, when the royal party came to hunt the Exmoor stags. The Prince's host was Mr. G. F.

Luttrell of Dunster Castle. Nine thousand spectators watched the meet of 2,000 riders at Hawkcombe Head. This time Russell did not hack thither. He sat next to the Prince in the royal carriage, and when it passed through Porlock, Russell waved "Good day" to the hostess of the Ship Inn, who thereafter became the talk of her town.

One tends to regard Jack Russell as the last of the hunting parsons, yet his kind died hard. During the 1930s the Reverend E. A. Milne, a Dorset parson, was still maintaining the tradition. At Cambridge he had followed the Trinity Beagles; then he became Master of the North Bucks Harriers. In Dorset he hunted six days a week, wearing pink instead of clerical black. For thirty-one years he was Master of the Cattistock Hounds, claiming that in the course of 5,000 hunting days he had killed 4,000 foxes, with another 4,000 marked to ground.

When Russell was 84 years old and a widower, he received from Lord Poltimore the offer of Black Torrington, a richer and less exacting living; but the new parish lay well beyond the moor, and Russell was torn between a love of home and the need to provide for himself when he could work no longer. Despite his hard labours there, Swimbridge could scarcely support him. To his old coxswain curate he confessed: "I cannot live on £220 a year. . . ." In the end, he decided to accept the parish and to enliven his loneliness by mastering yet another pack of foxhounds. One day he fell heavily, while jumping a bank, and for half an hour lay without speaking. Suddenly he recovered his voice, asked for his horse, mounted, and rode the six miles home.

That incident poses a question which has long interested me: why are West Countrymen as hardy as Northerners, yet less brusque and aggressive? Having so to say a gene in both camps— West and North—I am perhaps able to achieve some detachment in this emotional matter. A clue was dropped in 1969 when a sociologist classified regional differences in diet, recreation, religion, reading and so forth. One difference concerned the rearing of children. Northern mothers, it seems, are harsher than western mothers in the task of house-training their young; which recalls the late Doctor Ian Suttie's deeper studies, citing two neighbouring tribes whose nursery attitudes were respectively harsh and lenient. Males in the harsh tribe became suspicious and therefore aggressive; but males from the lenient tribe were trusting and therefore friendly, without any lack of courage or of independence. The house-training of young children is not the sort of market research that I am either willing or competent to undertake; yet the fact remains, a northern crowd—whether in the pub or at a football match—is markedly more militant than its Exmoor counterpart.

Russell, at all events, did not last long in Black Torrington. Aware that he was sinking, he went to stay at East Anstey, hoping that his beloved Exmoor air might brace him. It was not to be. To his old coxswain curate he wrote: "I don't gain strength as I fancy I ought; and overwhelmed as I am by letters, it is pain and grief for me to write at all." Not even Exmoor's air could mend the body, but it did blow away the cobwebs of an uncharacteristic melancholy, for Russell was soon telling a friend: "I want to send the Prince of Wales a brace of hunted hares. He sent me a basket of game last week."

On the way home from East Anstey, a few weeks before his death, Jack Russell revisited Swimbridge. He was too weak to walk, so they half-carried him into his old church. Next day he described how the people of Black Torrington had greeted him: "We got here at 6.30 last evening and met half the village, about 500 yards from home, carrying flags etc. etc., in procession, and entreating us to allow them to remove the horses from the 'fly' and draw us to the door of this house. . . ." Such love must surely shrive a multitude of venery sins. No man could wish for a surer passport to eternity.

XXI

THE HIGHEST HILL

As Mr. Lear remarked:

> 'Ere the days of his pilgrimage vanish,
> How pleasant to know Mr. Lear!

We are all either Lears or lunatics, and some of us are both.
We covet the esteem of our fellows, and wish that, being all
things to all men, we may thereby win a universal approval. The
wish can become so strong that it makes us weak, and then we
fear to speak out lest we ripple the surface of our civil reputation.
Myself, I wish heartily that I *could* heap praise, and nothing *but*
praise, on every one of the 1,705 feet which compile Dunkery,
our highest hill. Confronted by its austere beauty, I am tempted
to tilt *de mortuis* by saying nothing evil of the living. But the
living themselves would confound me. Therefore I make two
comments: first, Dunkery Hill is spoiled by August crowds;
second, there are still some people who feel that some places
really are spoiled by crowds. Most people who visit Dunkery
with the crowd, have not come to see Dunkery; they are there in
order to swell the crowd. They make friends with total strangers,
bless them, and then sit down, discussing food prices in Halifax
or their average speed from Walsall. Unfortunately, a road
passes within a mile of the summit. Fortunately, few people
ascend the summit. They prefer to sit *en famille* in the car, where
some of them snore. The poignancy of all this—the paradox
whereby pilgrims despoil their own Mecca—is emphasized by a
cairn on the summit, bearing a plaque which states that much of
the surrounding countryside, and the summit itself, were given to
the National Trust "for the benefit of the nation by Sir Thomas
Acland, Bt., Col. Wiggin and Allan Hughes Esq.". Perhaps,
after all, we are fortunate, and ought not to complain. Even in
August I have never seen more than ten cars parked beside the

path to the summit; but at Box Hill, they tell, nothing short of 1,000 creates a crowd; and in Lakeland even 1,000 is considered bad business by the lollipoppers and lucky-charmers. On most days of most months Dunkery is as uninhabited as the North Pole. Although he visited Exmoor for only a few days, the solitude of Dunkery so impressed Llewelyn Powys that it became a talisman which sustained him in foreign hands: "In after years," he wrote "when I rode across land in Africa devastated by a bush fire it was always to the fells around Dunkery Beacon that my dreams would go . . .".

Jan Ridd's servant was right when he described Dunkery as "the haighest place of Hexmoor". It is a Celtic name, probably from the Welsh *din* or hill fort and *creic* or rock. When Queen Victoria's Jubilee was celebrated, in June 1897, forty-four beacons were sighted from Dunkery. Unlike the Worcestershire Beacon, from which it can be seen, Dunkery does not achieve an over-weening dominance. It remains *primus inter pares*, up to its neck among near-neighbours. This may diminish the complacency of a climber, but it enhances the view from the summit, for Dunkery rises out of woods beside the sea, and then looks down on them like an eagle. South-west, Plymouth is visible. Eastward loom the Quantocks and beyond them the Mendips. Astern, Exmoor is corrugated with green fields and purple heather. Seaward stands Wales, Monmouthshire to Pembrokeshire. And at your feet the birds seem smaller than they did to Edgar in *King Lear:*

> The crows and choughs that wing the midway air
> Show scarce so gross as beetles. . . .

If you know what to look for, you need not be able to see it in order to savour it from the summit. Selworthy is there, white and thatched. Cloutsham is there, waiting for the staghounds. Luccombe hides among trees. Horner Wood is clear, watered by a stonebridged stream. So dazzling is the prospect that the Victorian guidebooks described Dunkery as a mountain; but that was before we had accepted Sir Hugh Munro's dictum that a British mountain must attain at least 2,000 feet, except in Scotland, where the minimum is 3,000. Among those Scottish giants, on top of Ben Lawer in Perthshire, you may see the remains of a cairn that was built by Malcolm Fergusson shortly before the 1914 war. Fergusson measured his cairn precisely: it stood fourteen feet high, that being the distance by which Ben Lawer

Exmoor ponies
Journey into the interior

fell short of 4,000 feet. Having made his cairn, Fergusson climbed it, crying: "It's a guid round number!" Dunkery lacks such a cairn, but it does carry traces of a beacon below the summit. Lorna Doone's maid, Gwenny Carfax, tells of the preparations for lighting a beacon on the hillside; the men, she says, "had been three days hard at work, clearing, as it were, a cockpit for their fire . . .".

When Jan Ridd was being escorted home from Blundell's, his servant, John, warned him to keep quiet lest the Doones should hear: "Us be naigh the Doone-track now, two maile from Dunkery Beacon hill . . . so happen they be abroad tonight, us must crawl on our belly-places, boy," Years later, when he had become a man, Jan watched that beacon from his snowbound farm: "The Doones are firing Dunkery beacon, to celebrate their new captain." It was an awesome sight, "blazing red and white and yellow as it leaped. . . . And the light danced on the snow-drifts with a misty lilac hue."

Exmoor is not a habitat of very rare plants, but on Dunkery you will find the yellow-flowered marsh St. John's wort (*Hypericum elodes*), the blue ivy-leafed bell-flower (*Whalembergia hederacea*), the red round-leafed sundew (*Drosera rotundifolia*) and the pink bog pimpernel (*Anagallis tenella*).

There are no trees on Dunkery; the wind would regard them as squatters, to be uprooted. The sky above, and the sea below, are as wild as Swinburne's:

> The wind is as iron that rings,
> The foam-heads loosen and flee;
> It swells and welters and swings
> The pulse of the tide of the sea.

When a gale strikes from the north-west you must turn away if you would breathe freely. All talk is swept aside in the utterance. Shout into the wind, and your call ten yards away will be a whisper. Walk into the wind, and you must either crouch forward or be toppled backward. Birds are hurled past, out of control; I have seen one dashed to pieces against the cairn. In such weather the difference between a lee and a weather side can seem almost incredible. I have stood on the summit, unable to stop my teeth from chattering; but when I walked a short way below the summit, into a hollow under a bank, I unbuttoned my coat while the February sun seeped through.

13

England's smallest parish church, Culbone
Wagons on the Moor

There are times when I think that Dunkery looks best on a calm and moonful night. True, the sea here is narrower than at the Haven, so that the lights of industrial Barry mar the beauty, like coughs at a concert. Even so, the moon sets a silver fan upon the water, the fairways wink, the Welsh hills emphasize the stars. When a stag roars, the echo ricochets among the combes and is lost on the heights. A gentler music arises when you overhear the stream which you cannot see, reciting to itself beneath the heather. Such nights compose a silver-and-sable version of Samuel Barber's Adagio for Strings. But when clouds dim the moon, then Victor Hugo's night appears, "ageless and without shape, a chiaroscuro of spectres":

> . . . quelle nuit! Là, rien n'a de contour ni d'age;
> Et le nuage est spectre, et le spectre est nuage.

If I time the homeward journey carefully, I return with the dayspring lighting my footsteps and the trees before them, so that a beech turns from grey to olive-green, and each leaf is translucent. The sea paints itself, borrowing the sky's brightest blue, transmuting Victor Hugo's mirage into Thomas Carew's oasis:

> Now do a choir of chirping minstrels sing,
> In triumph to the world, the youthful Spring:
> The valleys, hills, and woods in rich array
> Welcome the coming of the long'd-for May.

Dunkery juggles with our notion of Time. In one sense it is old, touched but not marred by men; in another sense it is young, like a child's face on a crone's body. Perhaps that is why it invites the portrait to look ahead as well as behind and all around. In whose hands does Exmoor's future lie? Not in yours nor in mine; neither with the State nor with Mammon nor with Mars. No man knows why the Goths marched westward to capture the future of Rome. Living space, aggressiveness, tedium, climate; each may have played its part, but the dramatis persona excels the sum of its parts, and thereby eludes identification. Even fifty years ago a man could have assumed that his great-great-grand-children would see Exmoor as he saw it. Such assumptions are no longer tenable. In 1969 the State announced that neither the National Trust nor the National Parks could any longer regard their jurisdiction as inviolate. If gold is found on Ben Nevis, then that part of the Highlands must be defaced. If water is needed from Windermere, then that lake must be drained or diverted. The same sort of thing occurred in 1940 when graceful ships were filleted in order to cope with a vast population of Britons on the Dunkirk beaches. The only certainty is uncertainty. Did Owain Glyn Dwr think it possible that the green valleys of Wales would one day become black? Did Edmund Spenser think it possible that the "sweet Thames" above Sonning would one day flow through an industrial Golgotha? Did Wordsworth think it possible that Cross Fell would one day be crowned with tin shacks and radio masts? Did Jan Ridd think it possible that the Knights would one day so nearly change Exmoor into a Black Country?

At present the outlook seems hopeful. Encroachments, enclosures, afforestation, new plantations; these are urgent problems; but neither singly nor together do they threaten a countryside whose depth and height offer something richer than a pretty view.

Coleridge once said to Hazlitt: "I must be alone if either my imagination or my heart are to be excited and enriched." That was an overstatement and therefore untrue. But if Coleridge had said "enriched by what Wordsworth called 'the depth and not the tumult of the soul'," he would then have spoken for some who seek those heights on Dunkery Hill.

XXII

THE SMALLEST CHURCH

There is no road to it. You must walk. Most people come from
Porlock Weir, following a seaside path among woods; a splendid
route, but in wet weather so slippery that two miles may take one
hour. I approach from the Devon border, likewise along a path
so slippery that in wet weather two miles an hour seems good
going. The last half-mile is the best, along a track between high
hedges with gates that reveal the sea. Away to the right, the hills
need no gate; their wooded arcs tower above everything under
the sun.

Soon the track becomes a footpath, tiptoeing steeply into a
wood where a stream arrives, offering an audible signpost at
night or when mist has hidden the next tree. In autumn and
in winter the path becomes so quiet that when you tread on a
twig the crackle runs all round the world. Faithful indeed were
the generations of moorfolk who from their isolated farms walked
this way to church and home again.

Now the path emerges from the wood, revealing a narrow
valley whose topmost trees climb half out of sight; and in the
foreground a building which you might mistake for the gatehouse
to a castle on the Rhine. This building is made of local stone, in
two parts that are joined by an archway. There, in 1970, lived a
craftsman and his wife, making pottery beside the stream. If
you stand under the archway, you will see the tip of Culbone
steeple, on a level with the doorstep of a cottage above. There is
no other building. Edmund Spenser imagined just such a place:

> A little lowly hermitage it was,
> Down in a dale, hard by a forest's side,
> Far from resort of people that did pass
> In travel to and fro. . . .

The guidebooks have written much fiction about Culbone

church. Most of them imply that it is the smallest consecrated building in England, which it is not; others claim that the Lakeland churches at Wythburn and Wasdale are smaller, which again they are not, because they never were churches, but only chapelries. Several guidebooks either guess or crib the size of the church; one says that it is thirty feet long; another, thirty-three feet; a third, thirty-five. Equipped with a tape-measure, I came to agree with the Reverend Dr. Charles Cox who said: "I have measured Culbone church many times, its length is 35 feet; length of nave 21ft. 5in. Width of nave 12ft. 8in. Width of chancel 10ft. Width of chancel arch 2ft. 6in." Culbone is the smallest parish church in England.

Lost among the grandeur of the hills, swathed in a stillness deepened by bird-song and the stream, you will say of this place what Wordsworth remarked of Seathwaite church in the Cumbrian mountains: "Time, in most cases, and nature everywhere, have given a sanctity to the humble works of man, that are scattered over this peaceful retirement. As it glistens in the morning sunshine, it would fill the spectator's heart with gladsomeness ... he would feel an impatience to rove among its pathways. ..." And if you would know what Culbone is like on a summer evening, Wordsworth will tell you that also;

at evening, when the sun is set, and a pearly light gleams from the western quarter of the sky ... when the trees are dusky, but each kind still distinguishable; when the cool air has condensed the blue smoke rising from the cottage chimney; when the dark massy stones seem to sleep in the bed of the foaming brook; *then*, he (the spectator) would be unwilling to move forward, not less from a reluctance to relinquish what he beholds, than from an apprehension of disturbing, by his approach, the quietness beneath him.

The interior of the church is whitewashed, airy, and—for its size—lofty. The walls, two feet thick, are eight centuries old; the screen is six centuries old. I would say that about thirty-eight people can occupy the pews, some of which are two-seaters. Again Wordsworth sets the scene by likening it to his native Westmorland:

How sacred the spirit by which our forefathers were directed! The *religio loci* is nowhere violated by these unstinted, yet unpretending, works of human hands. They exhibit generally a well-proportioned oblong, with a suitable porch, in some instances a steeple tower, and in others nothing more than a small belfry. But these objects, though pleasing in their forms . . . derive their interest from the sentiments of piety and reverence for the modest virtues and simple manners of humble life. . . .

As at Seathwaite, so at Culbone:

A man must be very insensible who would not be touched with pleasure at . . . its diminutive size, how small must be the congregation there assembled, as it were, like one family; and proclaiming at the same time . . . the depth of that seclusion in which the people live, that has rendered necessary the building of a separate place of worship for so few.

Those few are even fewer than they used to be. If you turn the soil near the church, you will uncover the foundations of cottages that crumbled and were buried in the grass.

The average visitor regards Culbone church as a quaint relic of something which, because its vocabulary contains the words Thou Shalt Not, is a hindrance to his right to go to the Devil in whatever way he chooses. There, I fancy, lies the deepest difference between the past and the present of this portrait. Somerset folk today are healthier, kindlier and less fearful than were their ancestors; and the improvement is due chiefly to the influence of Christianity. You can, of course, present an apparently unanswerable case to show that Culbone church preaches a false because an illusory metaphysic; you can compile a litany of the anti-Christian acts which men have committed in the name of Christ; but you cannot deny that our forefathers pondered man's ultimate destiny more deeply and more often than we do. Even a century ago the majority of moorfolk agreed with the author of *Ecclesiastes* when he wrote:

To every thing there is a season, and a time to every purpose under the heaven: a time to be born, and a time to die; a time to plant, and a time to pluck up that which is planted; a time to kill, and a time to heal; a time to break down, and a time to build up; a time to weep, and a time to laugh; a time to mourn, and a time to dance. . . .

Among those times—even for the busiest man, even for the simplest—was a time to look back and then forward; not as the seller of life insurance looks forward and back, but rather as a man adrift at night on a stormy sea, searching the clouds for a star that shall steer him in his belief that land does exist and can be reached.

Many visitors to Culbone assume that its church, or some other in England, will soon become the last white elephant of a half-forgotten superstition. That time may indeed arrive, but not until men have ceased to say to themselves and one another: "what does the Lord require of thee, but to do justly, and to love mercy, and to walk humbly with thy God?" Meanwhile, the portrait must present a paradox of its time: on the one hand, orthodox Christianity, the most esoteric religion of which we possess record; and on the other, two or three—or thirty-eight —countryfolk gathering together, assured that in the midst of them is the Way, the Life, and the Truth as they were promulgated 2,000 years ago world without end *nil obstat imprimatur etcetera*. And all that paradox is contained within *The Book of Common Prayer*, not as an archaic ornament, to be donned briefly once a week, but as a talisman that spans all the days of man, his everydays and the days that dawn but once in a lifetime.

At Culbone and throughout Exmoor—despite the wailing of their infant at the font—young parents still "Hear the words of the Gospel, written by Saint Mark in the tenth chapter and the thirteenth verse. . . . Jesus said unto them . . . Suffer little children to come unto me, and forbid them not; for of such is the kingdom of God." When they grow up, some of those infants will answer a question: "Wilt thou love her, comfort her, honour, and keep her, in sickness and in health; and, forsaking all others, keep thee only unto her as long as ye both shall live?" One day the man or his wife may fall ill, and then the priest coming into the sick person's house, shall say, "Peace be to this house, and to all that dwell in it." If, unlike Jan Ridd, the man himself serves with the Royal Navy, he will daily hear: "Preserve us from the dangers of the sea, and from the violence of the enemy; that we may be a safeguard unto our most Sovereign Lady, Queen Elizabeth, and her Dominions, and a security for such as pass on the seas on their lawful occasions. . . ." And when at last the day comes, "The Priest and Clerks, meeting the corpse at the entrance of the Church-yard . . . shall say . . . I am the resurrection and the life, saith the Lord: he that believeth in me, though he were dead, yet shall he live: and whosoever liveth and believeth in me shall never die."

Such, then, is the present state of affairs on Exmoor; in other words, a few people still say their prayers; and many say that all prayers are useless. Granted, a Rolls-Royce is unlikely to arrive solely because we have knelt down and prayed for one; yet many people—uncountable millions, both past and present—have felt less afraid solely because they did kneel down and ask for courage. Faith really can move mountains metaphorically; and the physicists—those of them who are not moonstruck—may one day discover that faith exerts also what we call a physical effect, as witnessed daily in many village surgeries. Scepticism creates its own superstition. In the presence of mystery, only arrogance and foolishness are dogmatic.

One afternoon I visited Culbone with a friend, during Evensong. The church door being open, my friend entered, leaving me in charge of the dog. Presently an old woman appeared at the porch, beckoning me to come inside. I pointed to the dog. Still the woman beckoned: "Bring 'en with'ee, midear," she said. The early Fathers debated whether women have souls, *Habet femina animam*, but Mrs. Cook thought it possible that there are dogs in Heaven.

The Cooks—husband and wife—occupy the cottage above the church. In a sense they *are* the church, and the moor also, for they serve as sextons, guides, custodians; and have lived in the valley above eighty years. If you know Mrs. Cook well, you may use her Christian name, Liz. By any name she and her husband will seem the most vivid features of our portrait, at any rate to visitors who, like Max Beerbohm, "have always been less greatly interested in books than in people."

We have already noted some of the resemblances between Exmoor and Lakeland; their inaccessible valleys, their sheep walks, their small churches and whitewashed cottages. But when Wordsworth described Westmorland two centuries ago, he revealed one profound difference between Lakeland and Exmoor; the former, he said, was "a community of shepherds and agriculturalists, proprietors, for the most part, of the lands which they occupied and cultivated". Exmoor, by contrast, was chiefly a community of tenant farmers and their workpeople, together with others who served a landed family. The Cooks served the Lovelaces, an ancient family, some of whom had been Kentish landowners in 1368.

A Tudor Lovelace acquired his fortune by looting Spanish galleons. Having retired, he built himself a mansion, Lady Place, at Hurley beside the Thames. One of his descendants, Lord Lovelace, used Lady Place as the headquarters of a plot to dethrone James II. The plot failed, and Lord Lovelace went to Gloucester jail. A more famous Lovelace was Richard, the poet, who was imprisoned on the eve of the Civil Wars:

> Stone walls do not a prison make
> Nor iron bars a cage;
> Minds innocent and quiet take
> That for an hermitage.

But all that seems far away and long ago when I sit by the kitchen range at the Cook's cottage, hearing news from a less distant past, and seeing it, too, because the parlour walls are draped with pale brown photographs of soldiers on horseback, of women in bonnets, and one of the Countess Lovelace when she was four years old. Here lives the moor as it was, as it is, as it will remain awhile.

"Mr. Cook," I said. "Your whole life has been with horses. You must know Exmoor backwards."

"I know it backwards all right." Cook winked at Liz. "Be about forty years ago now. I took some fellas out, to round-up the ponies. Well, we got away on the top there, and down comes a mist. 'Twasn't no use trying to peer ten yards ahead' cause you couldn't tell where the head was. I'd never known such a mist. Still, I did know the moor, so every now and again I'd stop, and shout to 'em, 'Come on, you fellas, this is the way.' And then I'd gallop again, and up they'd come. And then again they'd fall behind. Well, I stopped once more, and I stood up in the stirrups, and I shouted, 'Come on, my lads! We'm nearly in Porlock.' And next minute . . . what do 'ee think? A voice calls out o' the darkness, 'You'm bloody well not in Porlock. Another ten yards and you'll be in Brendon.' " Cook spoke to the bowl of his pipe. "That's the kind o' mist it was. And that's the kind o' trick a mist plays when you'm young and think you know all the answers."

One would expect the Cooks to be praisers of years past and of nothing else. But they have outlived that occupational hazard of growing old. Time after time they use the same metaphor: "In our day the clock was slow. Now it's racing 'cause the pendulum's swung too far." They are the heirless heirs of a long tradition of service which Baring-Gould described: "the daughters of farmers, the cleanest, most thrifty, most obliging, reasonable, and altogether admirable domestics that ever were. They were conscientious, they took an interest in the family, their mistresses liked—even loved them." Then at last the old order began to change: "the farmers became too grand in their ideas to send their girls out to service." It is interesting to see the situation as it appeared to Baring-Gould in 1890:

> We are in a condition of transformation in our relations to servants; we no longer dream of making them our friends, and consequently they no longer regard us with devotion. But I am not sure that the fault lies with the master . . . when the servants shift quarters every year or two, how can master and mistress feel affection for them?

'Service' having become a comic word, 'servant' also raises a smirk (and from some people a snarl). The Cooks do not share that low opinion of their own lifework, nor do they regard themselves as the only servants whose master or mistress was lovable, generous and just. Something more than a social order changed when service became despised. Mankind repeated its familiar pattern of Either-Or. Slavery was replaced by the folly which now compels refinement and education to squander much of its leisure on tasks that were better and more fittingly performed by those who are not, and do not wish to become, educated and refined. Sugar may be refined, and no one laughs; but when anyone suggests that human nature likewise needs to pass through a sieve, he is howled-down by those who believe that a bigger car and a costlier bathroom will enable them to wallow in the mire without stinking: "Seek ye first the kingdom of comfort, and everything else will soon cease to matter."

Those simple facts of life are well known at Culbone; so also are some other facts: "I saw the very first car as ever went up Porlock Hill. Ah, and I saw 'en come down again 'cause her couldn't make it, not even though she'd two strong men heaving at the stern-post. And I'll tell 'ee something else. My old grandmother saw the first *cart* as ever went up. And that come down again, too, and went on coming down till another horse arrived to haul 'en hup agen. I suppose folks still do walk Porlock, but I'm damned if I would. Not the rate some o' them motorists come down. What a world, eh? Do you know what my Dad used to say? . . . 'If you want to get down Porlock alive,' he used to say, 'just you creep slower than if you was going to your own funeral.' "

While Cook was repairing the cottage roof one morning, his

wife reminded me of another difference between the past and present of this portrait. In her younger days it was not necessary to lock the church door against vandals; but in 1969 some louts stole the candlesticks from the altar. Having chased and caught the criminals, Mrs. Cook admonished them: "I don't say I swore, but by golly I tore 'em off a strip o' my mind and no mistake."

After a pause, and much pipe-tapping, Cook or some other veteran will resume the remembrance of things past: "Three days ago I sent a letter to Lynton. Cost me fivepence. And when I didn't get no reply, I spent another bob, phoning to ask why. Well, you can guess why. The letter hadn't arrived. God dammit, I said, if you pointed a tortoise there, her'd arrive afore three days."

Then someone else says "T'ain't all that while ago since you could post a letter from Porlock at seven o'clock in the morning, and at eight o'clock it was popped through a letter-box away to Bossington. That is, if you knew the postmaster. As for the postman, he'd a pony, you understand. It didn't need twelve horsepower for one postman. Not in them days it didn't. Ah, and it didn't need five pence neither. Two postcards a penny, that's what you could send. *And* they arrived next morning."

Life at Culbone is a vivid proof that countryfolk live longer than townspeople; that they get drunk less often, go to jail less often, fall ill less often, are divorced less often, commit suicide less often. No matter what shape of evolutionary things are to come, mankind has not yet adapted itself healthily to the indoor routine of a mechanised existence. Planners may devise towns that will in time stabilise the people who have been able to send roots therein; but architecture never will transmute cement into humus. A municipal park, swathed in petrol fumes, is no substitute for a village street; a civic shopping centre, silently serving itself, lacks the *camaraderie* of a country town. In London or Glasgow or Cardiff the crowds are strangers; but when the Cooks visit Porlock they meet friends by the way, friends at the counter, and friends on the way home. Shopping on Exmoor is a sociable pleasure, not a solitary chore. Not without reason do the 'progressives' pare away the power of the parish and the county. Villagers must be persuaded, but a herd can be driven.

Not even the Cooks can live forever. Someday a new cottager will appear. I hope that he is an Exmoor man, one perhaps of those middle-aged cottagers who are already mellowing into the worthy heirs of a lovable tradition. And before he too disappears, his own heirs may sit by his fireside, hearing tales of the old times: "You'm too young to remember. It was in the days afore everyone came yere by haircraft. . . ."

XXIII

THE FINEST WALK

Within an hour-and-a-half of the Haven I can walk with leisure
through every aspect of Exmoor: the heights, the heath, the
combes, the meadows, streams, deer, ponies, woods. I like best
to go when a June sun stands well to the west, etching light with
shade. If you care to join me, I will walk with you.

From the Haven we turn left, up the one-in-three lane, where
a stream chimes in, tumbling downhill with water music that
spurs you on while the miniature waterfalls—rainbows in their
own spray—slake an arduous ascent. After a few hundred yards
the trees close-in, forming a bower of beech and oak and ash.
Soon a red signboard reminds you that walking up is sometimes
safer than driving down: "Danger," it says, "If In Trouble
Turn Left." But when you are charging downhill at the wheel of a
runaway car, have you the nerve to spin your helm hard a-port
in the hope that it will carry you *uphill* along a track among trees?

The trees themselves have stepped back by this time, revealing
a skyline that is indeed stiffnecked, for only the sheep would
choose to scale those fern-floored slopes. It is easier to admire the
bluebells, foxgloves, violets, ragged robin, snow-in-summer and
many other small calendars that tell their own time of year.

After about ten minutes' climb, the lane swerves left-and-
right by a drystone wall. Here the unwary motorist pulls his car
across the tide, and then tacks ten times in order to advance five
yards. Below the wall, in a combe on the left, hidden by summer
foliage, Mannacott Farm leads a good life despite the world's bad
news. Meanwhile, an explorer braces himself for the last few
yards to the summit, or so he supposes; but the lane suddenly
becomes so steep that a white farmhouse, fifty yards away,
resembles a child's exercise in perspective, the far end of it reced-
ing into the ground.

Having passed this farm, the gradient slackens, the lane veers left, and the stranger halts; partly to enjoy the view, partly to recover his breath. But I never do halt. I proceed for another 300 yards, to a crossroads with a signpost that flashes like an inland light-house, white against blue. One of its fingers—pointing to Cherryford and Kemacott (they are farms, not villages)—utters a warning: "Unsuitable For Cars." Our own lane bears left, overlooked by a telephone kiosk so lonely that it must have been set there for the benefit of those in perils on the steep. Not once during the last three years have I seen anyone using it.

Just beyond the kiosk, on the right, we reach a gate: and there I do halt, to greet and to be greeted by what James Thomson called:

A gaily chequered, heart-expanding view.

Leftward loom the green domes of Parracombe; rightward the sea shines bluer than the sky. Ahead, above Trentishoe, rump upon rump of moorland heaves like a pontoon of purple whales; in the middle distance the spurs of lesser hills interlock, graceful as a swan's neck, their lower flanks densely wooded; in the foreground the combes delve too deep to be quizzed.

We can walk from the gate to Martinhoe in seven minutes, but the journey takes longer because, all the while, we are glancing sideways at the view. I once tried to discover the number of people in Martinhoe, but gave up when I had counted ten and saw no prospect of reaching twelve. Several guidebooks say that Martinhoe was named after Martin of Tours, or one of his descendants who held the manor; in fact, it seems to have been named after an earlier lord, Matta. A document of 1228 spells the name as Mattingeho, the *hogh* or high place occupied by Matta's people. Thomas Westcote summed it up: "Here the land is so uneven that you shall have the words of hoe and combe often repeated, which signify hills and valleys."

Martinhoe contains a church, a church hall, a farm with cottages, one sizeable house and the old schoolmaster's cottage. Twenty years ago the rector described Martinhoe church as "a windswept light house of the Faith". Few churches stand closer to the cliffs. Dedicated to St. Martin in the eleventh century, the building is small, even by Exmoor standards; it was smaller still until 1866, when a north aisle was added. The Victorians removed many of the ancient amenities, but a Tudor altar table survives, and two bells (one is inscribed *Maria*, the other, *Santa*

Maria). There is a 1683 memorial to Margaret, daughter of Squire Whichehalse of Combe Martin, who married Richard Blackmore.

Martinhoe had a famous parson, James Hannington, who arrived during the 1860s to read with the rector. Having graduated, he became a deacon, and returned as curate. In 1884 he was translated overseas as Bishop of Eastern Equatorial Africa. One year later he was murdered by order of Mwanca Kabaka of Uganda. His Exmoor memorial is a church hall whose foundation stone was laid (1933) by Earl William Cecil, Bishop of Exeter. An inscription says: "To the glory of God and in memory of the Right Rev. Bishop James Hannington." The eighteenth century might have erected something more pretentious, but only the twentieth century could have achieved such squalid plainness. The place resembles a public lavatory, stuccoed and weed-ridden. Its gate is hitched-up with string. A notice-board advertises Bingo. This is the only blemish on our walk, and I have learned to pass it with my right eye shut. The martyr himself was a more pleasing feature of the landscape. He described his workaday uniform as follows:

A pair of Bedford cord knee-breeches of a yellow colour, continued below with yellow Sussex gaiters with brass buttons. Below these, a stout pair of nail boots, four inches across the soles, and weighing nearly four pounds. My upper garment was an all-round short leather jerkin of black cloth, underneath which an ecclesiastical waistcoat, buttoning up at the side.

Thus attired, he walked vast distances across the moor, and achieved local renown as an intrepid cliff-climber.

Beyond Martinhoe the lane again comes face-to-face with every aspect of the portrait. Starboard the sea unfolds a blue carpet; on the port side is another kind of sea, a surge of green pasture, grazed by sheep that shine because they were lately shorn; midships a more distant surge stops short of the dramatic cliffscape and becomes moorland twinkling with gorse.

Here we leave the lane, striking a path across a heathy patch to the sea and three promontories poised like a runner for the race. Each is grazed by sheep, and all are wooded, whence the name of the first, Woody Bay, where three or four houses shelter among trees and rhododendrons near the top of the cliff. If Mammon had prevailed, those houses would have been a town because some Victorian financiers plotted to 'develop' this majestic and inaccessible rampart of the moor. They built a road thither—on the brink of the cliff—and a pier too, hoping that the pleasure-cruisers would bring many shekels; but the pier was swept away a few hours before the top hats arrived to open it. In the end their cash petered-out and the plot with it. Today both the National Trust and the National Park stand guard against Burke's "sophists, economists, and calculators".

Hitherto we have been climbing eastward, with the sun behind; now we steer due west into the glory of early evening and the fellowship of the sea, for this is a coastal path, always narrow, sometimes dizzy. Few people walk it, though some do venture part of the way; the majority are like the man in Shakespeare, who was daunted because

> Those high wild hills and rough uneven ways
> Draw out the miles and make them wearisome.

My companions are the gulls and the waves. Throughout the year a blossom of gorse bends to the wind, as though confirming an old saying, that gorse-time is kissing-time; in other words, just as there are always some people in love, so there is always some gorse in flower. Among shaded places the bluebells may live long enough to greet the foxgloves. Day and night the sea murmurs to itself, hundreds of feet below.

But now another sound is heard, coming from the left, where a stream has flopped four feet down a bank, and then disappears underground, gurgling, tinkling, plashing. A few yards more, and the stony track becomes a grassy path through a tunnel of trees. At the far end of the tunnel, the sea winks a blue eye. Having emerged, the path walks as it were a tight rope; on one side the ravines plunge into the waves; on the other, they climb to the heather and thence to meadows grazed by the hardiest sheep south of Westmorland. Seen against the sun, two promontories ahead gleam like ebony, their jagged silhouette miming a castle that has slithered into the water. If you peer down, the ravines— scarred like the face of a Sioux—will turn your stomach.

Now the path becomes stony again, zig-zagging past a copse whose roots protrude below the ledge of the cliff. Every year a blackbird builds his nest in an oak tree here, rocked by gales, rinsed by spume, interminably harried. Between February and June I halt awhile, listening to the loveliest music ever uttered by

Above Heddon's Mouth

a wild creature, with a beck singing *sotto voice*. Often a ship passes by: and although she lacks a sail, her bow-wave poses the question that Robert Bridges asked:

> Whither, O splendid ship, thy white sails crowding,
> Leaning across the bosom of the urgent West,
> That fearest nor sea rising, nor sky clouding,
> Whither away, fair rover, and what thy quest?

The sea itself remains unapproachable except by water.

Suddenly the path alters course, climbing steeply into the shade of a plateau. A stone clatters, and is followed by a little landslide. Looking up, you see a sheep that has come to sample the pathside herbage. Looking down, you notice that the sun, having found a chink through the plateau, is transforming a grassy headland into a green groin.

Soon the path turns into the sun once more, and then you feel that you have stopped not only from another time of day but also from a different time of year. Within one pace the temperature leaps by eight degrees. As though to greet this new-found warmth, the path turns green again and begins its long descent. More ruined castles loom ahead, archaic and Arthurian, carved by Time and the elements. Far above, the Romans built an outpost.

Guidebooks make much of this ancient monument, but all I ever found was a shadow in the scrub, which may have been anything at all. And in order to find even that, I had to arm myself with compass, map, gumboots, gloves and a billhook to hack a way through briers. Why, one asks, did Rome condemn her soldiers to serve amid such solitude? True, there were some silver mines at Combe Martin, two hours' march to the west; but this was no place from which to defend them. If the outpost were attacked, it must either advance and prevail or retreat and be drowned. No, the site was a signal station with its back to the moor, and its eyes towards Wales, for there lurked the menace, among turbulent Celts. How the Romans must have hated this post, even as the British soldiers of 1914 and 1939 hated Alaska, or Iceland, or Scapa Flow. Most of the Romans came from a sunny climate; some, no doubt, dreamed of warm skies in Provence while they trudged through damp mists in Devonshire. What letters they must have written home, cursing the uncouth natives, the immense distance from a town, the lack of hot baths. How

14

Sunset, Woody Bay

hard it must have seemed to fulfil Livy's boast that "a Roman is by nature brave and hardy". *Et facere et pati fortiter Romanum est.*

Perhaps the outpost was a penitentiary for old lags and young laggards, with discipline enforced by a passed-over centurion and two disgruntled NCOs. In spring and summer, though, even the forgotten few may have nodded contentedly when bees droned in the heather, and warlike Wales shone like an emerald brooch on a blue toga. In such weather the look-out had a simple task, for if the Welsh did sail across the sea, their ships would be sighted soon after they had embarked, and the beacons could blaze a warning. No such invasion occurred.

Seventeen centuries later an invasion did occur, watched by many people, some of whom did not know what it was they saw. The story begins during the French Revolution, when a renegade American artillery officer, William Tate, persuades the French to give him command of a force that shall seize Bristol, and march thence into the Midlands. The invaders are not required to capture England; their task is to cause havoc and consternation.

William Tate is already 70 years old when he assumes the rank of Colonel of Chef de Brigade. His fleet seems efficient, under the command of an ex-pirate who has become Commodore. The troops, however, are less satisfactory, being chiefly a collection of jailbirds who have volunteered to serve in exchange for their liberty. One of them delays the invasion by trying to incite a mutiny. When at length the commandos do sail, the wind carries them to Lundy Island, where they capture an English fishing boat and compel one of her crew to act as pilot. By wearing the Dutch colours they pass unsuspected through a convoy of English merchantmen. Now they bear north-east into the Severn Sea, past Ilfracombe, past the Hangmen, abreast of this Roman ruin, and so to Porlock Bay, watched perhaps by a shepherd on Dunkery Hill, an unsuspicious man, who, though he lives within sight of it, knows no more about the sea than did Jan Ridd himself: "I had been in a boat nearly twice: but the second time my mother found it out, and came and drew me back again. . . ."

At Porlock, however, the wind shifts and becomes a gale. Instead of sailing up to Bristol, the invaders are beaten back to Wales. By this time they have been sighted, but news travels no faster than a horseman, and they land unopposed near Carreg Wastad in Pembrokeshire. At once the jailbirds loot the cottages and farmhouses, delighted to find that many of them contain much liquor (a smuggling vessel had run aground there only a day or so before). Within a few hours the sons of Liberty are drunk as well as disorderly.

A small party of Welsh militia arrive, supported by some English bluejackets hauling their guns. Each side tries to persuade the other that vast reinforcements are imminent. After a comic opera interlude, Colonel Tate surrenders unconditionally, whereupon the British commander, Lord Cawdor, issues the prisoners with bread and cheese, their first meal for many hours.

When Tate is exchanged for English prisoners, he retires on half-pay to an expensive Paris hotel, accompanied by a lady whose tastes are even more extravagant. Soon the police begin to investigate the Colonel's debts. In an effort to make the best of a bad job, the American minister rescues Tate by paying his passage home to America. But whether Tate ever reached America remains unknown; and so also do the time and the place of his death. Like a meteorite, the last invader of Britain is lost without trace, having briefly stirred the chancellories of Europe.

Beyond the signal station our descent becomes steeper, and the ramparts of Exmoor rise up from the sea. As though unwilling to scale such heights, the path turns abruptly inland; but it is not unwillingness that caused the detour; it is a cove, a narrow ravine, called Heddon's Mouth, whose cliffs resemble the hull of a cap-sized warship, rusted with bracken, steel-grey with scree, flecked with gorse. Through that ravine the River Heddon flows beside green pastures and among wooded banks, passing under a timber footbridge and thence into the sea. Inland the moor reaches for the sky, summit on summit, with trees almost to the tops; a blend of grass and heather browsed by cattle and sheep, all woven into what William Camden called "a master-piece of Nature, perform'd when she was in her best and gayest humour. . .".

I have never met anyone on the further summit of Heddon's Mouth. No paths are there, only a series of sheep tracks, bright with heather and gorse that slope almost into the sea. If you follow those sheepwalks you will exclaim with Gonzalo:

> . . . here's a maze trod, indeed,
> Through forthrights and meanders.

Across the water, Wales bends northward out of sight, leaving the western horizon as empty as the Atlantic.

J. W. L. Page was impressed by the rugged grandeur of Heddon's Mouth; "the finest combe," he called it, "on the North Devon coast." Northwood you can see the Great Hangman, 1,044 feet above the waves: "the loftiest seaward hill," said Page, "in the west of England". He compared it with his other mountainous exploits: "I have done some of the worst of the Lake mountains, I have done Ben Nevis, but I know of nothing, except perhaps the screes of Rosset Ghyl, to equal the tremendous climb up the slippery slopes of the Great Hangman." Page was not exaggerating. The Great Hangman really does create the illusion which Barbour projected onto Ben Cruachan when he declared that no higher hills were to be found in Britain:

> I trow nocht in all Bretane
> Ane hear hill may funden be.

I sometimes pass a whole day on the cliff above Heddon's Mouth. Bees drone there, tirelessly making honey while the sun shines. Larks leap up, so loud and near that the dog is startled. Rabbits creep among the heather. Ships come and go. Gulls glide, all the while mewing. Far away, above Rhydda Bank, a soundless tractor crawls acutely up and down. Nearly 1,000 feet below, the sea repeats its monologue. If Thomas Westcote had lazed awhile at Heddon's Mouth in summer, he would never have dismissed Exmoor as a "coarse, barren, and wild object, yielding little comfort by his rough, cold, and vigorous complexion."

The last lap of our walk lopes down the remains of the coach road with which those Woody Bay businessmen failed to make their fortune. Yet some coaches did come this way, within a few feet of the cliff; and until recent times the last of the coachmen lived at Kentisbury, full of reminiscences: "I'd a gun on that coach. They weren't going to make me stand and deliver."

Down, then, and down, wheeling dizzily on the brink of destruction, protected only by two feet of stunted gorse; and as you descend, so the River Heddon seems to arise, until at last you hear it, tumbling over rocks, by-passing boughs, plunging into a coppice of springtime daffodils and high summer foxgloves. No longer face-to-face, you must crick your neck in order to see the rusty summit and its steel-grey scree. Step by step the sea disappears and becomes no more than a glimpse between the two arcs of Exmoor.

Presently the track turns inland through woods to the Hunter's Inn, which Page described as "a picturesque thatched hostelry at the foot of wooded heights . . .". The inn was favoured by undergraduates, for in those days a man did most of his reading during the summer vacation: "the young men from Oxford may often be seen sunning themselves on the seat in front of the Inn." You will seek them in vain today; their successors prefer a lighter programme. But when the world has gone home, Hunter's Inn becomes the pleasantest hotel on Exmoor.

And there we take leave of each other, in a steep valley beside a singing river among precipitous woods. We have sampled every aspect of the moor. Now it is time for me to climb toward the Haven.

XXIV

THE PLACE FOR ALL SEASONS

The author of *Hudibras* declared: "All countries are a wise man's home." Kipling agreed, but added a wiser postscript, saying that every countryman prefers his own homeland above all others.

There need not, and indeed there ought not to, be any vainglory in such a preference. I am not the only man whose great-great-grandfather was vicar of a country parish; nor is Exmoor the only region whose beauty begets kindliness. Though I do prefer Exmoor, and am faithful to it, I never have spent my days "forsaking all others". On the contrary, I retain humanity's roving eye, and could name a hundred places wherein a man might live and die content with his surfeit of good fortune. Toward Westmorland I feel an especial fondness because the land thereabouts was the land of my fathers. With the wooded Chiltern Hills of Oxfordshire and Buckinghamshire I have an acquaintance so old that it long ago became ineradicable. And has any Englishman sailed the Cornish waters without being baptized thereby? Unlike Mary Tudor, who died with one place-name carved sadly on her heart, I live among a roll-call that echoes happily from Land's End to John o' Groat's and back again by way of Rutland and Cardiganshire.

Yet Exmoor transcends them all, and never so superbly as when the Devon heights meet the Severn Sea. In most other parts of England even a well-loved landscape tends now and then to be taken for granted, or in some other way to lose its grip upon our gratitude. At the Haven no such faltering is possible. Grief fear, joy—the daily chore in a familiar round—all are enhanced by their dramatic background. I do not know of any other comparable area where such wildness and such softness are so closely interwoven. I recall no other area where, by climbing a lane, you can within ten minutes pass from a mild to a cold climate. Nor have I found any scene-shifting so vivid as the coast at Heddon's Mouth, the meadows of Oare, the heath above Withypool.

Moreover, I might call witnesses—men and women from distant regions—who came, and saw, and were conquered. Casting about for a romantic setting, Sir Walter Scott caught it near Charles. Shelley chose Lynmouth, seeking and there finding "The Spirit of Beauty". Richard Jefferies gazed with awe at Dunkery's purple skyline. On Combe Martin cliff Kingsley praised "the infinite variety of beauty". Beatrix Potter, a pilgrim from Lakeland, fell in love with Dunster and Selworthy ("perfect villages" she called them). Arriving one day at Malmsmead, Llewelyn Powys was so enthralled that in his age he confessed: "It was an adventure which influenced the whole of my life." But, of course, if this portrait has fulfilled its purpose, it will need no other testimony than the reader's.

Some countryfolk are at home in a domesticated landscape; others must have their diet braced by ingredients closer to the untamed aspects of mankind. There lie the moor's threefold claims on my inherited allegiance: the wildness, the sea, the softness. So, whenever I hear the stream, or watch the waves, or wander the heights, I find many facts which persuade me that mine is the most varied and majestic corner of what R. D. Blackmore called "the fairest county of England".

ALSO BY J. H. B. PEEL

POETRY
Time To Go
In The Country
Mere England
Frost at Midnight

ESSAYS
To Be Brief
Small Calendars
Country Talk (in preparation)

NOVELS
A Man's Life
Sea Drift
The Young Rector
The Gallant Story

COUNTRY BOOKS
The Chilterns: A Vision of England
Portrait of the Thames
Portrait of the Severn
Along the Pennine Way
England

GUIDEBOOKS
Buckinghamshire Footpaths
Discovering the Chilterns
North Wales

INDEX

Poltimore, Lord, 189
Porlock, 106–8
Potter, Beatrix, 143, 215
Powys, Llewelyn, 96, 144, 192, 215
Prayway Head, 49
Prior, Richard, 141
Prynne, William, 60–61
Pugsley, T., 183

Q
Quartly family, 132–3
Quiller-Couch, Sir A. T., 177

R
Raleigh, Sir Walter, 115, 146–7
Rawle, G., 182
Rhydda Bank, 212
Richards, G. S., 178–82
W., 183
Ridler, J., 182
John, 53
R., 182
Rose Ash, 138
Rossetti, Christina, 80
Ruskin, John, 102–3
Russell, Rev. Jack, 184–90

S
Sackville-West, V., 152
Sassoon, Siegfried, 114
Scott, Sir Walter, 100, 136, 215
Selworthy, 120–21
Shakespeare, William, 125, 151, 192, 211
Sharp, Cecil, 104–5
Shelley, P. B., 75, 152, 165
Short, John, 104–5
Shoulsbarrow Castle, 136
Simonsbath, 110–12
Slade, W. J., 148
Slader, Richard, 159
Smart, Christopher, 116
Snell, F. J., 54, 68
South Molton, 66–9, 185

Southcomb family, 138
Southey, Robert, 75, 76, 106
Spenser, Edmund, 124, 196
Stevenson, R. L., 73
Stogumber, 56
Stoke Pero, 119–20
Suttie, Dr. Ian, 189
Swimbridge, 185, 190
Swinburne, A. C., 50, 193
Sydenham family, 55–7
Synge, J. M., 94–5

T
Tame, Thomas, 117
Tate, William, 210–11
Taylor, John, 31
Temple, Archbishop, 71–2
Tennyson, Lord, 54, 59, 82
Thomas, Edward, 17
Thompson, Francis, 108
Thomson, James, 100, 206
Timberscombe, 119, 120
Tiverton, 69–72
Traherne, Thomas, 120
Tremayne, Rev. Richard, 129
Trentishoe, 138, 206
Tusser, Thomas, 27
Twitchen, 134

V
Vancouver, Charles, 133

W
Wamsbarrows, 114
Ward, J., 182
Watchet, 104–6
Watersmeet, 123
Watson, Sir William, 14
Wesley, Rev. John, 130, 160
Westcote, Thomas, 64, 69, 73, 75, 130, 132, 149, 157, 208
Wheddon Cross, 119
Whichelhalse family, 74, 207
White, Rev. Gilbert, 124, 143
Sir Thomas, 22